Basic Theology:
Applied

Basic Theology: Applied

Wesley & Elaine Willis
John & Janet Master

Editors

VICTOR BOOKS

A DIVISION OF SCRIPTURE PRESS PUBLICATIONS INC.
USA CANADA ENGLAND

Copyediting: Mary Horner/Robert N. Hosack
Cover Design: Scott Rattray

ISBN: 1-56476-442-7

Suggested Subject Heading: Theology

© 1995 by Victor Books/SP Publications, Inc. All rights reserved. Printed in the United States of America.

1 2 3 4 5 6 7 8 9 10 Printing/Year 00 99 98 97 96 95

CONTENTS

MAN: THE IMAGE OF GOD

SIN

JESUS CHRIST OUR LORD

SO GREAT A SALVATION

THE HOLY SPIRIT

INTRODUCTION

What a joy to honor Charles C. Ryrie on his seventieth birthday!

Charles has greatly impacted our lives as professor, mentor, friend, and associate. God has blessed his teaching and speaking ministries throughout the world. Millions have also benefited from Charles' writings, ranging from object lesson books for teachers to works of biblical and systematic theology, and *The Ryrie Study Bible,* which is produced in a variety of translations.

To honor Charles Ryrie we felt that it would be appropriate to compile a festschrift—a collection of articles written by students or colleagues. Traditionally festschrifts are scholarly works in which intellectual acumen provides the driving force. This volume seeks instead to reflect scholarship focused on relating the Word of God to our everyday lives, even as Charles Ryrie does. A work stressing application is appropriate to honor a man known for his clarity of thinking, for his extraordinary teaching skills and, above all, for his commitment to the Word of God as a guide for Christian living. With his keen mind, Dr. Ryrie can grasp the most complex ideas; with his gift of teaching he helps others understand biblical concepts and their application to life.

The seed ideas for how to approach and organize this volume grew out of our discussions with others, including our friend Paul Feinberg. We settled on a format that parallels Ryrie's book, *Basic Theology,* and consulted with Charles along the way. With his guidance, we invited contributors who have meant so much to him over the years. Some were unavailable for various reasons, but those who have contributed represent a cross section of persons who have studied under Dr. Ryrie and/or served with him. The involvement of our wives in the editing of this book was Charles' special request, reflecting his awareness of their great contribution, not only to this book, but to our lives and ministries as well.

This is a companion volume to *Basic Theology*, and we have asked each contributor to address how selected theological concepts discussed in that book relate to everyday life. Theology is practical, and good theology is very practical. The same is true of theologians, and Charles Ryrie is an outstanding theologian. As you read, rejoice with us in the gifts of God embodied in Charles C. Ryrie.

John and Janet Master
Wes and Elaine Willis

The Living
and True God

"A knowledge about God should deepen our relationship with Him which in turn increases our desire to know more about Him."
(*Basic Theology*, p. 26)

CHAPTER ONE

The Living and True God Present in Our Lives

Gary E. Vincelette

I walked across the aged hospital campus of the University of Freiburg in the Black Forest of Germany. I felt very much alone. Summer was giving way to fall. The brilliant colors of autumn would eventually drift to the ground and yield to winter. But my apprehension grew as I strode toward the neurosurgery building, where my wife, my most precious friend, companion, lover, sharer of the vision, mother of our four children, lay in intensive care. The day before she had undergone seven hours of delicate surgery to remove a large tumor lodged in her spinal cord. Now she lay paralyzed in her left leg, able to twitch only her right toes.

The neurosurgeon, a kind, grandfatherly man of international reputation, looked dismayed as I entered his office. We sat alone together as he spoke:

> I was unable to sleep last night. Parts of the tumor were as hard as glass. I had to drill away for hours with a diamond headed drill. There was no clear line of demarcation between tumor and spinal cord tissue. I could not remove all of the tumor. Presently she can twitch her right toes, but her left side is paralyzed. We have a few days to wait for some kind of signal, for some movement in the left leg. I'm deeply troubled.

Then the room was quiet—deadly quiet. I hurt for him, for my wife, for our children, for me. Communism had recently fallen in the former Soviet Union and Eastern Europe. Annette and I had returned to Europe just four weeks prior inspired with new vision and new opportunities for these rapidly changing mission fields. We had scarcely begun to unpack our boxes before our plans and years of preparation were dramatically intercepted. What about all of our plans?

I hurt for answers. Does there not exist a trustworthy point of orientation, an immovable anchor for us? Is there not more to life than birth, life, disease, death, decay? I must know.

The Apostle Paul reminded the Greek philosophers in Athens: "For in him we live and move and have our being" (Acts 17:28, NIV). The one, true and living God is present within life and around life. He alone is the epicenter of life. Because the living and true God has clearly revealed Himself in creation, in human conscience, and in the words of Scripture, men and women can know God.

Knowing God permits us to stand with Him on the mountaintops viewing life in its broad strokes, and to walk with Him in the valleys of life's ebb and flow. The illusion of no meaning disappears like the morning haze when we realize "in him we live and move and have our being." The knowledge of God does not solve the mystery surrounding life's storms, but knowing the living and true God will enable us to encounter the vicissitudes of life with endurance, purpose, and hope.

The Knowledge of God

"A full knowledge of God is both factual and personal" (*Basic Theology*, 26). I knew many facts about my wife before we married; I know substantially more after over two decades of marriage. However, objective knowledge alone limits a relationship. Healthy relationships must be based upon both a *factual* and a *personal* knowledge of the one loved. Thus it is in knowing God. A healthy relationship with God must begin with an intellectual knowledge of who He is, which then matures into a deeper personal experience of knowing God in life. God manifests Himself to us on the mountain peaks, in the valleys, in the swamps – in all aspects of our lives.

The Divine-human relationship might be illustrated as an ascending spiral. At the moment of belief we enter into an eternal life relationship with the true God (John 17:3). Thus begins a growing vitality in our knowledge of God and our experiencing His presence. As our knowledge of God grows, so also grows our trust. The more we know of Him, the more we desire to know, and the deeper we trust. As life progresses in a fallen, sinful world, both the beauty and the ugliness of life constantly encourage us – even force us – to trust, and to experience God more fully.

The picture of the ascending spiral of growth in relational knowledge of the living God is painfully beautiful. For we must go against gravity, pulled and pushed by both our deepening relationship with the glorious God, our own weak nature, and the harshness of life. Even more beautiful is the truth that the sovereign God is continually reaching down to us in the midst of real life to progressively reveal more of Himself to us. He knows what He is doing and where He is headed. "In him we were also chosen, having been predestined according to the plan of him who works out everything in conformity with the purpose of his will, in order that we, who were the first to hope in Christ, might be for the praise of his glory" (Eph. 1:11-12). Mysteriously, God and people work together according to God's plans and purpose, to the end that we may grow in the true knowledge and image of the living God and bring praise to Him by reflecting facets of His glory now and forever.

Healthy Theology—Healthy Living

People eventually become like whatever god they worship. The psalmist writes, "Those who make [idols] will be like them, and so will all who trust in them" (Ps. 115:8). The Bible teaches us about the one living and true God.

Romans 5:1-8 explains one of the means by which Christians develop a healthy knowledge of God in the center of life. Here we discover a life cycle revolving about the character of God. By faith we have entered into a right relationship with God (v. 1). We now enjoy the benefits of this new relationship, experiencing harmony with God, receiving the grace and spiritual blessings which Christ offers.

In addition, we have been given hope in which to rejoice (v. 2), a hope more certain than the sunrise tomorrow. The believer's life now rotates toward the majestic hope that God will manifest His glory in the believer in the days ahead. Death and decay will not strike the last blow. Christ will return and those who have gone to the grave believing in Christ will rise, be transformed, and enter into indescribable glory in the presence of God. This hope of the revelation of the glory of God's person and work becomes an anchor, a source of joy. Charles Ryrie writes, "The glory of God means the awesomeness, splendor, and importance of God seen in some way. . . . It is God seen in some or all of His characteristics. . . . God has a number of facets to His character, and His glory may be seen sometimes through one facet and sometimes through another" (Charles C. Ryrie, *Transformed by His Glory* [Wheaton, Ill.: Victor, 1990], 18–19). What a splendid hope. Christians will both see and participate in the glory which God will manifest.

Before believers can reflect God's glory, we must first be transformed. God begins refining Christians with "sufferings" (Rom. 5:3). As the pressure of suffering bears down upon us, we become unbalanced, and are forced to grab for something or someone to help us regain equilibrium. We will, in faith, reach out toward the God we are coming to know. The more intimately we know Him, the more we will trust Him. We seek inner strength and wisdom to bear up under the pressure of suffering. Later, usually in hindsight, we discover that this very process, rather than crushing us, is developing perseverance and character. Life rolls on relentlessly, rotating the wheel of life from hope to suffering to perseverance to character (Rom. 5:3-4).

The Christian who has been tested by suffering and has come through it displays tried and proven character. He or she comes forth as gold (Job 23:10). Proven character rolls on to hope once again, which is where the life cycle begins. However, now hope radiates with a capital "H." Our sufferings "help to produce character, and approved Christian character finds its ultimate resting place in the presence of God, not in a grave" (Everett F. Harrison, "Romans," in *The Expositor's Bible Commentary*, ed. Frank E. Gaebelein [Grand Rapids: Zondervan, 1976], 57). Pain encourages us to listen to God and to seek a deeper relationship with Him. The psalmist writes, "It was good for me to be afflicted so that I might learn your decrees" (Ps. 119:71). Affliction drives us to make certain that our theology about God and ourselves is correct. This promotes healthy living.

The chain of events in Romans 5:1-8, beginning with hope for the believer and rotating through suffering, perseverance, character, and back to hope, spin around a stable hub. The believer's hope is not destroyed in the inequities of life because it is based upon the *character of God*. The character of the living and present God is the hub about which the Christian's life must revolve, the rim which holds life firmly intact in the middle of a hostile society. Healthy theology about God produces healthy living.

How is the Christian certain that his hope is not simply a pious wish? God, knowing us, has anticipated our doubts and has deposited within us a guarantee to still our worries. He pours out His love (one of His perfections, 1 John 4:8) directly into our hearts by giving us the divine gift of the Holy Spirit (Rom. 5:5). The Holy Spirit assures the believer that God will not go back on His promise. God clearly demonstrated His love to the whole world when He gave His Son, Jesus Christ, to die for sinful people (v. 8), and He now pledges to Christians through the indwelling Holy Spirit that their hope will not be in vain. Our hope is as good as God—the Father, the Son, and the Holy Spirit.

The construction and the function of a wagon wheel illustrates the life cycle pictured in Romans 5:1-8. When wagon wheels rolled

17

over the rugged terrain of prairie and mountain, the outer rim would have collapsed if it had not been securely attached to a stable hub and surrounded by a solid iron rim. The solid hub and strong metal rim gave the wheel its strength to withstand the bumps, boulders, and blows as it rolled. The spokes connected hub and rim into a single, tight unit. Likewise our lives roll along from hope to suffering to perseverance to approved character. The triune God in all His glory serves as both the hub, giving support, and the rim, giving protection and strength.

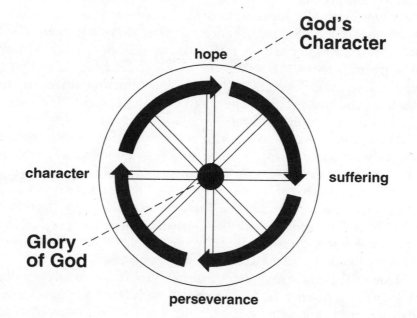

As Christians encounter affliction, they will hold tightly to the hub of their lives, the stable hope that God will not disappoint them. God is present now and will manifest His glory in the days ahead. By faith we rely upon the love and hope expressed to us by God the Father, demonstrated by the Son, and guaranteed by the Holy Spirit. In so doing we find strength to endure today's tribulations and tomorrow's uncertainties. The very character of God surrounds our lives, assuring us that "God is faithful; he will not let you be tempted beyond what you can bear" (1 Cor. 10:13).

As we roll through life's experiences, we continue to grow in the knowledge of God. We find God to be not a severe taskmaster, but a Father, who has only allowed suffering to draw Father and child into a closer relationship. Our faith is strengthened, our knowledge of God and our own human nature is refined, and our character is proven.

Living and Growing in the Knowledge of God

Was I really alone as I walked across that hospital campus in Germany toward my wife in intensive care? No; God was with me. There is no place in all of creation where I can escape the ever penetrating presence of God (Ps. 139:7-10). "God is everywhere present with His whole being at all times" (Ryrie, *Basic Theology*, 41). God is *omnipresent*. I began to interact with Him in prayer. I told Him I was fearful. He told me, "Even though [you] walk through the valley of the shadow of death, [you] will fear no evil, for [I am] with [you]" (Ps. 23:4). My wife and I were entering a valley that we never had visited before, but we were not in it alone. The Triune God in all His perfection was with us.

Did He know that this was going to happen before we entered the plane headed for Germany? Did He know how I hurt for my wife and children, and how numb I felt? Without doubt. "O LORD, you have searched me and you know me. . . . All the days ordained for me were written in your book before one of them came to be. How precious to me are your thoughts, O God!" (Ps. 139:1, 16-17). God is *omniscient*. "God knows everything, things actual and possible, effortlessly and equally well" (Ryrie, *Basic Theology*, 41). I found solace in this knowledge of God in the midst of my pain. My wife lay paralyzed in intensive care; my two older children were studying in Boston; my two younger children were entering new schools elsewhere in Germany; and I, husband, father, missionary, stood hard pressed in the middle. God was knowingly present with each of us spread out on two continents. None of us was separated from Him by time or space. My heart needed the inner assurance that my Father was with me in all of His person, knowing not only the facts but also my feelings.

But could God have prevented this from happening? Can He

change the situation; heal my wife? Yes, He could; yes, He can! He is God Almighty, *El Shaddai*. He is *omnipotent*. "God is all-powerful and able to do anything consistent with His own nature" (Ryrie, *Basic Theology*, 40). I was reminded: "I will be a Father to you, and you will be my sons and daughters, says the *Lord Almighty*" (2 Cor. 6:18). Therefore if God could have prevented this tumor, or suddenly healed my wife, but has not chosen to do so, He must have a purpose in all of this. I bow to His sovereignty.

"God is the chief Being in the universe . . . God is the supreme power in the universe. . . . Ultimately God is in complete control of all things, though He may choose to let certain events happen according to natural laws which He has ordained" (Ryrie, *Basic Theology*, 43). His plan remains all-inclusive (Eph. 1:11). I gain new hope, for life has not spun out of God's control. God has not been surprised by a health oversight. There is a purpose in the midst of all this pain. God, who is filled with mystery, may choose never to reveal His purposes either to me or to my wife, just as He did not disclose them to Job. Nevertheless, I do believe that He can bring good out of the afflictions of life. "And we know that *in all things God works for the good* of those who love him, who have been called according to his purpose. For those God foreknew he also predestined to be conformed to the likeness of his Son, that he might be the firstborn among many brothers" (Rom. 8:28–29).

Ten months later my wife remains partially paralyzed in a rehabilitation center in Switzerland. For now she lives in a hospital world with other paralyzed women. These include a bubbly teenager suddenly stricken by an automobile accident, a wife and mother paralyzed after jumping out of the window of a blazing house, a young woman shot in the spinal cord in war-torn former Yugoslavia, and another severely paralyzed from a stumble while hiking. Many of them cry out, "I would commit suicide if I could move my arms enough to do it." "How can God be good? Look at us!" God's ways may be a mystery to us, but God remains sovereign. His character remains unchanged in its *goodness*, and is the same, yesterday, today, and forever. "You are good and what you do is *good*" (Ps. 119:68).

Even though I do not understand God's ways, I nevertheless submit in the fear of the Lord. Let God be God. Let Him choose the suffering and pain of life to transform my wife and me, so we may reflect His goodness to those around us. How else will they ever come to know the God we know? He can use tragedy to give birth to glory and goodness!

God remains faithful. We are not forsaken. The knowledge of God gives us strength and stability as we travel through this personal valley. The facts are taking on deeper meaning; the relationship is growing, becoming more intimate. I want and need to know the true, living God present in life even more. I continue to pray as Paul did: "I keep asking that the God of our Lord Jesus Christ, the *glorious* Father, may give you the Spirit of wisdom and revelation, so that you may *know him* better. I pray also that the eyes of your heart may be enlightened in order that you may know the hope to which he has called you, the riches of his *glorious* inheritance in the saints" (Eph. 1:17-18).

"The Christian's conscience operates
to prod him to do what is right in
various relationships of life."
(*Basic Theology*, p. 199)

C H A P T E R T W O

A Christian Witness
in the Midst of Controversy

Charles C. Tandy

A ndrew Young, former mayor of Atlanta, tells a wonderful
story about a man in Georgia who had spent a lifetime
breeding gaming chickens. He finally developed what he
believed to be the two best gamecocks that could be produced. It
was time for the state fair, and he decided to enter his prized cocks
in the competition. He placed the two cocks in a cage and carefully put them in the back of his old pickup for the trip to Atlanta.

When he arrived at the fairgrounds, he walked to the back of his
truck to unload the birds. Unfortunately, all he could see were
feathers and blood everywhere. Realizing that the cocks had killed
each other, he covered his face and exclaimed, "My goodness, I
forgot to tell them that they were on the same side!"

More often than we would like to admit, we also forget which side we are on and fight against those with whom we should be cooperating. Working together to spread the Gospel and to promote the well-being of fellow human beings ought to be a high priority for all Christians.

Leading in public life had never been on my agenda, but after repeated requests I finally consented to serve as a member of the Dallas City Council. During six years on the city council, I often found myself in an ever-increasing swarm of controversies. How to maintain a Christian attitude and demeanor was a constant challenge in the midst of differing personalities and political agendas. We struggled with the monumental problems that face modern American cities: crime, a decreasing tax base yielding less revenue, bad decisions made by predecessors, homelessness, racial tensions, and countless others.

Early in my term of service I recognized that there were certain unresolved controversies in my own life that I believed God wanted me to settle, before I could go to work on the city's problems. First, I needed to resolve a long-held smoldering grudge I had with a prominent architect and business leader in Dallas. This had resulted from a bad multi-partner business deal which, in retrospect, probably neither of us could have prevented. Years of avoiding each other had become increasingly unacceptable to me. We agreed to get together, and he welcomed me warmly as I arrived at his office. That meeting began a healing process and a relationship, one which he too had longed for and prayed about, that continues to bless us both.

Another problem area for me concerned a person who was the consummate fund raiser and activist for any good cause in our community. Years before, when he was a political candidate, I had strongly opposed his election because of his style and personality, and he had been defeated then. It seemed apparent that if I were to serve effectively in the public arena, I wanted this man as my friend, not my enemy. A late afternoon appointment in a local coffeehouse provided the opportunity to ask forgiveness for harsh feelings in the past. And thus began a friendship with one whose personality is totally different from mine, but whose commitment to do the right thing is tireless. Even now, as he is dying with

23

cancer, we have been able to share God's love and provision together.

At the time of my election to city council, we had to deal with one of the most controversial political activists in decades. Knowing I would have to interact with her, I called and invited her to breakfast. I opened the conversation with, "You and I do not know each other, and all I have heard about you is bad. But I don't believe that and want to know you better." Her style of confrontation never changed, but it never was directed at me. We actually found many areas on which we could agree and we chose to disagree on others without the venom that others perceived.

As I reflect on these early days of public service and on who I am, I conclude that I was uniquely chosen of God to do a work that no one else could. Second Timothy 1:12 demanded that I take a positive stand: "I am not ashamed, because I know whom I have believed and am convinced that he is able to guard what I have entrusted to him for that day" (NIV). Likewise, 2 Timothy 2:23-25 had to be addressed:

Don't have anything to do with foolish and stupid arguments, because you know they produce quarrels. And the Lord's servant must not quarrel, instead he must be kind to everyone, able to teach, not resentful. Those who oppose him, he must gently instruct, in the hope that God will grant them repentance leading them to a knowledge of the truth.

This review of a few of my experiences focuses on one particular segment of my life. During that period I learned many lessons that have generated the following theme or personal mission statement toward which I work daily. Things I want to be true of my life:

To be faithful to God and my family
Having loved God and in turn those whose lives I touch

To be a physician who honored Christ in and through all my activities

To be a wise mentor and leader

To love my neighbor as myself

A man of honesty and integrity

Secure with my wife and family, ensuring God's love for them through me

At peace with all men, and that there be no one I had not forgiven or who had not forgiven me.

These are lofty goals that can only be achieved through a daily walk with Christ. But they are truly worth the effort as we approach the next chapter in our lives, whatever that may be.

My involvement in public service impelled me first to deal with my own weaknesses and failures before trying to help others. I learned the scriptural admonition to avoid giving offense to others (1 Cor. 10:32; 2 Cor. 6:3). The biblical way is always the best way if we desire to serve God and to help others.

"Christ died for all.
What should we be telling the world?"
(*Basic Theology*, p. 323)

CHAPTER THREE

The Sovereign God
and the Sinner

Robert P. Lightner

T he salvation of the sinner from eternal condemnation is a
work of the Triune God—Father, Son, and Holy Spirit.
The sinner contributes nothing to salvation. It is all of God.
To be sure, God has established a human condition which must
be met before the sinner can receive eternal life: faith or trust in
Christ alone as the sinner's substitute for sin. This condition,
however, adds absolutely nothing to the gift of eternal life. From
beginning to end, the deliverance from sin's condemnation is
God's work.

Benefits of God's saving grace do come in response to our
obedience to God and His Word, but life from above is a gift from
the sovereign God. To put it another way, eternal life is what God

26

alone gives to the believing sinner; living out that life in a way that is pleasing to God involves cooperating with Him.

Charles Ryrie has been a champion of God's marvelous saving and keeping grace. Following are some practical applications of the great contribution he has made to our understanding of "so great a salvation" (Heb. 2:3, NASB).

The saving relationship between the sovereign God and the sinner involves the Father's love for sinners, the Son's death for sinners, and the Spirit's regeneration of sinners. These truths form the foundation for practical suggestions on how to share the sovereign God's salvation with others.

God the Father's Love for Sinners

Like all of the other attributes or characteristics of our great God, His love belongs to His whole being. It is equally true that His divine essence is in His love. All His divine perfections belong eternally to His essential being. God's attributes must never be thought of as appendages, or parts of God tacked onto Him. This means that God's love is not merely something He possesses as much as it is something He is (1 John 4:8).

The Bible speaks in universal terms of God's infinite love for sinners. Without doubt the most familiar verse in the entire Bible serves as a pattern for dozens of other passages. "For God so loved the world that He gave His only begotten Son, that whoever believes in Him should not perish but have everlasting life" (John 3:16, NKJV).

God's love is given much attention in the New Testament, and it is repeatedly demonstrated in the Old Testament as well. God's sovereign choice of Israel as a nation for His special use was based upon His love for them (Deut. 7:7-8; Hosea 11:1). Hosea 1–3 illustrates God's love even for those who rejected Him.

Scripture makes no distinction between sinners in their unregenerate state when it comes to God's love for them. The sovereign God loved and still loves them all. In addition to the clear statements of Scripture, proof of God's universal love is also found in His universal provision for the "ungodly" (Rom. 5:6-8) without any restriction.

The universal, sovereign love of God is also seen in Paul's description of Him as the Savior "who desires all men to be saved and to come to the knowledge of the truth" (1 Tim. 2:4, NASB), or again, in Peter's statement that He is "not willing that any should perish but that all should come to repentance" (2 Peter 3:9).

No, Scripture does not say that God is benevolent to all people but loves only the elect. The sovereign God's love for sinners is not a truth for believers alone. Of course, the Bible teaches that God hates sin and will indeed pour out His wrath on sinners not saved by His grace. But the sovereign God's hatred of sin does not mean He does not love all sinners.

God the Son's Death for Sinners

Did the Lord Jesus Christ die in the stead of every member of Adam's lost race? Or did He die as a substitute only for those who believe in Him?

On the one hand, there are some passages of Scripture which speak of Christ's dying for specified groups:

Isaiah 53:5 — "He was pierced *for our transgressions.*"
Matthew 1:21 — "He will save *His people* from their sins."
John 10:15 — "I lay down My life *for the sheep.*"
Acts 20:28 — "*the church of God* which He purchased with His own blood."
Ephesians 5:25 — "Christ also loved the church and *gave Himself for her.*"

On the other hand, many passages of Scripture tell us He died for all:

Luke 19:10 — "The Son of man has come *to seek and to save that which was lost.*"
John 1:29 — "Behold! The Lamb of God who takes away *the sin of the world.*"
Romans 5:6 — "Christ died for *the ungodly.*"
2 Corinthians 5:19 — "God was in Christ *reconciling the world to Himself.*"

1 Timothy 2:6— "[Christ] gave Himself as a *ransom for all*."
Hebrews 2:9—"[Christ tasted] death *for every one*."
1 John 2:2—"[Christ is] the propitiation for our sins . . . and *for those of the whole world*."
1 John 4:14—"The Father has sent the Son to be the *Savior of the world*."

What are we to make of this twofold teaching that the sovereign Son died for specific individuals, and yet He died for all? It should be noted that nowhere does Scripture teach that Christ died *only* for certain individuals. He certainly died for Israel's transgression, to save His people, for His sheep, and for the church, but that does not mean He died *only* for these. The same Scripture teaches He died for all. Jesus came to call sinners to repentance (Luke 5:32). He came to seek and to save the lost—whoever they may be (Luke 19:10). He died for all the ungodly (Rom. 5:6).

The Gospel message we are to share with sinners includes three essentials: (1) the sinner's lost condition, (2) the Savior's death in the sinner's place, and (3) the need to trust the Savior alone for eternal life.

Those who believe that Christ died only for *some* people cannot and should not, in all honesty, fully personalize the entire Gospel message. They can personalize the first element of the message, saying to the person they are seeking to win to Christ, "Everyone is a sinner and guilty before God, including you and me." But when it comes to the second essential element, they cannot say, "God loves you and sent His Son to die for *you*." Honesty requires them to say, "God loves sinners and sent His Son to die for elect sinners." This aspect of the message cannot be personalized because the messenger does not know whether or not the sinner being addressed is elect. The third essential part of the Gospel message *can be* personalized: "If you acknowledge yourself as a lost, hopeless, helpless, guilty sinner before God and trust His Son as your Savior, He will give *you* eternal life."

Limited redemptionists cannot totally personalize all aspects of the Gospel. They can personalize the sin part of the Gospel message since they believe all are sinners, just as the unlimited redemptionists do. They must generalize part of the second essential

29

element of Christ's substitutionary death, because no one knows before salvation who the elect are except God. They may again personalize the third element of faith in the Gospel message.

Is it important to personalize the Gospel of God's saving grace? Isn't it enough to personalize the sin part and the faith part? Does it really make that much difference? Yes, it does make a difference. It is very important to personalize all aspects of the Gospel message. If Christ did not die for that person with whom we are sharing the Gospel, how can we genuinely offer them a Savior? According to the limited view, Christ is not their Savior if they are not elect. Our message must be truth: Jesus Christ is the way, the truth, and the life for everyone. To be consistent, those holding a limited redemptionist view should tell an individual, "Jesus, as the Savior, died only for the elect."

The Bible stresses the need for sinners to trust the finished work of Christ in their stead. No one has ever passed from death unto life because they believed that they themselves were guilty sinners but that Christ died for *others*. As we share the Gospel message, we must be convinced that we are making a legitimate offer to all. Christ personally died for everyone we meet. Personal response to that offer results in the marvelous gift of salvation.

God the Holy Spirit's Regeneration of Sinners

Apart from God the Father's love for sinners and God the Son's death for sinners, there would have been no provision of salvation. Apart from God the Spirit's application of the finished work of Christ, there would be no saved sinners.

The Spirit of God convicts sinners, showing them their need of Christ, breaking their stubborn wills, and making them willing to believe. In short, the Spirit regenerates us. He imparts divine life to those who are dead in trespasses and sin, without God and without hope. And He performs this marvelous work of grace through the Word of God.

While the Father and the Son are both said to give life to believing sinners (James 1:17-18; John 5:21-24), the work of regeneration seems to be especially related to the Holy Spirit. When Nicodemus asked how a person could be born again, Jesus told him, "Unless one is born of water and the Spirit, he cannot enter into the kingdom of God" (John 3:5). In the same way Paul told Titus the sinner's salvation was true because "He saved us . . . by the washing of regeneration and renewing of the Holy Spirit" (Titus 3:5).

How good to know that God the Spirit gives life to sinners. The ambassador for Christ does not have the responsibility of convicting the sinner or of saving him and giving him life; that is the sovereign God's work. Our role is to share the Word of God which He then uses sovereignly and supernaturally to bring sinners to Himself. The witnessing believer draws upon the power of the omnipotent God. We do not minister in our strength alone, but we trust in His power to melt the most hardened heart.

Sharing God's Message of Salvation with Sinners

Daily the news media is crowded with bad and sad news. We Christians, however, have the best and greatest news in all the world: God loves all sinners; Christ died for all sinners; the Spirit of God will give eternal life to each sinner who receives the Lord Jesus Christ as his/her substitute for sin.

The Human Messenger

The sovereign God has been pleased to call upon His people to be laborers together with Him. In fact, it is His sovereign will that each born-again child of God be a witness for Him. The Bible describes believers as ambassadors for Christ (2 Cor. 5:20). Serving as an ambassador is a high and holy privilege; it is also an awesome responsibility.

Believers are not asked if we want to be ambassadors for Christ. We already are His representatives in an antagonistic world. God has said so. The questions before each of us are these: What kind of an ambassador am I? How can I be a better ambassador?

If we would follow the Apostle Paul's example, we would be motivated to be God's witness by the command of Christ. It was "the love of Christ" (2 Cor. 5:14) which constrained him to take the message of God's saving grace to those who had not heard.

31

Paul was brought to the place where he saw himself as a debtor to those outside of Christ (Rom. 1:14). God's love for all and Christ's death for all brought Paul to the place where he could say he was "ready to preach the gospel" (Rom. 1:15) and was "not ashamed" to do it (v. 16).

The believer, like the surgeon's glove, must be *empty* of self, *cleansed* of "all defilement of flesh and spirit" (2 Cor. 7:1), and *filled* or controlled by the Spirit to be used most effectively in the salvation of sinners. A believer does not need to have formal training in the Bible and in theology to be a good witness for Christ. Although formal training makes us better tools in God's hand, we need only to know and to articulate the three essentials which we embraced when we trusted the Savior: All are sinners by nature and by choice and stand guilty before the holy God (Rom. 3:23; 6:23); God loved the world of sinners so much He sent His Son to die in their place (Rom. 5:8; 1 Cor. 15:3); when the sinner accepts the finished work of Christ as the payment for his/her sin, God gives eternal life (John 1:12; 3:16; Acts 4:12).

The Divine Message

The Scriptures present the Savior as both substitute and sovereign Lord. To deny either one of these truths is to put one's self outside the historic orthodox Christian faith. Christ *is* God's substitute in the sinner's place and He *is* God's eternal sovereign Son. He could not have been the former if He had not been the latter.

No one is called upon to make Christ the divinely appointed substitute for sin. God the Father has already done that. In the plan of God, the Son was slain from the foundation of the world (Rev. 13:8). Christ came to seek and save the lost (Luke 19:10). At His death on the cross, He was made to be "sin on our behalf, that we might become made the righteousness of God in Him" (2 Cor. 5:21). There on Golgotha's hill He bore "our sins in His body on the cross" (1 Peter 2:24).

When an unsaved person trusts the Savior for salvation, that person does not, by an act of faith, *make* Christ his or her substitute for sin. That work was completed 2,000 years ago when Christ died. At the moment of faith, when the sinner trusts the

Savior alone for salvation, God the Father graciously applies the finished substitutionary work of Christ to the individual trusting sinner's account. The substitution was finished at Calvary. The application of that finished work takes place when, in response to the Spirit's convicting work, Christ is received for all that He already is—the sinner's substitute.

Jesus Christ is, and has always been, the sovereign Son of God—the Lord. If He is not the *Lord* Jesus Christ, He cannot be the sinner's Savior. To put it another way, if He is not God, He cannot be our Savior and our sin substitute. He had to be God to make the perfect sacrifice and He had to be man to die, to shed His blood. Since He is God, He is Lord.

Today some sincere, well-meaning people believe that to be born again, the unsaved must not only accept Christ as their substitute for sin, but must also accept Him as Lord of their life. Old sinful habits must be surrendered before Christ will give eternal life. Or at the very least there must be the promise, the intention, the willingness to give them up. Some view this surrender to Christ's lordship over every area of life as a part of the nature of faith. They insist that Christ must be received as the sinner's substitute for sin and also be made absolute Lord of the sinner's life.

Does the Bible teach that Jesus' rightful lordship must be realized in a person's life *before* that one can be saved? Does it really teach that *before* a man can be saved he must stop living with the woman he is not married to? Or must occasional drunkenness be stopped *before* a person can become a Christian? Maybe it's just a habitual liar or cheater who wants to become a Christian. Must these sins be abandoned before the sinner can become a child of God? Lusting after a person of the opposite, or even same, sex is sinful too. Would the one under the control of lust have to stop lusting or at least promise to stop lusting *before* he or she could get saved?

Does the Christ of Scripture, the Christ we share with those who do not know Him, make such demands upon the one outside of Him? What, exactly, must a person do to inherit eternal life? How are we to share Christ and the way of salvation with those who do not know Him?

33

Rather than call sinners to make Jesus their Lord, we need to encourage them to accept Jesus as their Savior. As they accept Him as Savior, they then will be in a position to recognize His claims of lordship in their lives. Eternal issues are at stake here. If there is only one way of salvation for all mankind, how important it is that we know that way and that we articulate it clearly to the lost.

Communicating the Message

We can conclude from Scripture that every believer is to bear witness for Christ. There are two ways to do this—through our manner of life and through what we say, or by life and by lips.

Several qualities should characterize our lives if we would attract people to Jesus. To begin, we need to be *friendly,* showing a genuine interest in people. *Kindness* is an outgrowth of friendliness. Expressions of love and interest are not easily forgotten. We need to win the confidence of those we seek to win to Christ. *Tactfulness* is another important trait to cultivate. We need to be sensitive to the Spirit's leading and people's needs as we relate to them. Jesus began where people were; we must do the same. Finally, we must show *personal interest* in those we want to reach. Again, the example of Jesus as He dealt with the woman at the well (John 4) should be our pattern.

With the way prepared by our actions, what words may we use as we bring a person to the point of decision? The message is threefold. Imagine you are talking to John or Mary who is very interested in knowing how to become a Christian. Here are suggestions of what you may say:

First, "John/Mary, the Bible says, 'All have sinned and fall short of the glory of God' (Rom. 3:23). This sin brings spiritual death, separation from God (Rom. 6:23). Do you believe you are a sinner and cannot save yourself?" After a yes answer, proceed to the next point.

Second, "John/Mary, Christ died for sinners (Rom. 5:8; 1 Cor. 15:3), and that means He died for you. He paid the debt your sin incurred against God. Jesus is the only one who could pay the debt. Because He is the Lord, He could serve as a perfect sacrifice; and because He was a man, He could die. Proof that God the Father accepted Christ's payment is that He arose from the dead. Do you believe this, John/Mary? Do you believe He died for you?"

Third, "John/Mary, you can have a right relationship with God. The Bible says that whoever receives Christ, trusting His finished work as payment for their sin, will never perish but will have everlasting life (John 3:16). Would you like to have this relationship with God and assurance of everlasting life right now? You can have it by receiving Christ, by faith, as your substitute for sin."

Each of the Scripture passages used should be read clearly and slowly from the Bible. Then, ask the person to thank God for their salvation based on the promises in His Word.

The sovereign God saves sinners as saved sinners share the salvation message. This is God's way, and it's a great way. God gives His children the wonderful opportunity to participate with Him in His work. We can see and experience His power in bringing sinners into a right relationship with Himself.

The Bible:
God-Breathed

"Inspiration can only be
predicated of the original writings."
(Basic Theology, p. 72)

CHAPTER FOUR

Biblical Inspiration
and Bible Translation

Richard E. Elkins

C harles Ryrie gives the following definition of biblical inspiration: "God superintended the human authors of the Bible so that they composed and recorded without error His message to mankind in the words of their original writings" (*Basic Theology*, 71). He then asks us to note the key words in that definition.

(1) The word "superintend" allows for the spectrum of relationships God had with the writers and the variety of material. His superintendence was sometimes very direct and sometimes less so, but always it included guarding the writers so that they wrote accurately. (2) The word "composed" shows

that the writers were not passive stenographers to whom God dictated the material, but active writers. (3) "Without error" expresses the Bible's own claim to be truth (John 17:17). (4) Inspiration can only be predicated of the original writings, not to copies or translations, however accurate they may be" (pp. 71–72).

This is a fully adequate definition of inspiration in all points. Yet Bible translators must address a question which is not often considered: Is there *anything* inspired about an accurate translation of the Bible? No. In a strict theological sense, no translation or copy is inspired.

As a result, today and throughout most of the church's history, none of the world's Christians have had access to a text of the Bible which is inspired in the sense Ryrie describes. Even the earliest Christians had only copies or translations of the Old Testament autographs (original manuscripts), and probably only a few of them ever saw any of the New Testament documents. Today all Christians must rely on copies or translations. Of course, a few Christians are able to read biblical texts in the original languages. Even these texts, though, are the product of a long history of textual criticism. Copies of the autographs have been made repeatedly and thus have no absolute theological claim to accuracy or inspiration.

In spite of this limitation, the Spirit of God does use the truth conveyed in our translations as He used the same truth which the autographs conveyed. Down through the centuries God has powerfully used translations of the Word (just as He used the autographs) to bring people to faith and to nurture them. We hide the Word in our hearts as did the psalmist, and we believe, with good reason, that it can keep us from doing wrong. We handle and revere our copies and our translations as if they were the original manuscripts. We derive our faith and Christian behavior from them just as if they were, indeed, the inspired autographs.

Only accurately translated meaning allows this effective use of Scripture. When a translation is faithful in all respects to the original source document, the meaning of that source document will have been transferred without loss or skewing. So, in handling

God's Word, accurately translated meaning is essential.

This requirement may seem obvious, but the history of Bible translation is replete with examples of translators trying to mimic the wording of the Greek or Hebrew text, but failing to transfer its meaning. Based on a wrong understanding of the nature of language, these translators have misapplied the doctrine of inspiration. Since the very words of the autographs were inspired, they merely reproduced those words as closely as possible, without communicating the message. But if reproduction of words is inadequate, how then is meaning accurately and faithfully transferred in translation?

All language (including the biblical languages when they were spoken) is composed of three formal systems. Every spoken language has a sound or phonological system, a grammar system, and a meaning or semantic system. A modern-day missionary translator of the New Testament into one of the many unwritten languages of the world must study and analyze all three of the systems of that target language before beginning translation. He must discover how speakers group the various sounds into what linguists call *phonemes,* each of which may be represented in writing by a symbol, a letter of the alphabet, so that the language may be written accurately. A translator must also study the grammar system of the target language and become thoroughly familiar with its intricacies.

More difficult and elusive, but even more necessary, is translating the meaning, or semantic system, of the target language. The meaning system of a language, like its phonological system and its grammar system, is idiosyncratic to that language. The formal meaning or semantic system of a language refers to the way its innate lexicon or dictionary is structured in the mind of a speaker. This lexicon is a mental list of words and word roots with information about their various senses along with facts about co-occurrence or collocational restrictions. The lexicon also includes idioms and figures of speech with their meanings and collocational restrictions.

A word with its particular senses in one language rarely has an identical match in any other language. For instance, the word *hand* in English has a number of senses. *Hand* may denote a body part (in "to have a cut on the hand"); it may mean "to help" or "to applaud" (in "to give someone a hand"); or it may be used as a synecdoche (in "all hands on deck"). In Manobo, a language of the southern Philippines for which I translated, only the first sense would have an equivalent in the semantic structure of belad (hand). To "give a hand" would seem gruesome and bizarre in that language.

Invariably a beginner tends to encode and decode statements in the new language using the formal semantic structure of his native tongue. I will never forget the howls of laughter from my Manobo friends when I observed that a particular board they were using in building construction was "weak." In Manobo the adjective *weak* can be used only to describe animate creatures. It was like saying in English, "That board is nervous." Imposing the semantic structure of *weak* in English onto the word for *weak* in Manobo led to a ludicrous skewing of my meaning. My intention could be expressed accurately only in terms of their own semantic system. Even when the source language and the target language are closely related, statements encoded according to the semantic rules of the source language are interpreted according to the semantic rules of the target language and are misunderstood.

A translator would never consider imposing the phonological system or the grammar system of a source language onto those same systems of a target language; but, in a formal translation, he often imposes the semantic system of the source language onto the target language with a resultant skewing of meaning. If a translator's goal is to transfer accurately the meaning of his source text, he must respect equally the semantic systems of the source language and the target language. This means that the meaning of the source text must be interpreted with respect to the formal semantic system of the source language and then re-encoded in the target language with respect to the formal semantic system of the target language. Even though these semantic systems do not match, if translation is done accurately, meaning will remain constant.

During the translation of the Western Bukidnon Manobo New Testament we found that biblical idioms and figures of speech, when rendered formally, were usually misinterpreted by speakers of Manobo. Early in my translation, because the words and phrasing of English translations (and often of the Greek text) were so familiar to me, I often tried to make a Manobo phrase resemble its Greek or English counterpart, without first checking to determine if it had the same sense as the Greek original. An example was our first rendering of a portion of the Revelation to the Apostle John. We translated:

> After that I saw a great number of people who, because they were so many, could not be counted. They had come from every kingdom and tribe and race and every language. They were standing before the seat of God and before the Lamb. They were dressed in white and held leafy branches in their hands. They shouted loudly saying, "Salvation to our God who sits on his seat of ruling and also to the Lamb" (Rev. 7:9-10).

When I read the passage to one of my neighbors, he responded, "It can't possibly mean what it says!"

"What does it say?" I asked.

"It sounds like all those people are concerned that God is not saved, and they are shouting that they hope that salvation comes to Him and to the Lamb."

The problem was that the phrase "salvation to our God" is a Hebraism, a praise idiom in Hebrew used in doxologies, which had come into common use in the Koine Greek of early Jewish Christians. This praise idiom, part of the meaning system of Hebrew and Koine Greek, could not be understood properly in Manobo when reproduced formally. We had to let the sense of the idiom be our guide.

In our final rendering we translated *soteria* (salvation) with a verbal expression. Since no Manobo verb stem meant "save" in the biblical sense, we chose the expression "free from punishment" for "save" here and in similar contexts throughout the New Testament.

In addition to the idea of "salvation," the idiom contained two other components: First, the people of the multitude were praising God and the Lamb. Also, the cause for praise was that God and the Lamb had saved them. So we translated: "They shouted loudly,

'Praise God who sits on his seat of ruling and praise also the Lamb because they are the ones who freed us from punishment.' "

Another example in which a disregard of the semantic structures of the source language and of the target language can lead to a misleading translation is in the Greek use of the preposition, *dia* ("through" or "by means of") with the genitive in Galatians 1:1. One modern translation of the verse reads: "Paul an apostle — sent neither by human commission nor from human authorities, but *through* Jesus Christ and God the Father, who raised him from the dead" (NRSV). The statement in question is "sent . . . through Jesus Christ and God the Father." In English, the preposition *through* means that the object of the preposition is either a location ("through the door") or an intermediary ("He made his request through John."). But in the above rendering of Galatians 1:1, the objects of the preposition cannot possibly have either sense. F.F. Bruce has written:

> Paul hardly means that Jesus Christ was the intermediary through whom he received his apostleship. One could indeed conceive his meaning to be that he received it from God the Father through Jesus Christ, but that is excluded in the present context because *theou patros* (God the Father) stands under the regimen of *dia* as much as does *theou Christou*. It may be concluded, then, that while *dia* before *anthropou* (human) means "through" in the sense of mediation, it is used in the more general sense of agency when it precedes "Jesus Christ and God the Father" (F.F. Bruce, *The Epistle to the Galatians: a Commentary on the Greek Text*, New International Greek Testament Commentary [Grand Rapids: Eerdmans, 1982], 72).

Burton also comments, "Taken together, therefore, the whole expression bears the meaning 'directly from Jesus Christ and God the Father' " (Ernest De Witt Burton, *A Critical and Exegetical Commentary on the Epistle to the Galatians*, The International Critical Commentary [Edinburgh: T & T Clark, 1921], 5). The Bauer, Arndt, and Gingrich lexicon lists one sense of *dia* with the genitive as "of the originator of an action" (Bauer, Arndt, and Gingrich, *A*

Greek-English Lexicon of the New Testament and Other Early Christian Literature, 2nd ed. [Chicago: Univ. of Chicago Press, 1981], 180). The translators of most English versions have understood and respected this particular aspect of the semantic structure of *dia* with the genitive case and rendered it with its proper meaning in English. The *King James Version* renders: "Paul, an apostle, not of men, neither by man, but by Jesus Christ and God the Father, who raised him from the dead." The *New International Version* translates: "Paul, an apostle—sent not from men nor by man, but by Jesus Christ and God the Father."

Clearly, a translation into Manobo or into English carries the same challenge. Meaning can be faithfully and accurately communicated in a language only in terms of its own semantic structure. Translations of the Scriptures are faithful, accurate, and fully usable by the Spirit of God to the degree to which the translators have respected the semantic structures of both the source language and the target language.

For the translator this requires careful study and exegesis of the biblical texts, with the help of the published studies of competent scholars. It also requires careful study of the semantic structure of the target language and the development of a sense of how things are said in that language. A translator must, to the best of his ability, discover what the source text means and then render it meaningfully and accurately in the target language. Meaning must be king for the translator. The formal structures of a source language are useful only as they offer guidance to what a text means in that language. Reproducing them in a target language translation can result in wrong meaning, ambiguous meaning, or no meaning.

It is the meaning of the biblical texts, accurately and faithfully transmitted, which the Spirit of God has always used among and through His people. It is our responsibility, therefore, to translate carefully and to choose the versions which we read and use for ministry with care. Rather than relying on one "favorite version" exclusively, often we should consult a number of excellent translations. Even the *Ryrie Study Bible,* for instance, is available in various versions. The Word in our day is still living and active, and we all desire to walk in the freedom which its truth offers by understanding its meaning most accurately.

"If God originated language for
the purpose of communication...
He saw to it that the means (language)
was sufficient to sustain the purpose."
(*Basic Theology*, p. 113)

CHAPTER FIVE

The Importance of Context in Biblical Interpretation

Howard P. McKaughan

Semantics is the study of meaning in language. But what is "meaning"? Lewis Carroll, in a well-known passage from his *Through the Looking Glass*, gives us an interesting insight:

"That shows that there are three hundred and sixty-four days when you might get un-birthday presents."

"Certainly," said Alice.

"And only one for birthday presents, you know. There's glory for you!"

"I don't know what you mean by 'glory,' " Alice said.

Humpty Dumpty smiled contemptuously. "Of course you don't—till I tell you. I meant 'there's a nice knockdown argument for you.' "

"But 'glory' doesn't mean 'a nice knockdown argument,' "
Alice objected.

"When I use a word," Humpty Dumpty said in a rather
scornful tone, "it means just what I choose it to mean—
neither more nor less."

"The question is," said Alice, "whether you can make
words mean so many different things."

"The question is," said Humpty Dumpty, "which is to be
master—that's all."

We tend to agree with Alice: words have their own meaning, apart
from the user's desires. But we would be mistaken were we to
dismiss Humpty Dumpty's final remark. Users influence meaning
of words.

The passage from Lewis Carroll brings into focus two major
divisions in semantics: lexical semantics and pragmatics. Lexical
semantics refers to word equivalencies—what words mean. Pragmatics is the study of the relationship between the speakers (and
hearers) and their use of words—what they mean by words. So
lexical semantics deals with the question, "What does this word
mean?" This is the study of dictionary meaning, the study of
words, phrases, and sentences from their structural use, meaning,
or content derived from form. Pragmatics, on the other hand,
answers the question, "What do you mean by this word?" It includes the speaker's (and hearers') backgrounds, attitudes, and beliefs, their understanding of the context in which a sentence is
spoken, and their knowledge of how language is used to inform,
persuade, and even mislead.

Semantics, then, is a large and very complicated field of research. Its study long predates the formation of linguistics as a
discipline. It has been the subject of philosophers for thousands of
years. Plato and Aristotle made contributions from ancient
Greece, and today's philosophers continue to struggle with the
subject. To understand semantics one should have knowledge
from logic, mathematics, and philosophy, and also from psycholo-
gy and linguistics.

It is impossible to summarize semantics here, or to even scratch
the surface of this fascinating area of research. But we can outline

a few things that will underscore, if not add, to what Dr. Ryrie has said about exegesis and hermeneutics in *Basic Theology*.

The Importance of Context

In language, meaning cannot be studied apart from context. Context may consist of individual words, of sentences, or of whole discourses and may involve the speaker's and the hearer's use of those words, sentences, and discourses.

Words in Their Immediate Context

It is surprising how much meaning we get from the immediate context of words. Take the word *run* as an example. Scripture uses this word not only in its primary sense of a person in rapid locomotion on his feet, but also in the following senses: a river runs (Ezra 8:15, NASB); branches run over a wall (Gen. 49:22); sores run (flow) (Lev. 15:3); one runs the way of the Lord's commandments (Ps. 119:32); feet run to evil (Prov. 1:16); those that wait on the Lord shall run and not get tired (Isa. 40:31); a nation shall run to you (Isa. 55:5); eyelids run (flow) with water (Jer. 9:18); tears run down like a river (Lam. 2:18); the eyes of the Lord run (range) to and fro throughout the earth (Zech. 4:10); we are enjoined in several places in the New Testament to run (live) as we ought (see 1 Cor. 9:24, 26; Gal. 2:2; 5:7; Phil. 2:16; Heb. 12:1; 1 Peter 4:4).

Words have multiple senses in their meanings, and we distinguish which sense is in focus by the context. If the context does not distinguish the meaning, then we have ambiguity. For example: *The captain corrected the list* may mean either that he corrected a list of the crew or that he corrected the angle of the ship. *The chicken is ready to eat* may mean that we are about to have dinner, or that the chicken has just hatched and is old enough to pick at the small seeds.

In the sentence *John ate locusts and wild honey*, John refers to a specific male individual. The position of the word John makes him the subject of the sentence; the meaning of the verb makes him the actor. The action depicted is past; at least John is not now eating.

The wider context, including this chapter about context in semantics and biblical interpretation, explains who John is. That context, plus the locusts and wild honey, immediately brings John the Baptist to mind. Further, the sentence suggests the location of the action. Certainly it is not in the city (although it could have been if we had only this one sentence). There were wild bees, for there was wild honey. That the diet was not ordinary is indicated by the very mention of the specifics.

The pragmatics of the situation of the sentence is also of interest. What is the intent of the writer of the sentence, and what does that tell us about John? Probably the intent was to give us a feel for this prophet in the wilderness by letting us know that John was living off the land, that he was not dependent upon others, and that he was a rugged individual (note the further description of clothing in the immediate context of Matt. 3:4). To understand any discourse, we must study the immediate and wider contexts.

Grammatical Context

Within lexical semantics we must deal not only with the referential characteristics of a word, but also with its grammatical context or syntactic meaning. The referential characteristics are the real world referents or concepts. *Tree* refers to the object in the real world so designated. Syntactic meaning refers to the grammatical relationships between words.

To get at the meaning of a sentence or paragraph, we must know the meaning of the syntactic (grammatical) structure. We must identify the subject and its role, the object and its role, each modifier and its role, and so on. The importance of grammatical context is best illustrated with an example of structural or syntactic ambiguity. For instance, *Richard saw the people with binoculars* could mean that: Richard had binoculars and he saw people as he looked through them, or the people Richard saw had binoculars in contrast to others who did not. In the first case, the prepositional phrase is adjunct to the verb while in the second case, *with binoculars* modifies the noun *people*. This example of ambiguity may give the reader an understanding of the need to study linguistics in order to translate the Bible meaningfully.

Principles of Biblical Interpretation Presuppose Context

Dr. Ryrie has given us several important principles for biblical interpretation:

1. *Interpret grammatically.* Since words are the vehicles of thoughts, and since the meaning of any passage must be determined by a study of the words therein and their relationships in the sentences, determining the grammatical sense of the text must be the starting point of normal interpretation.
2. *Interpret contextually.* Words and sentences do not stand in isolation; therefore, the context must be studied in order to see the relation that each verse sustains to that which precedes and to that which follows. Involved are the immediate context and the theme and scope of the whole book.
3. *Compare Scripture with Scripture.* The dual authorship of the Bible makes it necessary not only to know the human author's meaning but also God's. God's meaning may not be fully revealed in the original human author's writing but is revealed when Scripture is compared with Scripture. . . .
4. *Recognize the progressiveness of revelation.* . . . In the process of revealing His message to man, God may add or even change in one era what He had given in another. Obviously the New Testament adds much that was not revealed in the Old. What God revealed as obligatory at one time may be rescinded at another (as the prohibition of eating pork, once binding on God's people, now rescinded, 1 Tim. 4:3) (*Basic Theology*, 114).

These hermeneutical principles parallel the role of context in semantics. Context for semantics is primary. Though Charles Ryrie mentions the grammatical sense of the text and then the contextual sense, every one of his four principles is actually contextual. The grammatical meaning is derived from the grammatical context. The lexical sense of the words comes from the immediate and wider word context. Even the pragmatics, which Ryrie's third and fourth principles address, is based on the context of the situation. Ryrie's third principle deals with the authors' intent (both the human and the divine). Progressive revelation must consider the wider context of the entire Bible. Readers seeking to rightly divide the Word of Truth (2 Tim. 2:15) are required to carefully study meaning in context.

Language Presupposes Normal Interpretation

The complications of context in semantics may discourage the biblical interpreter. With syntactic meaning, multiple word senses, author intent, cultural background differences, and conversational maxims to consider, how can we reach the real meaning? Consider the following statements that help to explain the purpose of language in the first place.

> God gave man language for the purpose of being able to communicate with him. God created man in His image which included the power of speech in order that God might reveal His truth to man and that man might in turn offer worship and prayer to God.
>
> Two ramifications flow from this idea. First, if God originated language for the purpose of communication, and if God is all-wise, then we may believe that He saw to it that the means (language) was sufficient to sustain the purpose (communication). Second, it follows that God would Himself use and expect man to use language in its normal sense. The Scriptures do not call for some special use of language, implying that they communicate on some "deeper" or special level unknown to other avenues of communication (Ryrie, *Basic Theology*, 113).

These insightful observations again directly parallel the linguistic approach to the study of semantics. We do not look for hidden meanings when the primary sense of a word makes sense in its context. Ryrie concludes:

It is God who desired to give man His Word. It is God who also gave the gift of language so He could fulfill that desire. He gave us His Word in order to communicate, not confound. We should seek to understand that communication plainly, for that is the normal way beings communicate (*Basic Theology*, 115).

In God's desire to give us His Word, He did more than give us language in order to communicate through the written Word; He also gave us His Son, the Living Word. Jesus is the very expression of God and the ultimate communication in revealing God to us. That is why He is called "the Word" in John 1:1. The Greek term *logos* signifies more than our English language unit *word*. It is closer to what linguists refer to as *utterance* — any stretch of speech bounded by pauses. This Word, or utterance, existed before language, but He became flesh and lived among us. In doing so, John 1:18 says, "He has explained Him" (Jesus has explained God). Furthermore, when Jesus left the world physically, He sent the Holy Spirit to teach us (John 14:26).

We should not hesitate to read the Bible because we are afraid to interpret its meaning. But we do need to give it more than a cursory reading. We must look to the immediate and wider contexts, seeking out the correct biblical interpretation. We must look to the Holy Spirit as our teacher in rightly dividing the Word of Truth.

Contextual Illustration

Let me cite one more illustration of the importance of studying meaning in context. In Luke 14:26 Jesus says, "If anyone comes to Me, and does not hate his own father and mother and wife and children and brothers and sisters, yes, and even his own life, he cannot be My disciple" (NASB). In order to understand what "hate" means in this passage we should look at its use elsewhere in Scripture. Hate in this passage is used in contrast to love, and in this specific context, hate means "not to love, to love less, to slight" (*Robinson, Greek and English Lexicon of the New Testament* [New York: Harper & Brothers, 1872], 505). Robinson cites Matthew 6:24, Luke 16:13, John 12:25, and Romans 9:13 as other examples of this usage.

The wider biblical context clinches the meaning of *hate* in Luke 14:26. Matthew 10:37 reads: "He who loves father or mother more than Me is not worthy of Me; and he who loves son or daughter more than Me is not worthy of Me." This verse is in the context of Jesus telling His disciples that He did not come to bring peace, but a sword. He says He came to set a man against his father, and a daughter against her mother (Matt. 10:34-36). So if a person listens to family and thereby refuses to accept Christ, he or she cannot be worthy of Christ. An individual must accept what Jesus says above what his or her family may say. *The Ryrie Study Bible* note on Luke 14:26 reads: "This saying does not justify malice or ill will toward one's family, but it means that devotion to family must take second place to one's devotion to Christ." And on Matthew 10:34, Ryrie notes, "Christ's mission involves tension, persecution, death. The gospel divides families (Micah 7:6). The world will experience true peace only when the King returns again to rule (Isa. 2:4)."

Thus the specific and wider contexts help us understand the word *hate* in Luke 14:26. The intent of the divine and human authors here is to declare that Christ Jesus must be placed before even family in deciding to accept Him as Savior or in living the Christian life.

Conclusion

The principles of utilizing context in semantics, in both lexical and pragmatic aspects, not only assist greatly in biblical interpretation, but are essential for it. These principles support Dr. Ryrie's approach of following a normal (literal) path of meaning (interpretation), holding to the primary sense of words and sentences unless the context demands otherwise.

The nature of language reflects the character of our God who longs to communicate with us. The Bible is a loving gift of God who wants us to understand His truth. He has created us and language in such a way that we are able to understand the Bible, His instrument of communication to us.

"Theology is the discovery,
systematizing, and presentation
of the truths about God."
(Basic Theology, p. 15)

CHAPTER SIX

Theology and Exegesis

Elliott E. Johnson

T
he truths of God's Word form the foundation for our lives now and throughout eternity. Through systematic correlation of the biblical teachings on any given subject, we are able to derive a clear understanding of what the Bible teaches on that topic. However, God has not chosen to reveal His truth in the format of systematic theology. So it becomes necessary to correlate "the data of biblical revelation as a whole in order to exhibit systematically the total picture of God's self-revelation" (Ryrie, *Basic Theology,* 14).

When a particular doctrine becomes a focus of debate, biblical scholars must be especially careful to examine its source. Is the doctrine a valid teaching found in the Bible or merely a derivation from a system of truths? For instance, does the Bible teach a limited or unlimited atonement? Is the time of the Rapture directly stated in Scripture or is it an inference drawn from a dispensational system? Can the Spirit's role in spirituality be specified from the Bible?

The tension between theology and exegesis appears in Ryrie's treatment of the doctrine of the filling of the Holy Spirit. How can a believer be filled with the Spirit? (Eph. 5:18) The biblical answer to this question is not spelled out but must be inferred through the use of other passages which specify the condition of true spirituality. A Bible student who grapples with such an issue might follow Ryrie's approach in handling this doctrine. His model may give the student of Scripture some of the insights necessary to use the Word of God to develop theology through exegesis.

The Tension Between Theology and Exegesis

In *The Holy Spirit* (Chicago: Moody, 1976) Ryrie writes, "Of all the outlines on the conditions for the filling of the Spirit, none is more simple, scriptural, and to the point than Lewis Sperry Chafer's in *He That Is Spiritual.* It is this outline we follow in detailing what is meant by obedience as the condition for being filled with the Holy Spirit." The issue in question features the use of three Pauline texts in specifying the conditions of true spirituality: Ephesians 4:30 (KJV), "grieve not the Holy Spirit"; 1 Thessalonians 5:19, "quench not the Spirit"; and Galatians 5:16, "walk in the Spirit." Chafer's adoption of the view of these as "conditions" raises two questions: (1) Is spirituality conditioned on human response? and (2) Do these scattered verses specify conditions of spirituality? Ryrie addresses both questions. His subsequent writings show development in his thought, but his choice of "filling" as the basis of "spirituality" in practice remains unchanged.

In response to the question of spirituality being conditioned on human response, Ryrie states, "God does not ask believers either to tarry or to pray for filling. This does not mean, however, that filling is given without conditions. In a simple word the condition is obedience" (*The Holy Spirit*, 95). Later, in *Basic Theology*, he writes:

If filling relates to the control of the Spirit in one's life (whether in the sense of God's sovereign seizing of a person or of a sustained control that results in character), then filling is related to yieldedness. . . . I can check my willingness but I cannot manipulate His activities. As one matures, his knowledge and perspectives will deepen and broaden. New areas that need to be yielded will come to light (p. 378).

Is this development based on exegesis, or on theology, or both?

In discussion of the second question of whether the scattered verses specify conditions of spirituality, Ryrie's early writings reflect some tension. Chafer uses 1 Thessalonians 5:19 to epitomize "dedication of life." Ryrie responds, "Exegetically and contextually the verse primarily has to do with quenching prophesyings in the public assembly of the church. . . . Though this is the meaning exegetically, Chafer has taken the verse to stand for the theological truth that dedication is . . . the basic policy of one's relation to the will of God *in toto*" (*The Holy Spirit*, 95). In what sense does 1 Thessalonians 5:19 stand for a truth it doesn't express?

Again, Ryrie captures Chafer's use of Ephesians 4:30 as a summary of victory over sin in daily experience. He then adds, "Exegetically the verse does concern the effect of certain sins in the person's relation to the Spirit. . . . It is clear that sins of speech are those that particularly grieve the Spirit so that His ministry in the believer's life is hindered. Theologically we may permit the verse to represent and remind of any sin which grieves the Spirit. . . . When He is grieved by sin, He is not in control" (*The Holy Spirit*, 98). How valid is it to use exegetical messages to represent broader theological meanings? What is the basis for such a theological representation? This is an important consideration since we need to know how to use the Word of God in our lives.

A Historic Consideration of Theology and Exegesis

At the turn of the seventeenth century, a sharp division emerged in the perception of the task of interpretation which has influenced twentieth-century hermeneutics, and may shed some light on the problem at hand. A division arose between Johann S. Semler and Johann A. Ernesti, now regarded as the fathers of "general" biblical hermeneutics. Both sought to draw up general rules for the interpretation of all writings, including the Bible. They disagreed, though, on how to handle historical considerations.

To Semler, historical factors distinguished the ancient view of a given subject shared by an author in that culture from a modern view of the same subject interpreted by a reader. Ernesti, on the other hand, considered historical factors only to the extent that the author addressed a subject in the text. While Semler's position claimed the vast majority of scholars in his day, and formed the basis of a historical-critical reading of a text, Ernesti's view has been perpetuated in what is called a historical-literary reading.

Hirsch builds upon Ernesti's distinction between the understanding of *meaning* and the explanation of *significance*. For example, when Joshua (10:13) says "the sun stopped," meaning affirms that God acted miraculously to allow Joshua to complete the conquest. It doesn't consider the action as related to an ancient cosmology or to a modern cosmology. But meaning does include more than simply "God acted miraculously." The actual action of God is in question based on the language used.

Ernesti and Hirsch would see exegesis as an understanding of a text's meaning, and would see theology as an explanation of a text's significance. In Joshua 10:13, exegesis would consider whether "the sun was eclipsed" or "the sun stood still," but theology would consider the significance of the passage in relation to miracles (subject matter). Thus a person who seeks to derive doctrine from the passages mentioned above in the discussion of the Holy Spirit, must determine not only what the words say grammatically but also what significance they reflect. It is important to recognize that until we have done legitimate exegesis on a passage, we cannot address its theological significance. This approach must be applied to the topic of spirituality, a subject in which believers have a vital interest yet which is addressed comprehensively in no single passage.

A Summary of the Issues in Tension

Exegesis is the most direct use of the Bible and its authoritative message, but careful attention must be directed to what is meant historically.

Statements limited by the historical. First Thessalonians 5:19 is a part of Paul's final instructions, referring both to an immediate situation in the church (5:12-22) and to Paul's relationship with the believers (5:25-27). So Ryrie's conclusion is valid that "exegetically and contextually the verse primarily has to do with quenching prophesyings in the public assembly of the church. . . . The church in Thessalonica was frowning on any manifestation of the Spirit that was in any way out of the ordinary" (*The Holy Spirit*, 95). According to Semler, the text's meaning would be identified in the extended historical consideration of the problem. According to Ernesti, the text would refer to the Thessalonian experience, but only as a type of problem.

In such a literary-historical view of the epistle, what type of problem is it? While the problem is particular, it is expressed in terms of quenching the Spirit's manifestations in public prophecies. Rather than quench, they are to test and discern whether it is good or evil (5:21-22). So the "quenching" is due to a lack of discernment.

This is a different type of meaning than Chafer develops: "The Spirit is 'quenched' by any unyieldedness to the revealed will of God" (*He That Is Spiritual* [Grand Rapids: Zondervan, 1974], 86). This "quenching" results from a lack of yieldedness or an unwillingness. Chafer uses the verse for its wording rather than its meaning. The theology is undoubtedly true, but not because this verse says so.

Statements directed to a historical situation. Ephesians 4:30 is also related to a specific reference in the church's experiences. Again Ryrie recognizes the context: "Exegetically the verse does concern the effect of certain sins . . . of speech. Useless speech (v. 29), bitterness, wrath, anger, clamor, and evil speaking (v. 31) are mentioned" (*The Holy Spirit*, 98). But is the list intended to be an exclusive reference to what grieves the Spirit, or is it only an occasional reference to what is hindering the Spirit? May not any sin hinder the working of the Spirit? The fact that it is an occasional reference to what hinders the Spirit is supported on the basis of the introductory command against unwholesome talk (4:29). That was a particular problem in this church at Ephesus. The reason this sin is so dangerous is that it grieves and thus hinders the Spirit's ministry, even though He seals us until the day when redemption will be completed. In other words, a grieved Spirit is grieved in the very ministry of sealing for which He permanently resides. Can such conflict with the Spirit possibly support the will of God? Here the textual statement readily supports the general theological truth that the Spirit who indwells the sinning believer must turn from His blessed ministry through the believer, to a pleading ministry to him.

Theology is the more comprehensive treatment of the subject matter of the Bible than is exegesis. A theological discussion of the subject matter correlates the many treatments of the subject in various passages with which exegesis commonly deals. The subject of spirituality presents an example of the problems that theology must address. After the exegesis is complete, the significance and correlation must be determined.

Chafer addressed this central subject in his classic work, *He That Is Spiritual.* He chose 1 Corinthians 2:15 as the basic discussion of a spiritual man, and from logic, he affirmed that spirituality is the product of "a real adjustment of the Spirit" (*He That Is Spiritual*, 22).

J.I. Packer, in his book *Keep In Step with the Spirit,* identifies a different set of choices in pursuit of the same practical goal. The idea of "keeping in step" reflects Paul's thought in Galatians 5:25: "If we live by the Spirit, let us also walk by the Spirit" (NASB). In this verse, "walk" is not *peripateo*, as in verse 16 . . . but *stoicheo*, "which carries the thought of walking in line, holding to a rule, and thus proceeding under another's control" (*Keep in Step with the Spirit* [Old Tappan, N.J.: Revell, 1984], 11). This different set of choices while dealing with the same subject matter will result in a distinct emphasis.

Charles Ryrie follows the same set of choices which Chafer first made and clarifies the distinction in emphasis more sharply in *Basic Theology.* In addition, he builds upon Chafer's logical analysis of spirituality, while demonstrating greater attention to the exegesis of the textual statements involved. Ryrie first of all unfolds a basic facet of spirituality from 1 Corinthians 2:15. "If the spiritual believer judges or examines or discerns all things, yet himself is not understood by others, then spirituality means a mature, yet maturing, relationship to God" (*Basic Theology*, 375).

This is an exegetical implication. He again treats the fullness of the Spirit as a close synonym of spirituality. Then he gives greater attention to the full range of textual uses and distinguishes Spirit possession of someone for special activity (*pimplemi pneumatos hagiou*) from extensive Spirit influence and control (*plere* or *pleroo pneumatos hagiou*). This latter use is the sense of the Pauline statement (Eph. 5:18). Ryrie then analyzes the subject of spirituality exegetically: "If filling relates to the control of the Spirit in one's life (whether in the sense of God's sovereign seizing of a person or of a sustained control that results in character), then filling is related to yieldedness. When I am willing to allow the Spirit to do what He wishes, it is up to Him to do or not to do with me whatever is His pleasure. I can check my willingness but I cannot manipulate His activities" (*Basic Theology*, 378).

The distinctions between Chafer and Packer are now clarified exegetically. Chafer emphasized "walk in the Spirit" (Gal. 5:16, KJV), while Packer emphasized "walk by the Spirit" (Gal. 5:25, NIV). While both are biblical and both stress obedience, they do so in different ways. Chafer was faulted for treating obedience as a "condition," but that is more a result of his logic rather than exegesis. Ryrie has clarified that obedience is the result of yieldedness to the Spirit in the same sense as Romans 6:12-14. And that has an emphasis distinct from Packer's. In Packer, obedience is the result of the Spirit's rule, while in Chafer obedience is the result of the Spirit's empowerment and control. This strong underlying theme of grace in Chafer and Ryrie warms any responsive heart who deeply desires to keep in step with the Spirit but knows he or she is unable apart from Spirit enablement.

This brief exercise in theology and exegesis has validated the distinction which Ernesti recognized. *Exegesis* unfolds the meanings of passages while *theology* correlates the significance of these meanings. While no correlation can claim the authority of "thus says the Lord," the correlated system which corresponds most broadly and naturally to the Bible's meanings is certainly to be favored.

What makes Bible study so exciting is that, by God's grace, we can understand His Word. Once we have understood it, we have the truths necessary to help us live pleasing to our loving God. When theology and exegesis kiss, God is glorified.

Angels:
Ministering Spirits

"If one accepts the biblical revelation
then there can be no question about
the existence of angels."

(Basic Theology, p. 121)

CHAPTER SEVEN

The Real but Unseen Ministry of Angels

Renald E. Showers

T he Scriptures indicate that, although the holy angels have heaven as their dwelling place (Mark 12:25; Luke 2:13,15), they have access to earth and become involved in the affairs of humans and of nations. Because angels are invisible (Col. 1:16), humans are usually oblivious to the impact of angels upon their lives in many significant ways and on numerous occasions. What are some of those ways and occasions?

Angelic Involvement with Nations

The Book of Daniel gives a few brief, tantalizing indications of angelic involvement in the international affairs of Planet Earth

(10:13, 20-21; 12:1). These passages relate how Michael, a holy archangel of God (Jude 9), helped another holy heavenly being fight against "the prince of the kingdom of Persia" and later against "the prince of Greece."

In this revelation to Daniel, Michael is called "one of the chief princes," "your prince," and "the great prince which standeth for the children of Thy people" (KJV). It appears from these designations that Michael, as a holy angelic prince, has been assigned by God to a special relationship with the nation Israel.

Since Michael was assigned to Israel to fight against the princes of Persia and Greece, we might infer that these other princes were evil angels assigned by Satan to the kingdoms of Persia and Greece to influence these nations to threaten Israel. Michael was responsible to protect Israel from their policies.

While Persia exercised ruling authority over Israel, Haman advanced to a high position within the government (Es. 3:1). Being strongly anti-Semitic, Haman succeeded in persuading the king of Persia to pass a decree that all Jews be put to death on the thirteenth day of the month Adar (Es. 3:8-9). Thus, the entire nation of Israel was to be annihilated in one day. In the providence of God a young Jewess, Esther, became the favorite queen of the Persian king (Es. 2:17). Through her influence the king passed another decree permitting the Jews to defend themselves on the day of their slaughter (Es. 8:7-13). The Jews did defend themselves and Israel was spared. Every year Jews around the world keep the Feast of Purim to celebrate this deliverance (Es. 9:26-27).

The Book of Esther records both the Persian policy which threatened Israel and the means by which God delivered the nation, but it makes no mention of angelic involvement. In light of Daniel 10, however, we may assume that the Persian decree which required the annihilation of Israel reflected the invisible influence of the evil angelic prince of Persia. Likewise, Michael may have played a strategic role in the deliverance of Israel from Persian destruction.

Greece, the other nation mentioned in Daniel, also brutalized Israel. During part of the time that Greece dominated the ancient world, Antiochus Epiphanes, a Greek-Syrian ruler, tried to force the Jews into pagan idolatry by outlawing their worship of Jehovah and by commanding them to worship the Greek god, Zeus. He plundered and defiled God's temple, rededicated it as a worship place of Zeus, had a pagan altar built over the altar of God, and commanded that the regular sacrifices be replaced by the sacrifice of pigs. He burned and tore down large parts of Jerusalem, killed many Jews, and had women and children carried into slavery.

Eventually the Maccabees, a priestly family of Israel, were successful in leading a band of Jewish men to liberate their nation from this Greek-Syrian oppressor and his forces. Then the Jews cleansed the temple and restored the worship of Jehovah. Every year Jews around the world observe the Feast of Lights (Hanukkah) to celebrate this deliverance of their nation. In light of Daniel 10, perhaps Antiochus Epiphanes' brutal policies against Israel were motivated by the evil angelic prince of Greece. Once again the deliverance of Israel may have involved Michael, Israel's holy angelic prince, fighting against the prince of Greece.

Revelation 12 indicates that during the second half of the Tribulation period Satan will again pursue Israel with a vengeance, trying to annihilate the nation. According to Revelation 16:12-16, Satan, Antichrist, and the false prophet will send forth demonic spirits (evil angels) throughout the world to influence the rulers of all nations to bring their armies against Israel. These severe demonic attacks against Israel will prompt Michael's action in the middle of the Tribulation to prevent Israel's total annihilation (Dan. 12:1). Thus, in the future as in the past, Satan and God will assign angelic princes to nations to influence their policies in favor of satanic or divine purposes for history.

Has similar angelic involvement with Gentile nations taken place in the twentieth century? Perhaps it has. World War II may provide an example of such angelic activity in international affairs. Recent books and television documentaries have chronicled the interest of Hitler and the Nazis in the occult, which may have exposed them to intense demonic influence. In light of Satan's pattern of assigning evil angels to nations to influence them to threaten Israel, Satan may well have been behind Hitler's attempt to annihilate the Jews through the Holocaust. Surely the utterly inhumane, systematic liquidation of some 6 million Jews suggests demonic work. Perhaps God assigned Michael and other holy angelic princes to fight against these evil angelic princes, uniting the allied nations to crush Hitler and his forces.

When we listen to the world news, we hear only the human side of the affairs of nations. What is hidden from us is the incredible, invisible angelic warfare which transpires behind the scenes and which greatly impacts international events and, therefore, our lives.

Angelic Involvement with the Church

The Scriptures indicate that angels watch the affairs of the church. Angels observed what happened to the apostles (1 Cor. 4:9), and Paul implied that holy angels were watching Timothy when Paul told him to be careful how he exercised his ministry (1 Tim. 5:21).

One fascinating aspect of angels who are watching the affairs of the church is presented in Ephesians 3:10. There Paul indicated that angels in heaven are gaining knowledge concerning "the manifold wisdom of God" by watching the church. In the context Paul talked about how God through Jesus Christ removed the entrenched hatred which had divided Jews and Gentiles for centuries, and brought these former enemies together as equals to form one body, the church. Only God possesses the wisdom to accomplish this seemingly impossible task. Paul's point was that as the angels watch God build the church by bringing sworn enemies together with mutual love and respect, they learn things about God's wisdom which they could not learn in any other way.

An amazing current example of this aspect of God's wisdom recently took place in Israel. A Jewish man in Jerusalem came to a saving knowledge of Jesus Christ through the Gospel witness of a local church in that city. Some time later this new believer brought another man with him to one of the services of that church. At the conclusion of the service the two men walked to the front of the meeting place and faced the congregation. The Jewish believer introduced the other man and said: "This is my friend. He wants to trust Christ as his Savior. He is an Arab. This is the man who murdered my mother." What a demonstration of the wisdom of God and transforming power of the Gospel of Jesus Christ which can replace hatred with such loving concern for an enemy! I can imagine that, when angels in heaven witnessed this, some of them must have exclaimed, "Wow! Did you see that? How incredible is God's wisdom to accomplish such a feat!"

Another intriguing aspect of angels observing the affairs of the church is found in 1 Corinthians 11 where Paul addressed order in worship services. The apostle began by presenting a functional authority structure which God has ordained for the universe (1 Cor. 11:3). In that authority structure God the Father is the functional Head of Christ. Although they are equal in personhood and nature, Christ is subordinate to the Father's functional headship. Next, Christ is the functional head of the man. Finally, the man is the functional head of the woman. Although they are equal in personhood and nature, the woman is subordinate to the functional headship of the man.

To respect this order, the man was not to have a covering on his head while ministering publicly in a church service, but the woman was to have one on her head while ministering publicly in the church service (1 Cor. 11:4-9). Paul called the covering on the woman's head "power" (1 Cor. 11:10) or a symbol of authority. When the covering was placed upon the woman's head, she was (literally) under that symbol of authority. The point of Paul's instruction to the Corinthian church was this: When a woman ministered publicly in the church service, she was to put this symbol of authority on her head to acknowledge that she ministered under the functional headship authority in that church; she was not subverting or usurping that God-ordained functional headship.

Interestingly, women were to wear this symbol of authority on their heads "because of the angels" (1 Cor. 11:10). Angels are not part of the church, so what conceivable relationship could they have to this issue? Since Paul mentioned the angels immediately after relating the covering to authority, it would appear that the issue of authority is significant in the angelic realm.

Satan and the other evil angels fell away from God by rebelling against the functional authority structure which He ordained for the universe. They were the first of God's creatures to rebel against that authority. The goal of their rebellion was to overthrow God's functional headship over the universe so that Satan could usurp His position.

Paul's point is that as angels look on, Christian women should be examples of creatures of God who are willing to submit to His functional authority structure in the church. As examples, they should not rebel against or try to usurp the functional headship authority which God has ordained.

Paul's instruction implies that angels are present in church worship services, observing how the church functions. We do not see them, but they are present nonetheless.

Angelic Involvement with Individual Saints

Hebrews 1:14 declares that holy angels are "all ministering spirits, sent forth to minister for them who shall be heirs of salvation." This means that God sends His angels to minister to us as individual saints. There are at least three ways in which they minister to believers today.

First, holy angels guard and preserve the saints. Psalm 91:10-12 promised that God would give His angels charge over His people to guard and protect them from harm. In keeping with this promise, the Lord sent angels to deliver Lot and his family from the destruction which was to come upon Sodom (Gen. 19:1-25); God sent an angel to protect Daniel from the fury of lions (Dan. 6:22); and He sent angels to free the apostles from their imprisonments (Acts 5:19; 12:7-11).

Is each individual assigned his or her own personal guardian angel for life? Perhaps so. The early church saints apparently believed in personal angels. After Peter had been released from prison, he went to the home of Mary and John Mark where the believers were holding a prayer meeting. Hearing him at the gate, a young woman interrupted the meeting by announcing that Peter was there. The believers insisted that it was not Peter, but "his angel" (Acts 12:12-15). Their use of the possessive pronoun "his" seems to indicate that they believed that Peter had his own angel. In addition, on one occasion, when Jesus talked about little children, He referred to "their angels" in heaven (Matt. 18:10). His use of the possessive pronoun "their" may signify that each child has his or her personal angel.

Whether or not each person is assigned a personal guardian

68

angel for life is really not that important. What is crucial is that each person who inherits salvation is guarded and preserved through angelic activity, whether it be by just one or by several different angels throughout life. When believers get to heaven they will probably be amazed to learn how many times they narrowly missed harm or premature physical death because of angelic protection.

Second, holy angels assist the prayers of saints. John saw angels in heaven with golden vials filled with the prayers of saints and an angel offering incense with the prayers of all saints upon the golden altar before the throne (Rev. 5:8; 8:3). These passages seem to indicate that angels perform a ministry of gathering the prayers of saints in heaven and offering them to God. In that sense, they assist the prayers of saints. It also appears that angels carry out or execute some of God's answers to the prayers of saints (Acts 12:5-12).

Third, holy angels carry saints to heaven. In Jesus' account of Lazarus and the rich man, He declared that when Lazarus died, angels carried him into Abraham's bosom (Luke 16:22). Perhaps today also, when a saint is separated from his or her earthly body through death, angels transport that saint into the presence of the Lord in heaven. When a believer dies, he or she is not left alone. What a comforting truth!

There is a ministry of angels, usually invisible to believers today. Spiritual forces lie behind all that happens in life, whether internationally, nationally, corporately, or individually. There is far more to life than what the limited vision of the secular scientist is able to see. Angelic activity is another aspect of God's grace toward us.

> "Of course, God is not obliged
> to use angels; He can do all these
> things directly. But seemingly He
> chooses to employ the intermediate
> ministry of angels on many occasions."
> (*Basic Theology*, p. 133)

CHAPTER EIGHT

Child-Rearing and Angelology

Wesley R. Willis

A worthy goal for Christian parents is to see their children grow up with deeply held convictions based on the revealed Word of God. We long for our children to love and obey God and to place a high value on other people. We want them to be men and women of integrity, not succumbing to temptations of spiritual compromise to relieve the pressure of a difficult situation.

How can we as parents lead our children to place their trust in Christ and then to grow to maturity in Christ? This is not a new problem. Long before the time of Christ, godly parents knew the importance of teaching their children the Law of God. Indeed, when Jewish parents were faithful the nation of Israel prospered.

And when parents neglected their responsibility the nation fell away from God, and He visited judgment upon His people. "And all that generation also were gathered to their fathers; and there arose another generation after them who did not know the Lord, nor yet the work which He had done for Israel. Then the sons of Israel did evil in the sight of the Lord, and served the Baals" (Jud. 2:10-11, NASB).

The failure of parents in Israel during the time of the Judges apparently was twofold. The parents failed to teach their children about God and their responsibilities to Him ("another generation . . . who did not know the Lord"); and they failed to teach their children about what God had done for His people in earlier times ("nor yet the work He had done for Israel"). Because the parents neglected their responsibilities, their offspring also failed to follow godly ways.

In a similar way, many Christian mothers and fathers today fall short in their parenting. Identifying the problem is a good place to begin, but we need to move beyond diagnosis. What solution can we prescribe? We can examine how God directed Israelite parents to rear godly children. Through His servant Moses, God said that if parents and their offspring would fear the Lord and keep His statutes and His commandments, He would give them long life, prosperity, and national growth (Deut. 6:2-3).

God explained that this meant parents were to teach their children important doctrinal truths about God. "Hear, O Israel! The Lord is our God, the Lord is one!" (Deut. 6:4) In addition to accurate facts about God, the children needed to develop a deep love for God that would totally dominate their beings. "And you shall love the Lord your God with all your heart and with all your soul and with all your might" (6:5).

Virtually all Christian parents would agree with these instructions and see the wisdom in teaching their children about God and cultivating in them a deep love for God. But the question remains: How do we help our children to know the truth about God so that they love and obey Him? In Deuteronomy 6, before explaining the methods to accomplish these worthy goals, God gave one more word of admonition. The parents needed to be the kind of people that they desired their children to become. "And these words which I am commanding you today, shall be on your heart" (Deut. 6:6). It was imperative that the parents did more than talk about spiritual truth; they needed to "incarnate" it—to live it out before their children.

Teaching Our Children

If parents are committed to God, love Him with all their hearts, and obey Him, then they are ready to teach their children. Of course, in the absolute sense none of us would qualify because no adult loves God with total heart, mind, and soul. And certainly not one of us obeys Him perfectly. But since God stated this as His normal expectation for parents, it seems fair to assume that God's intent is to describe a spiritually growing person who genuinely loves God and seeks to obey Him. For that kind of a growing person, the explanation of how to teach our children is given.

Talk about God's Word

All of us know that effective parenting requires more than simply talking about spiritual truth. But it is equally wrong to go to the other extreme and never talk about spiritual things. Parents were instructed to discuss the Law of God. They were to talk about it when they went to bed at night and arose in the morning, and when they stayed at home or were on the go (Deut. 6:7-9).

Verbal communication of what God has taught us is the starting point for teaching our children. Since most of us get up and also go to bed at least once a day, it would appear that the emphasis is on regularity and consistency in verbal instruction. Just as regularly as we get up and go to bed (and perhaps specifically at those times), we should discuss spiritual truth. Most parents come to recognize early on that bedtime is a good time for thoughtful, reflective conversation. Reading Bible stories and praying, talking about the events of the day, reflecting over lessons and experiences can be done effectively with our children as we put them to bed.

But God also indicated that parents should talk of His Law at home and on the go, "when you sit in your house and when you walk by the way" (Deut. 6:7). There are many daily occasions to talk about God's Word. This involves more than taking our children to Sunday School once a week, and requires parents to thoughtfully spend time with their children and actively seek opportunities to discuss spiritual things.

Put God's Word into Practice

Effective parenting also includes demonstrating that we truly believe what we talk about (Deut. 6:6). When God told the Israelites to "bind them [the Law of God] as a sign on your hand" and that they should "be as frontals on your forehead," they took these commands quite literally. Many of the Jews wore phylacteries, small boxes containing a portion of the Law, tied to their arms and their foreheads. Did God have more in mind than decorative wearing apparel? It is likely that He was instructing Jewish parents, and us too, that our heads and hands need to be directed by His Word. Our very actions (God's Word on our hands) and our thoughts (God's Word on our foreheads) should be controlled by God. This instruction leads us to tell our children about God's Word and then to demonstrate by our actions what we believe.

Teach through the Atmosphere of the Home

Another guideline for teaching our children relates to our home environment. "And you shall write them on the doorposts of your house and on your gates" (Deut. 6:9). Again, the Israelites took this literally and attached a portion of the Law to their door frames. Even today Jewish homes commonly display a *Mezuzah*, a tube containing a portion of the Law that is written on a small scroll.

This wasn't meant as a home decorating tip; rather this instruction was given to direct God's people to teach their children about Him through the very atmosphere of the home. When a person enters our house, it should be obvious that our home is a place where God is honored. The values expressed in our home, the attitudes of family members, and our relationships with each other should communicate what we believe.

We often assume that children cannot grasp difficult concepts. Yet sometimes their simple faith enables them to accept theological truths more easily than adults often do with our sophisticated reasoning. Recognizing our responsibility to transfer biblical doctrine to our children, let us consider how to teach them some of the relevant truths about angels.

Children and Angelology

One common fear expressed by young children is a fear of the dark, ranging from occasional mild anxiety to deep-seated terror. Many children want a light left on in their bedroom and may plead with their parents not to leave them alone in the dark because they are afraid of "something" in their room.

Often parents try to convince their children that these fears are groundless and that there is nothing really there. But we found that this situation was a good opportunity to teach our children about angels. We recognized that what parents often tell children ("nothing is there") really is not true. While we may not see what is there, we must not confuse *visibility* with *reality*. The invisible spirit world is real. When our children expressed fear of the dark, we taught them about God's angels, and about their missions on earth from Him. We spent time together learning about the characteristics of angels and how they serve God and help us.

Psalm 91 is a good passage to share with fearful children. It talks about those who might want to hurt us. It explains that we don't have to be terrified by the dark, for God provides angels to guard and protect us. We combined this Psalm with Jesus' correction of Satan's misapplication of Scripture when he tempted Jesus in the wilderness (Matt. 4:5-7; Luke 4:9-12), and we taught that when Jesus was tempted, angels ministered to Him (Matt. 4:11; Mark 1:13).

A complementary passage is Jesus' teaching about children's angels: "See to it that you do not despise one of these little ones, for I say to you, that their angels in heaven continually behold the face of My Father who is in heaven" (Matt. 18:10). There are two commonly held interpretations of this passage. One is that each child has been assigned a "guardian angel" who watches over that child; the other is that God sends angels to provide specific services to children. We concluded, with our children, that this referred to guardian angels. And we talked together with our children about this expression of God's love in providing angels to watch over them. We could assure our young children that even in the dark, angels were watching over them and protecting them.

Biblical Examples of Angelic Ministry

Certain Bible narratives focus our attention on how God has provided angels to minister to His people. An exciting biblical account in 2 Kings 6 records Elisha's house being surrounded by the large army of the king of Aram. Elisha's terrified servant cried out to his master, but Elisha responded, "Do not fear, for those who are with us are more than those who are with them" (2 Kings 6:16). Then, turning from his servant, he asked of God, "O Lord, I pray, open his eyes that he may see." In answer to Elisha's prayer, God revealed the reality that the servant could not previously see. "And the Lord opened the servant's eyes, and he saw; and behold, the mountain was full of horses and chariots of fire all around Elisha" (2 Kings 6:17).

Other Scripture passages can help children recognize the reality of unseen angels. Numbers 22:21-35 is an interesting narrative of Balaam's donkey seeing the Lord's angel before God made the angel visible to Balaam. Angels visiting Lot (Gen. 19:1-16), and an angel bringing food and drink to Elijah after his victory at Mount Carmel (1 Kings 9:1-8) are other Old Testament accounts that we can draw on to teach our children about angelic activity. The New Testament includes accounts of angels who came to Mary (Luke 1:26-38), Joseph (Matt. 1:18-25), and the shepherds (Luke 2:8-18) to announce Jesus' birth; an angel who delivered Peter from prison (Acts 12:5-11); and many others.

Contemporary Accounts of Angelic Ministry

When our sons were young, our family spent many hours reading aloud books; and some of these dealt with the subject of angelic ministry. *God's Tribesman* (Jim and Marti Hefley, Wheaton, Ill.:

Victor, 1977) which describes events of Rochunga Pudaite (founder of Bibles for the World) as he grew up in India was one of these titles.

One account that particularly fascinated our boys was a description of the time that Ro traveled to his home from high school, which was a two-day walk after traveling partway by boat. As Ro started along the five-mile trail through heavy jungle, he saw signs that a dreaded Bengal tiger had crossed the trail only seconds earlier. In great terror he saw the tall grass moving beside the path and once caught a glimpse of the tiger walking parallel to his path. The longer Ro walked, the bolder he became, until finally the tiger turned off just before the village. Ro became bolder because he concluded that this was a messenger of God, perhaps an angel, whom God had sent to protect him from some other unseen jungle animal.

Another contemporary account described a Christian in another country who was being persecuted for his faith. After receiving repeated threats from local thugs, this Christian prayed that God would protect him. Throughout that night he heard people outside, but no one ever attacked him. Later, a group of men admitted that they had come several times intending to kill him, but each time were turned back by huge warriors guarding the house. There had been no one there, at least no one that the Christian had seen. But God had sent angels to protect his child.

Mrs. Alma Stanislaw, my wife's mother, recently experienced God's protection. She arrived to teach a women's Bible study at her church, carrying a plate of homemade cinnamon rolls. As she opened the church door, the plate began to slip from her grasp. While she tried to keep from dropping the plate, the door slammed into her. She lost her balance and fell backward down a flight of six concrete steps to the sidewalk below. The church janitor and a pastor who were standing in the foyer had seen her coming in and then noticed that she "disappeared." They knew that she had fallen and were about to call for emergency help. Instead they ran outside to find my mother-in-law sitting unhurt on the sidewalk. In her fall Mrs. Stanislaw never touched any of the steps and recounted that she experienced no fear. Rather, she felt as though someone was holding her and gently lowering her to the ground. She believed that God granted her protection in this instance, and it is likely that an angel was the means by which He provided it.

Recently I talked with Rev. Charles Walton, a Wycliffe translator serving in the Philippines, who had been abducted by rebels in November 1993 and held captive for twenty-three days. On one occasion during those days he felt as though he were nearing the end of his endurance following a period of especially intense harassment by his captors. Chuck related that as he was feeling most oppressed, the Lord provided encouragement in a strange way. A short, wiry fellow appeared whom Chuck never had seen before. This man walked right past the captors and no one seemed to notice. The visitor sat down on the bench with Chuck and still no one noticed. As he slid over close to Chuck, the man jabbed him in the ribs with his elbow, leaned over and simply said in English, "Praise the Lord." Chuck replied, "Praise the Lord," which seemed to greatly agitate his captors. After about five minutes, the little man left, and still no one took any notice of him. The visitor who provided such spiritual encouragement never was seen before or after that night, and to this day no one knows who he was or where he came from. But Chuck Walton is quite convinced that God sent an angel to comfort and to encourage him during his most difficult time. That conclusion certainly is compatible with biblical accounts of angelic ministry, and such contemporary accounts can help our children recognize that angels still are one means by which God ministers to us today.

We've seen that we have the responsibility to teach God's Word to our children. We do this through our own commitment to God and by talking about His Word, living in obedience to the Word, and showing God's truth through the ambiance of our homes. We need to teach what the Bible tells us about angels and help our children see how God ministered through angels in biblical times. But we should not stop there. We also need to teach our children that God still ministers to us today through His angels, and that we can expect Him to provide and care for us and for other Christians, even as He has done in times past.

Our Adversary the Devil & Demons: Unclean Spirits

"God has never, nor will He ever cease to exist; therefore His sustaining, providential control of all things and events is assured."
(*Basic Theology*, p. 37)

CHAPTER NINE

The World as Our Enemy

Kenneth Boa

Few people comprehend their mortality in the first three decades of life. It usually requires the sobering struggle of the midlife crisis (or midlife process, depending on the way we go through it) before we experientially grasp our mortality. As we discover the decline of our capacities and the increase of our responsibilities, we realize with clarity and force that we will not be able to fulfill many of our earthly hopes and dreams. This realization can be traumatic for those whose expectations are limited to this planet. But for believers, whose hope is in the character and promises of God, it can be a powerful reminder to transfer their affections and ambitions to their only true home, the kingdom of heaven. Again and again, the Scriptures drive these images

81

home to remind us that our stay on this planet is briefer than most of us are inclined to think.

> Time, like an ever-rolling stream, bears all its sons away;
> They fly forgotten as a dream dies at the opening day.
> The busy tribes of flesh and blood with all their cares and
>   fears,
> Are carried downward like a flood and lost in following years.

These verses from Isaac Watts' hymn, "O God, Our Help in Ages Past," are based on Psalm 90's contrast between the eternality of God and the brevity of our earthly sojourn. This psalm, written by Moses near the end of his own journey, counsels us to number our days in order to present to God a heart of wisdom (v. 12). David's meditation in Psalm 39:4-7 develops the same theme:

> Lord, make me to know my end,
> And what is the extent of my days,
> Let me know how transient I am.
> Behold, Thou hast made my days as handbreadths,
> And my lifetime as nothing in Thy sight,
> Surely every man at his best is a mere breath.
> Surely every man walks about as a phantom;
> Surely they make an uproar for nothing;
> He amasses riches, and does not know who will gather them.
> And now, Lord, for what do I wait?
> My hope is in Thee. (NASB)

Isaiah 40:6-8 uses a different metaphor to develop the same contrast between the temporal and the eternal (see also Ps. 103:15-18 and 1 Peter 1:24-25):

> All flesh is grass, and all its loveliness is like the flower of the
>   field.
> The grass withers, the flower fades,
> When the breath of the Lord blows upon it;
> Surely the people are grass.
> The grass withers, the flower fades,
> But the word of our God stands forever.

James adds, "You do not know what your life will be like tomorrow. You are just a vapor that appears for a little while and then vanishes away" (James 4:14; cf. 1:11).

This may seem to be a pessimistic and morbid way of viewing human life, but on further analysis, it turns out to be a realistic and hopeful approach. It is realistic because it is better to know things as they are than to believe things as they seem. It is hopeful because it informs us that there is more to life than what we presently see, and it assures us that our longing for more than this world can offer is not merely a pipe dream. The biblical vision of God's invitation to us is not only forgiveness, but newness of life in Christ, a new quality of relational life that will never fade or tarnish.

Though three dominant worldviews are vying for our allegiance, only one answers our longing for the eternal. The first claims that ultimate reality is material, and that everything in the universe is the impersonal product of time and chance. There are variations of this view, but it is best known as naturalism, atheism, and humanism. This view predicts annihilation.

The second worldview claims that ultimate reality is not material, but spiritual. However, this spiritual agent is not a personal being, but the "all-that-is." Variations of this view include monism, pantheism, transcendentalism, and the whole New Age movement. Though its teaching on reincarnation may sound hopeful, it is not. The religions of the East actually teach that reincarnation is undesirable, since it brings us around and around on the painful wheel of life. Instead, the Eastern vision of salvation is absorption into the ocean of being. But this is not a vision of personal consciousness or relationships; it is simply a spiritual version of annihilation.

Theism, the third worldview, distinguishes between the creation and the Creator and declares that ultimate reality is an infinite, intelligent, and personal Being. Christian theism affirms that this personal God has decisively revealed Himself in the person and work of Jesus Christ. Only the third worldview offers genuine hope beyond the grave.

Instead of annihilation or reincarnation, the Scriptures teach resurrection into an eternally new existence of light, life, and love characterized by intimacy with our Lord and with one another. Everything we go through now will be more than worth it in the end, because the divine Architect of the universe, the God and Father of our Lord Jesus Christ, never builds a staircase that leads to nowhere.

If we examine the heart's deepest longings, it becomes evident that these aspirations cannot be satisfied by any of the offerings of this transitory world. There is insufficient time, opportunity, and energy even to scratch the surface of our deep-seated hopes and dreams. A.W. Tozer put it well in his devotional classic, *The Knowledge of the Holy*, "The days of the years of our lives are few, and swifter than a weaver's shuttle. Life is a short and fevered rehearsal for a concert we cannot stay to give. Just when we appear to have attained some proficiency we are forced to lay our instruments down. There is simply not time enough to think, to become, to perform what the constitution of our natures indicates we are capable of."

Tozer goes on to add this important thought: "How completely satisfying to turn from our limitations to a God who has none. Eternal years lie in His heart. For Him time does not pass, it remains; and those who are in Christ share with Him all the riches of limitless time and endless years" (*The Knowledge of the Holy*, [New York: Harper & Row, 1961], 52).

The responsibilities and pressures of this world clamor for our attention and tend to squeeze out our inner lives and starve our souls. When this happens, we lose sight of the things that really matter and focus on the things that are passing away. Our value systems become confused when we invest more of our thought and concern in things that are doomed to disappear than in that which will endure forever.

The Apostle John warns us of this when he writes, "Do not love the world, nor the things in the world. If anyone loves the world, the love of the Father is not in him. For all that is in the world, the lust of the flesh and the lust of the eyes and the boastful pride of life, is not from the Father, but is from the world. And the world is passing away, and also its lusts; but the one who does the will of God abides forever" (1 John 2:15-17). James adds, "Whoever wishes to be a friend of the world makes himself an enemy of

God" (James 4:4). And Jesus admonishes those who are <u>more concerned with the opinions of people</u> than with the approval of God, saying, "That which is highly esteemed among men is detestable in the sight of God" (Luke 16:15). These are indeed strong words, but we would be foolish to disregard them. As St. Augustine observed, we must care for our bodies <u>as though we were going to live forever</u>, but we must <u>care for our souls</u> as if we were going to <u>die tomorrow.</u>

Some have accused Christians of ignoring the present life, even to the extent of being so heavenly minded that they are of no earthly good. In actual fact, it is precisely the opposite—when people become heavenly minded, they treasure the passing opportunities of this life and become <u>more alive to the present moment.</u> Rather than being overwhelmed with the problems and hassles of life, they understand that these too will pass, and that "the sufferings of this present time are not worthy to be compared with the glory that is to be revealed to us" (Rom. 8:18). Instead of taking things for granted, they learn to <u>savor blessings</u> and <u>joys</u> that are otherwise overlooked.

Instead of wasting time as though we had a million years to live on earth, we would do well to remember the Apostle Paul's exhortation: "Be most careful then how you conduct yourselves: like sensible men, not like simpletons. Use the present opportunity to the full, for these are evil days. So do not be fools, but try to understand what the will of the Lord is" (Eph. 5:15-17, NEB).

The Kingdom of God Versus the Kingdom of the World

It is difficult to convey the dramatic differences between the kingdom values of Scripture and the temporal values of the systems of this world. In a qualitative sense, they are virtually polar opposites. Choose any value in Christ's kingdom, stand it on its head, and you will have a good likeness of the corresponding value in the world's kingdom. A sampler of these contrasts may be the best way to express the profound spiritual, moral, and social discord between a temporal and an eternal value system.

The kingdom of the world (KW) is typified by the mentality of Thomas: "Unless I shall see in His hands the imprint of the nails, and put my finger into the place of the nails, and put my hand into His side, I will not believe" (John 20:25). By contrast, the kingdom ruled by Christ (KC) is portrayed in the words of our Lord a few verses later: "Because you have seen Me, have you believed? Blessed are they who did not see, and yet believed" (John 20:29).

In KW we always want to appear wise and sensible to others, but in KC we are willing to appear foolish for the sake of Christ. "Let no man deceive himself. If any man among you thinks that he is wise in this age, let him become foolish that he may become wise" (1 Cor. 3:18).

In KW we are told to save our lives by looking out for number one; in KC we are shown that the only path to finding life is by abandoning it for the sake of Christ. "For whoever wishes to save his life shall lose it; but whoever loses his life for My sake shall find it" (Matt. 16:25).

In KW we try to be first, but in KC we discover that the last will be first. "If anyone wants to be first, he shall be last of all, and servant of all. . . . Whoever wishes to become great among you shall be your servant" (Mark 9:35; 10:43).

In KW we seek to become rich, but in KC we are willing to be poor so that others may be rich. "For you know the grace of our Lord Jesus Christ, that though He was rich, yet for your sake He became poor, that you through His poverty might become rich" (2 Cor. 8:9). KW views money in terms of security, significance, and power, and thus encourages us to amass more and more without asking the question, "How much is enough?" KC views money as a responsible stewardship before God and encourages us to invest it in the service of others.

KW tells us to look to our own interests, but KC exhorts us to serve the needs of others. "Do not merely look out for your own personal interests, but also for the interest of others" (Phil. 2:4).

KW encourages us to exalt ourselves, while KC admonishes us to humble ourselves. "For everyone who exalts himself shall be humbled, and he who humbles himself shall be exalted. . . . Do nothing from selfishness or empty conceit, but with humility of mind let each of you regard one another as more important than himself" (Luke 14:11; Phil. 2:3).

KW values receiving, but KC tells us "it is more blessed to give than to receive" (Acts 20:35). "And if you do good to those who do good to you, what credit is that to you? For even sinners do the same. And if you lend to those from whom you expect to receive, what credit is that to you? Even sinners lend to sinners, in order to receive back the same amount. But love your enemies, and do good, and lend, expecting nothing in return; and your reward will be great, and you will be sons of the Most High" (Luke 6:33-35). The world tells us to be grabbers, but the Word tells us to be givers. KW teaches us to be manipulators; KC teaches us to be ministers.

KW prompts us to tell others about our good deeds, but KC directs us to keep good deeds secret. "But when you give alms, do not let your left hand know what your right hand is doing that your alms may be in secret; and your Father who sees in secret will repay you" (Matt. 6:3-4).

In KW, love is a feeling and is conditional; in KC love is a commitment and is unconditional. "A new commandment I give to you, that you love one another, even as I have loved you, that you also love one another" (John 13:34).

In KW, love often grows cold, but in KC, love never fails. The agape love of Christ is characterized by patience, kindness, a lack of jealousy or pride, a concern for others, a love of the truth, and a willingness to endure wrongs without being provoked or becoming cynical (1 Cor. 13:4-7).

People under the rule of KW naturally hate their enemies, but those who are governed by KC supernaturally love their enemies. "You have heard that it was said, 'You shall love your neighbor, and hate your enemy.' But I say to you, love your enemies, and pray for those who persecute you" (Matt. 5:43-44).

KW teaches us to seek revenge when we believe we have been wronged, but KC impels us to forgive others in the same way we have been forgiven through Christ. "Put on a heart of compassion, kindness, humility, gentleness and patience; bearing with one another, and forgiving each other, whoever has a complaint against anyone; just as the Lord forgave you, so also should you" (Col. 3:12-13).

We are told to cover our mistakes in KW, but KC exhorts us to acknowledge and confess our sins. "I acknowledged my sin to

Thee, and my iniquity I did not hide; I said, 'I will confess my transgressions to the Lord'; and Thou didst forgive the guilt of my sin" (Ps. 32:5).

KW encourages us to emphasize human power, while KC directs us to emphasize the power of the Holy Spirit. We must remember the word of the Lord to Zerubbabel: " 'Not by might nor by power, but by My Spirit,' says the Lord of hosts" (Zech. 4:6).

We are always tempted by KW to become institutionally religious, but in KC, we are called to grow in love for God and for others. Speaking to Israel through the Prophet Hosea, God said, "I delight in loyalty rather than sacrifice, and in the knowledge of God rather than burnt offerings" (6:6).

In KW, we seek to conform others to our way of thinking and acting, but in KC, we seek to conform ourselves to God's way of thinking and acting. "And why do you look at the speck that is in your brother's eye, but do not notice the log that is in your own eye?" (Matt. 7:3)

In KW, we say many things are impossible, but in KC, we acknowledge that all things are possible to those who believe (Mark 9:23).

KW counsels us to seek peace by trying to negotiate common agreements, while KC tells us that the greatest peace is achieved by becoming one in the Spirit (Eph. 4:2-3).

While recognition is important in KW, anonymity is a valued goal in KC. Jesus' words in Matthew 6:1-6 concerning almsgiving and prayer are often overlooked, but He warned us to beware of practicing our righteousness before others to be noticed by them. Even if others do not know what we have done, no good deed will be anonymous in the sight of God.

The Risk of Letting Loose

Any attempt to pursue both the claims of the temporal and the eternal is like holding onto two horses that are galloping in opposite directions. The simultaneous pursuit of the kingdom of the world and the kingdom of Christ is impossible; at any point, one or the other will prevail. Many have tried to have it both ways, but this can never be more than a matter of adding a thin spiritual veneer over the same furniture that is manufactured and promoted by the world system.

It involves great risk to let loose of everything we have been taught to clamor after. It is never comfortable or natural to treasure the invisible over the visible, the promises of God over the promises of the world, the things that will not be fulfilled until the return of Christ over the things the world says we can have here and now. We want control and security on our own terms. Yet the Scriptures tell us that the only true security comes from abandoning the illusion of control and surrendering ourselves unreservedly to the Person and purposes of God.

Part of the problem is that we often fail to review the nonnegotiables to which we claim to be committed. For me, the fundamental presuppositions that form the bedrock of my worldview are, as Francis Schaeffer put it, (1) God is there, and (2) He is not silent. That is, the Author of all creation is a Person who has revealed Himself to humanity in "many portions and in many ways" (Heb. 1:1), including the general revelation of creation, and conscience, and the special revelation of dreams, visions, prophets, apostles, and clearest of all, through His personal revelation in the Person and work of Jesus Christ. I see the Bible as God's declaration of His character and ways, His love letter to the people He sent His Son to redeem, and His blueprint for how to live life with wisdom, purpose, faith, love, and hope.

Since this is my fundamental presupposition about life, everything should flow out of it. It shapes my perspective on who God is, who we are, where we came from, why we are here, where we are going, and how we should relate to others. What are the logical implications of such a view? The most important is that life is all about God, and not about us. All things have been created through Him and for Him (Col. 1:16), and we exist to serve God and not to persuade God to serve us. In essence, the Bible reminds us again and again that "I am God, and you are not."

Also, since we were created for relationship with the Author of every good thing, we can have no higher purpose than to grow in the knowledge of God and, by His grace and power, to become increasingly like Him.

A final implication is that since the Bible was inspired by the living God, we would be wise to learn, understand, experience, and apply its precepts and principles. The Scriptures reveal that our brief earthly sojourn is designed to prepare us for eternal citizenship in heaven. Thus, it would be the heart of folly to become entangled and enmeshed in that which is "highly esteemed among men" but is "detestable in the sight of God" (Luke 16:15). Our ambition must be different from that of others; instead of pursuing position, power, prestige, or wealth, we should seek the approval of our God (2 Cor. 5:9), for that alone is eternal.

"Satan's aim is to create a system
that rivals God's kingdom but which
leaves Him out.... To achieve his aim,
Satan must try to make the values
of his godless system seem attractive."
(*Basic Theology*, p. 152)

CHAPTER TEN

The World and Spiritual Adultery

Glenn R. Goss

T his is my Father's world, and to my listening ears,
    All nature sings, and round me rings
    The music of the spheres.
  This is my Father's world; I rest me in the thought
Of rocks and trees, of skies and seas;
  His hand the wonders wrought.
—Maltbie D. Babcock, 1901

We sing of the world's beauty and we teach our children of its
wonders. Indeed, we should sing and teach of the wonders of
God's created world, for God "made the world and all things in it"
(Acts 17:24, NASB). "All things came into being by Him" (John

1:3), and "in Him all things were created, both in the heavens and on earth, visible and invisible, whether thrones or dominions or rulers or authorities—all things have been created through Him and for Him" (Col. 1:16). Our response to God's creation should be like that of David: "When I consider Thy heavens, the work of Thy fingers, the moon and the stars, which Thou hast ordained; what is man?" (Ps. 8:3-4) We must not place what was created above the Creator, for the creation is to point us to God (Ps. 19:1-6; Rom. 1:19-20), not to lead us to exalt humanity as self-developing, self-achieving beings who are masters of themselves and the world.

The Other Side of the World

Scripture also presents another picture of the world. The word for "world" in the New Testament is usually from the Greek word *cosmos,* and means the system of culture, government, society, and means of life directed by Satan. The cosmos is the enemy of God (1 John 2:15-16). Passion for physical and spiritual power and position for personal benefit, and craving for material things characterize the cosmos. It is, in sum, what Satan wants, not what God wants. This is the world most often mentioned by Jesus and the apostles.

The condition of the natural world pictures the true character of the cosmos. When Adam became a sinner, losing his initial position of fellowship with God, the ground was cursed (Gen. 3:17) and no longer freely provided the necessities of physical life. Instead, the earth became humanity's grudging master, demanding seemingly futile labor against weeds, thorns, and even poison ivy. Under this state of corruption the world now languishes (Rom. 8:19-22). Weeds and insects that devour our flowers and vegetables remind us that the world is no longer the perfect creation that it originally was. We see decay and destruction, and we fight to keep things alive. Nothing seems permanent. As John said, "Do not love the *cosmos* . . . for . . . the *cosmos* is passing away" (1 John 2:15, 17).

Two of my favorite flowers show the temporary character of the fallen creation. There is the daylily which flowers and fades in one day, no matter how beautiful the flower is, or how sturdy it looks when it first opens. Its name, "Hemerocallis" comes from two Greek words, *hêmera* (day) and *kalos* (beauty). And then there is the Phalaenopsis orchid plant which may keep five, ten, or more flowers open on one spike for three months! But sooner or later, even they fade away. What a picture of the world—beautiful and attractive, yet temporary and passing away.

Flowers are a natural part of the created earth. What human beings create illustrates the same principles of decay. Some automobiles run well for about 50,000 miles, while others still purr along after 200,000 miles. But sooner or later, all have to be replaced. That beautiful new car, the new home, the new suit, the new stereo system are all just like the flowers.

Like our surroundings, we too are temporary. We face a life quickly passing away. In an old song, Will H. Houghton observed, "The world moves on, so rapidly the living; the forms of those who disappear, replaced. And each one dreams that he will be enduring; how soon that one becomes the missing face." Isaiah put it this way: "All flesh is grass, and all its loveliness is like the flower of the field. The grass withers, the flower fades, when the breath of the LORD blows upon it; surely the people are grass" (Isa. 40:6-7).

But for the believer a better and eternal life awaits, very different from the present world. "Truly, truly, I say to you, he who hears My word, and believes Him who sent Me, has eternal life, and does not come into judgment, but has passed out of death into life" (John 5:24).

The World's Ruler Faces the Fire

Of greater significance than the temporary nature of the world is the one who wields authority over it. When Satan was tempting Jesus he took Him to a high mountain and said, "I will give You all this domain (*cosmos*) and its glory; for it has been handed over to me, and I give it to whomever I wish" (Luke 4:6). Jesus didn't disagree with Satan; in fact, he called Satan "the ruler of this world" (John 12:31; 16:11). As John noted, "the whole world lies in the power of the evil one" (1 John 5:19). John recorded the coming victory of the Archangel Michael over Satan, with Satan cast out of heaven (Rev. 12:7-9) and, ultimately, into the lake of fire which has been prepared for him and his angels (Matt. 25:41). The judgment of Satan is as certain as the consuming of the grass, which "is alive today and tomorrow is thrown into the furnace" (Matt. 6:30). The ruler and his realm face certain judgment.

The World Promotes Treacherous Living

Paul warns of the deceitful nature of this present world doomed for judgment when he writes, "Demas, having loved this present world (*aiòn*), has deserted me" (2 Tim. 4:10). *Aiòn* is "this present age," characterized as evil in Galatians 1:4. This present evil age seduced Demas to desert (*egkatelipen*) Paul and the Lord. The Greek Old Testament often translates this word as "treachery," using it for Israel and Judah's leaving God and turning to idols (Isa. 1:4; Jer. 2:13; 5:7; Hosea 4:10). What we may term "backsliding" or "a lapse into former practices," *Scripture labels "treachery."*

The world, like a manicured lawn, is deceitfully attractive, always seeking to enslave us. We water our grass, fertilize it, remove weeds from it, cut it, all in an effort to make it look beautiful. For our pleasure we plant it and cultivate it around our homes, public buildings, golf courses, and athletic fields. Now grass is not evil in and of itself. But grass is like the world: both are appealing and temporary. How many people expend time and money to develop something which is only temporary, and in the process miss out on what is eternal.

If Demas deserted Paul to enjoy the temporary but appealing things of the world in his day, how much more of material things, pleasure, position, fame, and power does the world offer to us in our day? For just as we feel pride and pleasure in manicuring our lawn to perfection, so we can feel pride and pleasure in the things of the world. And to get involved with the world we often desert God.

To Follow the World Is Spiritual Adultery

The world can also be deadly, for one who becomes a friend of the world has become an enemy of God (James 4:4), and one who is an enemy of God must look forward to judgment. How does one become an enemy of God? James is quite clear. "You adulteresses," he cries (4:4). This is the correct analysis, for believers are members of His body, the church, which is the bride of Christ (Eph. 5:22-33; 2 Cor. 11:2). The bride who leaves her husband for another man is an adulteress. James' readers were adulteresses, having left intimacy with Jesus to find a new love in the world.

Spiritual adultery is nowhere seen in more stark reality than through the eyes of the prophets of ancient Israel. Jeremiah proclaimed, "My people have committed two evils: They have forsaken me, the fountain of living waters, to hew for themselves cisterns, broken cisterns that can hold no water" (Jer. 2:13). Israel had turned away from Yahweh, her Maker and Husband (Isa. 54:5). Carving out broken cisterns pictures the worship of idols. Those cisterns held water that was collected from clay roofs and from ground seepage around the home and stable for use by the family and the animals. Jeremiah further said, "Have you seen what faithless Israel did? She went up on every high hill and under every green tree, and she was a harlot there" (Jer. 3:6). That was spiritual adultery, the worship of idols that often involved sexual acts with pagan priests or priestesses.

Ezekiel described Israel as a child, rejected by the nations (Ezek. 16:3-5), chosen by God (v. 6), and nurtured with royal provisions (vv. 7-14) until she became well known for her beauty and splendor. He detailed Israel's fall into spiritual adultery because of pride and because of the weakness of her heart—the inner control center of life (vv. 15-30). Her weak heart rationalized, "I know I shouldn't, but. . . ." Israel's spiritual prostitution was different from the prostitution normally practiced in that day. Israel, the adulterous wife, gave gifts to men (the gods of other nations) rather than receiving gifts from them. Though Israel got temporary pleasure from her spiritual adultery, what she loved became the agent of her destruction. Ezekiel detailed her coming judgment, mercilessly unleashed against her by those she sought for pleasure (vv. 35-41). And here is the principle: whatever Satan's world lays before us as beautiful, attractive, and pleasurable becomes a stinging viper. Satan never gives good gifts to those who choose to follow him. Like the cigar given by one clown to another, they always blow up in your face.

Hosea pictured Israel's spiritual adultery in a much more personal way. He obeyed God's command, "Take to yourself a wife of harlotry" (Hosea 1:2), and he became a living illustration of Yahweh having an unfaithful wife. His children's names described Israel's faithlessness: Jezreel (scattered), Lo-Ruhamah (not pitied), and Lo-Ammi (not my kin). Hosea's wife Gomer then left Hosea and lived as a harlot, picturing Israel's life in rebellion and spiritual adultery (3:1). Hosea purchased Gomer from slavery (3:2) and brought her back to himself. So she belonged to Hosea by choice (1:3) and by purchase (3:2). How well Hosea pictured the coming work of Christ to purchase those whom He had already chosen!

But our concern should extend beyond avoiding spiritual adultery. According to God's Word, believers are not even to be friends with the world (James 4:4). Friendship has the idea of "a spiritual affinity, a deeply shared unity, to be, in effect—one soul" (Luke T. Johnson, "James," in *Harper's Bible Commentary* [New York: Harper & Row, 1988], 1276). James declared that friendship with the world, or being "at one" with the things in the world, is more than just a minor wrong turn on the highway of spiritual development. It is a detour that leads to spiritual degradation. What one loves or is one soul with shows where adoration and intimacy are centered.

A poll recently reported in *The Wall Street Journal* stated that 38 percent of American men loved their cars more than women. What would a poll show if believers today were asked where God ranked in their priorities of love? What would push God out of first place? Car? Home? Bank accounts and investments? A person? What is it that urges us to leave the fountain of clear, sparkling, refreshing, pure water to go after the brownish, murky, smelly, polluted water of the cistern? Are the waters of the cistern tasty, healthful, and beneficial? Satan does his best to make us think so.

Family counselor J. Allan Petersen listened to the account of Doug's extramarital affairs, then asked, "Why these affairs? Like stolen apples?" Doug responded, "I'm sure it was stolen apples. The greener grass. The forbidden thing. I used to go behind the house and smoke when I was a kid because my parents wouldn't allow me to smoke otherwise" (*The Myth of the Greener Grass* [Wheaton, Ill.: Tyndale, 1988], 163). The grass is not greener on the other side of the fence, unless we look (which we do all too often) through Satan's glasses.

The ordinary housefly has nothing to fear from most plants except the Venus Flytrap. The alluring secretion draws the fly to entrapment and death. Satan has set out his strongest magnet to draw us into the world and the things of the world. But the ultimate power lies not with Satan, but with God. We are to be victorious overcomers, by faith, over Satan and the world (1 John 5:4). We were saved by faith (Eph. 2:8), we walk by faith (2 Cor. 5:7), we are sanctified by faith (Acts 26:18), and we live by faith (Gal. 2:20). And because of these great things God has done for us, our response to Him must be to follow what Jesus called the greatest commandment, "You shall love the LORD your God with all your heart and with all your soul and with all your might" (Matt. 22:37). Obeying this command leaves no room for spiritual adultery with the world and treachery toward God.

"It is our faith in Jesus that
makes us believers and thus overcomers,
sufficient to live Christlike
in the satanic cosmos."
(*Basic Theology*, p. 154)

CHAPTER ELEVEN

The Believer's Spiritual Warfare

G. Robert Kilgore

As believers, we are the focus of conspiracy. The world, the flesh, and the devil conspire to entrap us in lust, greed, anger, and the neglect of God's Word. Satan makes the world look so good and sin look like a legitimate option. How can we fight back?

Believers hear widely conflicting advice: "Ignore the devil and he will go away." "You should not be concerned about the devil; he is totally defeated." "You must confront the devil directly using the power God has given you." "You have authority over the demonic world—use it." Believers would like to be ready for the daily conflict experienced as a normal part of the Christian life but often are not sure how to prepare.

The New Testament clearly draws the battle lines (Eph. 6:11). Satan can cause believers to take the side of the world against God (Matt. 16:23), to lie to the Holy Spirit (Acts 5:3), and to lose self-control in sexual relations (1 Cor. 7:5). He may hinder the plans of Christians (1 Thes. 2:18) and use pride to cause the believer to be judged (1 Tim. 3:6). Satan can corrupt sound doctrine (1 Tim. 4:1; James 3:15) and prowls around looking for believers to devour (1 Peter 5:8). He also can be used by God to bring physical problems to the lives of Christians for beneficial purposes (2 Cor. 12:7) and as judgment for the purpose of restoration (1 Cor. 5:5; 1 Tim. 1:20). What can believers do?

Ephesians 6 specifically discusses the Christian's struggle with the devil in light of the victory over the spiritual powers of darkness presented throughout the book. Ephesians opens with an affirmation of Christ's supremacy "far above all rule and authority and power and dominion, and every name that is named, not only in this age, but also in the one to come" (Eph. 1:21, NASB). The Father has subjected these spiritual forces to Christ through His death and resurrection (Eph. 1:20-23). Christ was victorious over His enemies on the cross (Eph. 4:8-10; cf. Col. 2:15). Believers "formerly walked according to the course of this world, according to the prince of the power of the air" (Eph. 2:2), because they were "formerly darkness." Now they are "light in the Lord" and are to "walk as children of light" (Eph. 5:8). Ephesians concludes with a call to believers to struggle against the powers defeated by Christ, the powers that controlled their lives before salvation.

The first half of Ephesians is heavily doctrinal in emphasis. The second half of the book contains exhortations to Christian living, explaining how the believer can walk worthy in the battle (Eph. 4:1). Paul shows that the life of a believer in the Christian community (5:1-17) is a spiritual battle won only in the power of the protection provided by God. The battle involves the Christian's life at home (5:22–6:4) and in the work place (6:5-9). We should avoid immorality and ungodly speech, actions related to the darkness from which we have been transferred (5:8-13). We are to flee foolishness (5:17), avoid drunkenness (5:18), develop Christ-centered marriages (5:22-33), establish biblical child-parent relationships (6:1-4), and promote harmony at work (6:5-9). To help the believer resist the devil's attacks in these areas, God has provided the filling of the Spirit (5:18), our identity with and position in Christ (1:3; 2:6; 6:10), and the whole of the armor that is from God Himself (6:11, 13).

Ephesians 6:10-18 develops five commands to prepare us for spiritual victory. "Be strong" in verse 10 literally means "be made strong" rather than "make yourself strong." Earlier Paul had prayed that the Ephesians might be "strengthened with power through His Spirit in the inner man" (Eph. 3:16). Here he exhorts them to be strengthened by God's power by taking on His armor. The second command, to "put on" the armor of God, has the sense of being clothed in the armor. The third command, "take up the armor" (Eph. 6:13), displays the warrior's commitment to enter battle. To take up or put on the armor of God is a decisive act showing willingness to engage the enemy.

The fourth command, "to stand firm" (Eph. 6:14), echoes Paul's earlier exhortation to give no opportunity to the devil (Eph. 4:27) and Peter's injunction to "resist him [Satan], firm in your faith" (1 Peter 5:8-9). God's provision of complete armor provides the believer with protection to stand firm in the day of struggle. The phrases "stand firm" (Eph. 6:11, 13, 14) and "resist" come from the same root word in Greek, and are a call to be prepared for the inevitable struggle. It is not a call to initiate battle or to create power encounters. God has not called us to confront Satan and demand his submission to our exercise of divine authority. When Michael the archangel "disputed with the devil . . . [he] did not dare pronounce against him a railing judgment, but said, 'the Lord rebuke you' " (Jude 9). God has called on us to take up the provision He has provided, put it on, and develop it in such a way that we are able to stand firm in our warfare against the devil.

The fifth command tells us to "take the helmet of salvation and the sword of the Spirit, which is the word of God" (6:17). "Take" may mean to "receive as a gift" or "strap it on." In this context the latter meaning is more likely. The whole armor is a gift of God, yet God commands the soldier to accept the gift and strap it on in preparation for conflict.

Some have suggested putting on the armor daily through a prayer of faith. However, the aorist imperatives used here suggest a singular act. This verb form allows for development in knowledge and use of the truth, but it does not refer to often repeated action. It is like the command in Romans 12:1, "present your bodies a living sacrifice." We may need to grow in our understanding of serving as living sacrifices for God, but Paul's exhortation in Romans requires a decision about who will control my life and yours. Growth is needed in understanding the extent of God's provision, but we must take up the armor of God and keep it in place.

Paul delineates several ways for us to face the battle. We stand firm against Satan by putting on the belt of truth and taking the breastplate of righteousness (Eph. 6:14-16). "Having girded your loins" refers to a previous or simultaneous action. The believer can take no stand against the devil until belting the waist with truth. The belt or girdle in ancient times held the long flowing garments together so they would not trip the warrior. Since all of the armor is the provision of God, truth here has an objective sense. It is God's truth, but it is truth that must be put on, worn, and lived out.

Peter uses a similar expression, "Gird up [the loins of] your minds for action, keep sober *in spirit*, fix your hope completely on the grace to be brought to you at the revelation of Jesus Christ" (1 Peter 1:13). For the Roman soldier the belt was the last piece of the armor. Here it is first because truth is the foundation for the believer's defense. God calls on believers to confront Satan, the father of lies, with truth.

The Ephesians were accustomed to magic in their religions. But the belt of truth is not a magical force field or barrier thwarting the guile of the devil. It binds everything else together by the truth of God. Christ prayed that His own would be kept from the evil one: "Sanctify them in the truth; Thy word is truth" (John 17:17). God's truth holds the believer in a world opposed to God.

The exercise of God's truth allows the believer to confront the challenges to faith by providing biblical values for Christian families, business people, and churches. Part of the answer to moral decay in society is for Christians to stand on God's truth against this evil world system. We must be people who *live* the unchanging truth of God's Word—not just talk about it.

101

Next, our stand against the devil and his forces is aided by putting on the breastplate of righteousness. God declared us righteous and justified at salvation (Rom. 5:16-18); we were made the righteousness of God in Christ (1 Cor. 1:30; 2 Cor. 5:21; Eph. 4:24); and He is now making us righteous through sanctification (Eph. 5:9; 1 Thes. 4:3; 5:23; 1 Peter 1:15-16). In each case the righteousness is from God. Putting on the armor of righteousness restates Paul's instruction, "put on the Lord Jesus Christ and make no provision for the flesh in regard to its lusts" (Rom. 13:14). To be in Christ is to be clothed in His righteousness.

In Paul's day, this breastplate was a covering made of leather or metal to protect the vital organs of the body. The righteousness of God is the protector of all that is vital to the believer. It is a defense against the attempts of the enemy to draw us into sin. The believer is declared righteous, is made the righteousness of Christ, and is being conformed into the image of Christ. Our union with Christ and our understanding of this relationship protects us from Satan's temptations. Again, God provides this piece of armor, but the believer takes it up. Our weapons (the root word of "armor" in Eph. 6:11) are not of the flesh (2 Cor. 10:3-5) but of righteousness (2 Cor. 6:7). God's gift of righteousness and our exercise of that righteousness (cf. 1 Thes. 5:8) serve as a great defense in the struggle against the devil and his temptations. Satan can confront power but not God's righteousness.

The third provision of armor is for the feet: "Having shod your feet with the preparation of the gospel of peace" (Eph. 6:15). The footwear refers to sandals or boots. The military boots then had heavy soles to protect the feet of the soldier, and at times they were cleated to give better traction in hand-to-hand combat. There is a debate over the significance of the shoes. Are they a foundation for service to carry the gospel of peace (cf. Isa. 52:7), or are they simply part of the total protection of the Christian warrior? Considering the total context, and the command to "stand firm," the latter meaning seems better. The correct footwear keeps the combatant from slipping to his defeat. The Christian's foundation is the Gospel itself.

The gospel of peace is an unusual provision for spiritual warfare. This paradox occurs throughout the Bible. The Old Testament refers to Messiah's bringing peace through war. Messiah will battle with the wicked and will slay them, but the result of His warfare will be peace, for "the wolf will dwell with the lamb, the leopard will lie down with the kid, and the calf and the young lion and the fatling together, and a little boy will lead them" (Isa. 11:6). The Christian warrior must be prepared for conflict. This preparation includes the gospel of peace as an evidence of God's final victory.

Christians face a daily barrage of attacks (the flaming arrows of the devil) from the enemy, and need a shield of faith. The Roman shield, two and one half feet wide by four and one half feet long, was constructed of leather-covered wood or of metal and was used to deflect the arrows, swords, and spears of the enemy. Front-line soldiers often lined up shoulder to shoulder with their shields in front of them providing a wall of protection for the archers behind them. Properly used, the shield protected the entire body. The shield of faith is designed so that the Christian does not spend time unsuccessfully dodging temptations.

Faith is not some mysterious barrier that protects us, but it is a confidence based on clear, objective truth. The object of faith is the crucified, risen, and ascended Christ. Faith doesn't mean a blind hope or some intangible desire for gifts or blessing, but it is a total dependence on God and His Word.

In the Gospels Christ performed miracles of healing, feeding, delivering from evil spirits, raising the dead, and controlling nature. Yet Christ was no mere healer; He was no mere feeder of people; He was no mere helper nor exorcist. Christ's works were designed to call people to faith and sought to produce that faith in them.

The faith that shields the believer is total trust in God and His promises, resting in Christ's defeat of Satan on the cross. Habakkuk anticipated this when he said, "The righteous will live by his faith" (2:4), which was repeated in the New Testament (Rom. 1:17; Gal. 3:11; Heb. 10:38) and illustrated by the writer of Hebrews (chap. 11). By faith the "flaming missiles of the evil one" will be extinguished and his temptations turned away. As with the belt of truth and the sword of the Spirit, faith is related to the Word of God. Solomon tells us that "every word of God is tested; He is a shield to those who take refuge in Him" (Prov. 30:5). The shield of faith depends on God's promises. Faith represents the complete trust in what God has said and the promises He has made.

The helmet of salvation (Eph. 6:17) is the protection provided for the head—the center of thought and control of the body. The word "salvation" may refer to a past application of when we passed from death to life, or to the present application of salvation to daily victory, or to the future perfection of salvation in eternity. Here it appears that the present application of salvation is meant as part of Paul's exhortation for us to walk worthy of our calling (Eph. 4:1). The helmet includes our basic acceptance of God's salvation, our growth in understanding this salvation, and our living "in a manner worthy of the calling" of God.

Paul's explanation of salvation (Eph. 2:1-9) explains that we have been saved from the control of the devil by our identity with Christ. God has "made us alive together," "raised us up with Him," and "seated us with Him in the heavenly places, in Christ Jesus" (vv. 4-6). As a result, we are part of the family of God and are expected to walk in the good works He planned for us (vv. 9-10).

As a guard for our head, salvation is more than simply understanding all that God did in saving us. The truth that we have been saved by God's power and are kept by His power protects us from Satan's attacks on our thoughts about God and His salvation. Nothing, including principalities and powers (Rom. 8:38-39), can separate us from the love of God in Christ.

The final part of the armor is the sword of the Spirit (Eph. 6:17). The Roman infantry used a short, straight sword for thrusting. The sword of the Spirit is the Word of God, written under the direction of the Spirit (2 Peter 1:21) and taught by the Spirit of truth (John 14:17; 15:26), who guides us into all truth (John 16:13; 1 Cor. 2:12). While *logos* speaks best of the whole of the Word of God, *rhēma* used here refers to specific parts used in a specific situation. From this meaning many have correctly inferred that *rhēma* refers to spoken words—specific passages of Scripture used to answer specific temptations (including proper application combating the misuse of Scripture by Satan).

Christ used Scripture in just such a way when He was tempted

(Matt. 4:1-11; Mark 1:12-13; Luke 4:1-13). He could have confronted Satan in many ways. A simple "get away from Me," as an exercise of His own power or the power of the Holy Spirit would have been adequate. He could have "bound Satan," as many teach we should deal with temptation. However, the Lord responded with truth from the Scriptures. When challenged to turn stones to bread, He quoted from Deuteronomy, "Man shall not live on bread alone, but on every word that proceeds out of the mouth of God" (8:3). To the challenge "throw yourself down," and Satan's misuse of Scripture ("He will give His angels charge concerning you"), Christ again used Scripture, "You shall not tempt the Lord your God" (6:16). Satan, the liar, offered Him the kingdoms of the world in exchange for worship. He offered Him the reign without the cross. Christ's answer came from the truth, "You shall worship the Lord your God, and serve Him only" (10:20). For each temptation He gave a specific answer quoted from God's Word.

The means to answer the temptation of Satan is the use of the sword of the Spirit—the Word of God. Just as Christ was able to cite specific verses that reflected God's truth against Satan's lie, so we must be prepared to use specific biblical passages when tempted. God provides His Word but we must memorize, understand, and be prepared to use it against the devil. As the psalmist reflected, "Thy word I have treasured in my heart, that I may not sin against Thee" (Ps. 119:11).

Paul concludes his instruction about dealing with Satan by exhorting us to pray. While not a specific piece of armor, prayer should occupy a central place in our lives. We are told to accompany the whole armor of God with a fully developed prayer life. The prayer that allows us to stand firm includes prayers of worship, praise, thanksgiving, confession, personal petition, and intercession. As we pray, the Spirit helps our weakness by interceding for us according to the will of God (Rom. 8:26-27). We are to pray without ceasing (1 Thes. 5:17) and to pray that we not enter into temptation (Matt. 26:41). A prayerful attitude, not only for ourselves but "for all the saints," demonstrates that we are alert. Prayer undergirds all the spiritual armor so that we can "stand firm against the schemes of the devil."

We are engaged in a spiritual battle. Victory is no cliché. God intends that we experience victory over Satan's attacks and has provided all we need to resist temptation. The provision is His, yet He has commanded that we take up the provision. The more we resist temptation, the more we become aware that we are able to overcome.

Man:
The Image of God

"Since animals were not created
in the image of God, as was man,
there exists a clear distinction
between animals and man."
(*Basic Theology*, p. 189)

CHAPTER TWELVE

Animal Rights and Hunting

Joseph Y. Wong

I n an era where people's rights are emphasized as an ultimate
agenda, it should come as no surprise that animal rights are
becoming a primary battleground. If the animal rights or animal liberation movements succeed, our world would become dramatically different.

Owning pets would be questionable if not prohibited. We could
become forced converts to a vegetarian diet. Medical and other
scientific animal studies would be terminated. Ranching, dairies,
fur farming, and related trades, along with supermarket meat and
poultry counters, would become relics of the past. The implications are staggering, impacting all levels of society.

Conservative Christians find themselves bewildered. Some

might ask, "Why all the fussing, fuming, and fighting? And why change the rules of the game now?" Is there any validity to the charge that a complacent church has been brainwashed by a criminal cultural tradition of raising and using animals and eating meat? Is this an issue that the church should have addressed long ago?

Perhaps the only way to put these issues into perspective is through a biblically based study. God's people need spiritual insight to distinguish serious agendas from noisy absurdities and to show how relevant God's Word is to the issues we face and the times in which we live.

Why Now?

Several factors have come together to bring about the movement of animal rights. The post '60s "silent spring" pesticide concerns made us more aware of ecology, including animal protection. The '50s emphasis on civil rights was followed by feminist rights in the '60s and then by gay rights in the '80s. This "rights revolution," after addressing human needs, began to concern itself with nonhumans.

And so historic vegetarians and old-line anti-animal-experimenters came together with these new kindred souls to ride a modern bandwagon of animal sympathy into prominence today. Further help came from the media which ennobled the protectionist spokespersons by disseminating their sound bites and enshrining them as the darlings of mammal morality. All of this was done with no real concern for the teachings of God's Word.

Our post-biblical and post-Christian society furnishes a fertile setting for spreading such an animal rights agenda. The animal rights cause is not content with traditional animal welfare. Rather, this crusade champions the liberation of animals from any and all debilitating suffering. Such belief arises from respect for animals' co-creaturely rights shared with humans as joint-heirs of life. It is a natural result of rejecting God's creation of human beings as distinct from the rest of creation.

There seems to be little doubt that we sense a post-Christian bias today. Rejection of a Christian view of life and the authority of God's Word leaves our society with a totally secular worldview.

Who's Who and What's What in the Aggressive Animal Agenda?

Four names continually appear in discussions of animal rights and liberation. Each has his own agenda, and together they demonstrate the diversity (and even the contradictions) in animal rights thinking.

Peter Singer, philosopher and educator of Melbourne, Australia, broke ground for the birth of the animal liberation movement with his 1975 work. *Animal Liberation* (New York: Avon, revised 1990) is acclaimed as "the bible of the animal liberation movement." His gospel's great commission commands that we struggle against what he calls "the tyranny of human over nonhuman animals" as the "last remaining form of discrimination" to be conquered (from the 1975 preface).

The primary item on Singer's agenda is what he has called "speciesism" (pp. 18-23). He maintains that speciesism involves man putting his selfish interests above all others. "But to use *this* difference [membership in human species versus other species] as the basis for granting a right to life to the infant and not to the other animals is, of course, pure speciesism" (p. 18). Food production (pro-vegetarian) and experimentation (scientific and medical) are the *causes célèbres* of his book. He ignores any discussion of the cruelties of hunting, trapping, rodeos, zoos, and circuses as too self-evident even to address.

Tom Regan holds the position of University Alumni Distinguished Professor of Philosophy at North Carolina State University. His book *The Case for Animal Rights* (Berkeley: Univ. of California Press, 1983) has been lauded as "definitive," "monumental," "a modern classic in ethics." His "scholarship, originality and uncompromising rigor" apparent in this "most important philosophical contribution" and "best work on the subject," seem to push Regan ahead of Singer. He states that he intends to "lay the philosophical foundations of the animal rights movement as I conceive it," and thus "command the attention of my professional peers in philosophy."

Animal awareness or consciousness is what he calls "the subject of a life" criterion (chaps. 1–2). This elevates animals to man's moral level (chaps. 4–6), thus making them worthy of justice, equality, and rights (chaps. 7–8). Vegetarianism is "in," but hunting, trapping, and experimenting are "out" (chap. 9). Regan proposes that humans adopt the mandate of "a new generation . . . of service: of giving not taking, of commitment to principles not material possessions, of communal compassion, not conspicuous consumption" (*The Thee Generation*, Philadelphia: Temple Univ. Press, 1991).

Michael W. Fox, a veterinarian, is Vice President of the U.S. Humane Society. With the others, he contends that *Animals Have Rights, Too* (New York: Continuum, 1991, an interactive teaching tool), but more moderately than most animal rights and animal liberation activists. Arguing from a platform of "biological kinship" of animals with people as co-members of a "world ecological community," Fox demands "humane planetary stewardship" by humans as they relate to nonhumans.

He senses four rights for animals. "Our animal kin should be accorded . . . the right to life, to humane treatment, to freedom, and to responsible care" (p. 17). His moderation allows for pets (chap. 6), humane experimentation (p. 81, but ultimately to be phased out, p. 130), even hunting and trapping for subsistence by meeting the "responsible care" criterion (p. 89). Growing out of his belief in animal rights, Fox has proposed an animal bill of rights (p. 112) and an amendment to the U.S. Constitution (p. 109).

Chaplain Andrew Linzey directs the Center for the Study of Theology at the University of Essex. His importance in this discussion grows out of his *Christianity and the Rights of Animals* (New York: Crossroad, 1987), which builds on *The Status of Animals in the Christian Tradition* (1985) and ultimately his pioneering polemic *Animal Rights* (1976). In justifying the strongly polemical flavor of the initial work, he reveals his underlying theological assumptions on animal rights: "I defended, contrary to almost all Christian tradition as I saw it, the idea that animals had moral status and in particular that no convincing reasons could be advanced for denying rights to them" (p. 1). This is theology by reason, not revelation, even though he tries to build a case upon Psalm 104.

His current work, billed as "a comprehensive and well-argued theological case for the rights of animals," presents his major slogan and thought, "the Theos-Rights of Animals" (chap. 5) — that "God alone is the source of the value of all living beings."

What's What in the Arguments for Animals

Unfortunately, the discussion-frequently-turned-debate has been tainted by inappropriate excess on both sides.

Emotionalism and name-calling have been all too common. Each is convinced of the rightness of his or her position, so passionate exchanges take on fiery, confrontive, religious fervor. True spiritual insight may well be obscured by confrontative slogans and intransigent declaration.

Guilt-association terminology against traditionist positions and practices are freely employed. Historic animal welfare may be castigated as "slavery," and passed off as "sentimental, sympathetic patronage." Eating meat today is said to reflect a "vestigial carry-over" from our "animal heritage." Medical scientist-vivisectionists are accused of practicing "experimental torture" with "pathological morbidity." Our civilization is called "psychopathic."

Those who promote animal rights and liberation agree on whom they oppose. One major consensus is that the historic church, the Bible, and traditionalists of society (as well as any others who disagree with animal rightists) have been, are, and always will be wrong.

Ultimately animal rightists seem guilty of inconsistency as measured by their own premise and arguments. First of all, the argument that humans cannot have a distinctive species uniqueness breaks down in several ways. Extensive, unbridgeable differences exist between the highest, exceptional mammal-animals and the normal, average human. The highest of the animals cannot worship, develop language, examine agendas, and worry over what's right. Comparing the exceptionally dysfunctional, deformed, or degenerate humans with the exceptionally advanced mammal-animal does not solve the problem. It is valid only to compare norm with equivalent norm. Also, the movement judges humans alone as guilty of speciesism. Yet speciesism exists within the animal kingdom as animals kill and eat each other. Why are they innocent?

Secondly, the animal rights movement arbitrarily discriminates against other nonhumans. Why don't fish, insects, even vegetables deserve equal, fair treatment? Could we not conclude that they value their own lives?

Singling out some nonhuman animal life at the expense of others is based on the assertion that such creatures possess a consciousness of life, ability to suffer pain (sentience), some soulish (near moral) qualities, or some other value of life criteria. And yet by what authority are these declarations affirmed? Ultimately, most of these assertions sound more like religion than science—a puzzling position for self-proclaimed rationalists. Contrast such metaphysical subjectivism with Christianity and its base of divine revelation and biblical authority. From this source we derive a clear, consistently high picture of humanity's created uniqueness in God's image.

So What Does the Christian Hunter Do?

Proponents of the animal rights agenda and others are especially incensed with hunting. Their outrage centers on the cruelty of causing suffering while killing kinfolk animals and eating them as meat. They conclude that all so-called benefits or fulfilled human desires are self-serving, barbaric reasons for hunting. These benefits are viewed as optional, not absolute; elective, not essential to civilized man.

With any hobby or avocation, the question is one of value (Is there benefit?), rightness (Is it legal, regulated and restricted for humaneness, conservation-ecology benefit, and enjoyment?), and morality (Is it ethically justifiable?). The Bible provides teaching, regulations, and examples addressing these questions.

Is there a rationale for hunting? The development of America into urban concrete canyons has rendered subsistence-survival hunting skills and success an optional luxury rather than a common essential. The appeal and attractiveness of the animal rights agenda fits today's overly civilized human experience. Fully sanitized and separated from the daily cycle of life-suffering-death that is normal for all life—vegetable, fish, fowl, and field—urban people are foreign to hunting and killing game. Wildlife takes on a mystical, almost religious aura. Some have observed that as human life cheapens in the violence of the urban jungle, so the wilds of nature take on the status of icons, becoming more spiritual and sacred. And the hunter finds himself or herself forced to justify hunting.

Justifying Considerations

A fivefold rationale (with scriptural basis in example, exhortation, or permission) provides justification for continuing the traditions passed down over the centuries.

1. The biblical example clearly and directly assumes hunting, citing it as God-sanctioned and moral (Gen. 10:9; 25:27; 27:3-5; Lev. 17:12-14). Regulations specify proper handling and use of game. Hunting analogies occur in biblical moral-spiritual teachings. Neither Jesus Christ, nor the rest of the New Testament countermand, condemn, or limit hunting, the responsible taking of game, and meat-eating. Jesus sanctioned traditional use of wild and domestic animals, observed the sacrificial system, and ate fish and meat (Luke 2:8-11, 21-24; 15:22-24; 17:26-30; cf. Gen. 9:3; Luke 22:7-16; John 6:9-13; 21:1-14). The animal rights agenda can be accepted only if we reject the Bible, and if Christ be proved wrong.

2. Hunting has educational value for the hunter. Hunting is not just pulling the trigger, but includes woodsmanship, survival, and self-sufficiency along with physical exercise. Success hinges on full, applied knowledge of animal habits and habitat. (For hunting and educational references, see 1 Sam. 24:11; Job 10:15-16; Ps. 140:11; Prov. 6:26; Jer. 16:16; Ezek. 13:20; Micah 7:2). The hunter marvels at the wonder of God's creation which reflects the greatness of the Creator. Furthermore, he or she recognizes the unique role that God has assigned to humankind, created in the divine image.

3. Hunting has social and physical value. Life, relationships, and physical exertion around the hunting camp and in the field enrich the person, provide healthy exercise, and challenge the person (see 1 Cor. 9:27; 1 Tim. 4:8).

4. There is a sense of accomplishment. For humans to outfox and outmaneuver wild prey in its own habitat is a thrilling, fulfilling, adventuresome achievement (see Gen. 10:9; 25:27; Prov. 12:10-14; Ecc. 2:24–3:3, 12-13, 22; 5:18-20; Phil. 4:8).

5. Of course, hunting provides food. When successful, unwasted game and fowl constitute a healthy food source, approved by Scripture (see Gen. 10:9; 25:27-28; 27:3-5; Lev. 17:12-14).

Animal rights and animal liberation advocates ridicule these considerations as self-serving speciesism at its worst. But the critical question to be answered has little to do with justification for hunting and/or eating meat. It has to do with presuppositions and source of authority. As Christians we must understand that anthropology comes from the Bible and not from human reasoning. The Bible teaches us how we differ from all of the rest of creation. If there is no intrinsic difference between us and the highest (or the lowest, for that matter) creatures in our world, then we will view hunting and meat-eating in one way. On the other hand, if humans are markedly different in essence and not just in degree, then we should view this issue differently.

Conclusion

Based on the unique role that God has given mankind in His creation, Christians need not be intimidated by those who reject biblical revelation. Whether one chooses to hunt or to eat meat is a personal decision—neither action is moral or immoral. But whether one chooses to accept the animal rights *philosophy* is critical. Humanity is distinct from all other forms of created life. As those responsible to manage God's creation, one day we all will have to give an account of our stewardship.

The elevation of animals in a discriminatory fashion to the created, ordained heights of human beings made in God's image needs to be brought back down to reality. Only a proper view of God, of God's Word, and of people will balance normal, practical, and traditional life realities in the face of the animal liberation agenda. As one astutely concluded, there is no diet under heaven given among men whereby we will be saved!

"In the final analysis
one must believe evolution,
just as one must believe creation."
(*Basic Theology*, p. 179)

CHAPTER THIRTEEN

Evolution and the Origin of Man

Frederic R. Howe

Where did we come from?" "Why are we here?" Any worldview must address the deep questions about the origin of the universe, and the origin, nature, and destiny of man. In this century Darwinian evolution and its more contemporary variations provide an ideological basis to explain all of the phenomena of nature, and attempt to explain the origin of man without God. Charles Ryrie significantly and astutely dealt with aspects of the question of evolution and origins in *Basic Theology*, noting that "possibly no subject is more widely debated ... than this question of how man originated" (p. 171).

The topic still commands wide interest and still demands a scriptural answer. How is it being approached today?

Some Definitions and Descriptions

Let us define a few key terms carefully. By evolution we mean the total system of thought that postulates the chance beginning of the universe, the rise of organic life from inorganic sources, and the development of all forms of life from simple to complex entities, with man being the apex or highest level of life.

Paleoanthropology studies the discovery, classification, and placement of fossils interpreted as revealing the long history, over supposed millions of years, of the rise of the bipedal being classified as man, or *Homo sapiens.* The practical significance of discussions among paleoanthropologists becomes apparent when we consider exactly what the evolutionary view of man really means, in contrast to the position of special creation.

Evolutionists state flatly and dogmatically that man is an animal, and that his long history of development from higher animal forms is a continuing challenge for intellectual discovery. One writer, reporting on recent fossil finds interpreted by paleoanthropologists, describes humanity:

> No single, essential difference separates human beings from other animals—but that hasn't stopped the phrasemakers from trying to find one. They have described humans as the animals who make tools, or reason, or use fire, or laugh, or any one of a dozen other appealing oversimplifications. Here's one more description for the list, as good as any other: Humans are the animals who wonder, intensely and endlessly, about their origin (Michael D. Leminick, "Rewriting the Book on Human Evolution," *Time,* 14 March 1994, 81).

Recent Trends in the Study of Fossil Man

Interpretations of fossil evidence constantly change. Advocates of evolution frankly view this disarray of scholarly opinions as the battleground for hammering out the ultimate truth, from their vantage point, concerning the real history of man. These differences of interpretation, however, can easily reflect also on the relative scarcity of the fossil evidence, and the need for massive amounts of inference and even guesswork in analyzing fossil remains.

Paleoanthropologists work with fossil finds from many areas of the world. They classify fossils that they evaluate as leading to the rise of man, *Homo sapiens*, as hominid fossils, or fossils in the human family line of ascent. Popular treatments still show detailed artwork illuminating, from the artist's imagination, the rise of modern man from smaller, less humanlike beings. Much of the fossil evidence upon which these artistic efforts are based is fragmentary in nature.

To determine the age of these fossil hominid remains, scientists estimate the age of the rock strata in which the fossil remains are located. Other modern techniques used to assign dates to the fossil evidence involve the decay or change of chemical composition of the specimen in question. The assumptions in this method are that the rate of decay of one ingredient into another is constant, and that comparing amounts of material in the fossil with amounts of the same material in living organisms can give a time frame for determining the actual age of the fossil.

Searching for man's supposed evolutionary rise from lower forms, researchers generally look to the fossil finds in East Africa and Ethiopia. Classified as *Australopithecines*, specimens in this general category are believed to have walked in an upright stance and bipedally, thus marking an evolutionary advance from the stance of apes and other more primitive beings. One particular fossil find in 1974, called *Australopithecus* afarensis (designating the Afar desert in Ethiopia where Donald C. Johanson found it), is generally thought to be a transitional form leading on to modern man.

Fitting fossil evidence into a developmental pattern from simple to more complex beings is a task fraught with speculation. To be sure, workers in this realm are experts, yet they often disagree. Many currently believe that modern man arose through an evolutionary line from the *Australopithecines* into the line of *Homo habilis*, and *Homo erectus*. Of these latter finds, *Homo habilis* is described as living about a million years ago (discovered in 1961 in the Olduvai Gorge of East Africa, by Jonathan Leakey).

A final link in this line of human development postulated by many scientists is called *Homo erectus.* Various examples of this type have been found (among them an earlier find called Java man, also Peking man and others from Africa and Ethiopia). Factors that convince many evolutionists that this is indeed the forerunner of modern man include evidences of culture found with the various fossils, evidence of toolmaking, the probability that language could have been used by these beings as well as the making of skin garments.

The final transitions to modern man, *Homo sapiens,* include the possibilities of the now famous Neanderthal fossils, or more recent finds in Israel (in a cave at Skhul), pointing to a proposed evolutionary change from Neanderthal to modern man.

There are continuing uncertainties in this area of study. Commenting upon recent redating of fossil skull fragments from the island of Java, Michael Leminick states:

> Now it appears to be happening once again. Findings announced in the past two weeks are rattling the foundations of anthropology and raising some startling possibilities. Humanity's ancestors may have departed Africa—the cradle of mankind—eons earlier than scientists have assumed. Humans may have evolved not just in a single place but in many places around the world. And our own species, *Homo sapiens,* may be much older than anyone had suspected. If even portions of these claims prove to be true, they will force a major rewrite of the book of human evolution (*Time,* 14 March 1994, 82).

Major Problems with Evolution and the Origin of Man

The entire evolutionary framework or model is assumed by evolutionists to be absolute truth in all their discussions concerning the rise of man. This is a critical point for analysis. Massive amounts of inference and assumption are used to cover the key phases of the supposed transitions from one to another of the various assumed steps in human evolution. Yet, no scientific explanation is given for crucial steps in this process. Let us think this through logically.

The mechanisms or basic methods used to explain proposed evolutionary changes are adaptation to environment and adaptation to changing needs of the life form. In such realms as the matter of walking upright, of chewing and dental structure, and of the size of the brain, evolutionists assume that the vast differences between man and his supposed animal ancestors are explained by the intrinsic ability of the evolving creature to add new dimensions, to take on new traits, to actually develop the higher genetic structure necessary for such actions as walking, chewing, and even reasoning.

The overwhelming amount of sheer inference and speculation that is demanded to explain the evolution of the human brain, for example, is staggering. One is drawn to the inescapable conclusion that the evolutionist is forced to say of these major changes in such things as brain size and capacity: "They just happened!" Speaking about the uncertainties in this supposed evolutionary process, one scholar writes:

> The size of the human brain, however, is not its only distinction: the various areas of the brain have undergone specialized developments and the number of nerve cells have increased and their spacings altered. These and other changes have endowed the human brain with its enhanced capabilities. Unfortunately, the fossil relics of the cranium cannot provide reliable comparative material on many of these structural changes. Unlike other features already mentioned as adaptive to upright posture, enlargement of the brain is not immediately dependent upon a change in bodily posture, although conceivably there may be interactions between the two (Harry L. Shapiro, "Evolution of Man," in *Collier's Encyclopedia,* [New York: P.F. Collier, 1993], 9:483).

Even some who do not believe in creation recognize the stretch that this evolutionary position demands. Michael Denton, a molecular biologist and medical doctor, has written a major critique of evolution. His extensive expertise in molecular biology reveals the logical impossibility that random changes or even genetic adaptation to changing environment would produce the brain capacity of modern man. He states: "Is it really credible that random process-es could have constructed a reality, the smallest element of which — a functional protein or gene — is complex beyond . . . any-thing produced by the intelligence of man?" (Michael Denton, *Evolution: A Theory in Crisis* [Bethesda, Md.: Adler and Adler, 1986], 342)

In spite of such recent scholarly works as Denton's, however, the vast majority of scientists still hold to evolution. How should Christians respond to this pervasive view?

Theistic Evolution and Man's Origin

Some scientists and theologians assume that theistic evolution is the only position that can make sense of both Scripture and sci-ence. Theistic evolutionists believe that the abundance of evidence for evolution demands that they accept this evidence scientifically much as they accept the theory of gravity, and that they blend belief in God as Creator into this system. They stress that the Bible does not specify the method whereby God brought man into existence as a fully human person.

Theistic evolutionists state that evolution produced pre-humans, and then perhaps at some crisis point, or perhaps even through the long evolutionary process, God supernaturally added the dimen-sion of spirituality to the bipedal animal already existing. This animal then became human, in God's image.

Many theistic evolutionists do not interact with or even attempt to respond to the major criticisms of evolution, such as those previously referred to by Michael Denton. They simply grant to the evolutionist the entire evolutionary pattern of thought, fully aware of its Darwinian origins. They assume the scientific validity of evolution.

Yet this effort to maintain a commitment to Scripture while achieving scientific credibility does not meet either goal. One pop-ular evolutionist states:

> Divine creation is . . . the ultimate leap from inanimate clay to fully formed man. . . . The whole *point* of the theory of evolution by natural selection was that it provided a non-

miraculous account of the existence of complex adaptations. For what it is worth, it is also the whole point of this book. For Darwin, any evolution that had to be helped over the jumps by God was not evolution at all. It made a nonsense of the central point of evolution (Richard Dawkins, *The Blind Watchmaker: Why the Evidence of Evolution Reveals a Universe without Design* [New York: W.W. Norton, 1986], 248–49).

Conclusion

What difference does it make? Why make this an issue? Simply because Scripture makes it a major issue! Man is a distinct and separate being, created in the image of God. Genesis 2:7, taken seriously, demands special miraculous creation, not long evolutionary process, as the explanation of man's origin. Evolution of any sort must postulate a living entity existing prior to the actual arrival of man as a spiritual being. Yet Genesis 2:7 states categorically that man did not exist as a living being in any form whatsoever until the miraculous creative act described in Genesis 2:7. Put succinctly, evolution claims that a bipedal living animal became man, *Homo sapiens.* Special creation states that man became a bipedal living being, *Homo sapiens,* at the precise point or moment of the creative act. Assuredly, theistic evolutionists face many other major problems in attempting to blend evolutionism and a belief in some form of special creation, yet this matter of Genesis 2:7, taken straightforwardly and seriously, rules out any form of pre-human life into which God placed the element of spirituality.

Speaking of the work of our Sovereign God, Revelation 4:11 states, "For you created all things, and by your will they were created and have their being" (NIV). No wonder one writer, speaking of evolution, concludes: "How could God declare such a slow, wasteful, inefficient, cruel, and mistake-ridden process to be good? How could a God of love use natural selection, in which the weak lose out, to create his perfect world?" (L. Duane Thurman, *How to Think about Evolution and Other Bible-Science Controversies* [Downers Grove, Ill.: InterVarsity, 1978], 124)

The demands of sacred Scripture and the mandate for total

123

consistency call for evangelicals to resist carefully, cogently, and firmly the shift toward acceptance of evolution as a proposed mechanism for creation. Let us hold fast, with courtesy and determination, to the biblical truth of the special creation of all forms of life, and of man as created uniquely and supernaturally in the image of God.

Sin

"Words and sentences do not stand
in isolation; therefore, the context
must be studied in order to see the
relation that each verse sustains
to that which precedes and to that
which follows. Involved are the
immediate context and the theme
and scope of the whole book."
(*Basic Theology*, p. 114)

CHAPTER FOURTEEN

Kadesh Barnea in the Book of Hebrews

J. Dwight Pentecost

Few passages have disturbed readers more than Hebrews 6:4-6: "It is impossible for those who were once enlightened . . . if they shall fall away, to renew them again unto repentance" (KJV). Does this mean, as some have suggested, that a believer can lose his or her salvation? And if so, is he or she permanently lost? What would such falling away involve? Are these people believers at all?

These questions, so important to a believer's understanding of the Christian life, must be addressed through a study of context. In fact, consistent application of the hermeneutical principle of context often helps in dealing with problem texts of the New Testament. The warnings in the Book of Hebrews present a clear example of the importance of the immediate context, of the context of the book, and of the broader context of the Old Testament to understanding biblical truth.

Interpreting the difficult concepts of "entering into rest" (Heb. 4:1) and "it is impossible to renew them again unto repentance," will show the importance of broader context. The author of the Epistle to the Hebrews is writing to instruct, encourage, exhort, and warn a generation of believers who are losing patience in their circumstances. The recipients are viewed as believers, "holy brethren" (3:1), who have publicly identified with Jesus Christ through their baptism and "confession" (10:23), who have been grounded in truth (5:12), who in their past experience have suffered for Christ's sake (10:32-34), and who need patience to endure present persecutions (10:35-36; 12:1).

To encourage these believers, the author shows the superiority of the new arrangement (introduced through Christ) to the old arrangement (introduced at Sinai). This superiority is demonstrated by reference to many persons (Moses, Aaron, Melchizedek) and institutions (the Law, the sacrifices, the tabernacle, the priesthood) of the old order. The historical incident which took place at Kadesh Barnea provides background to much of the exhortation and warning of the book and, therefore, becomes a key part of the larger context.

God, through an eternal, unconditional, unilateral covenant, had given to Abraham and his many descendants title deed to the land of Canaan. Through this covenant they would experience His abundant blessings by faith. Though the covenant people later languished in Egypt, God remembered His covenant promises and delivered Israel from bondage, not through their own merit but by His divine grace (Ex. 2:24-25; 3:8), through blood (12:13, 23), and based on faith (12:28). God's purpose and promise was to bring His people out of Egypt into the land and life of peace and rest (3:8). On the night of Passover the nation of Israel by faith and through blood became a redeemed nation (Isa. 43:1) and began a journey by faith that would take them into their Promised Land.

At Sinai God revealed Himself to them in the Law. The Law was not given to redeem them, for they had been redeemed, but to

128

enable the redeemed nation to walk and to worship so as to please the Redeemer. After receiving and submitting to the Law (Ex. 19:8) the nation moved toward the Promised Land to possess their inheritance.

Prospect Based on Promise

As the nation approached Canaan, God instructed His servant Moses to send one representative from each of the tribes to search out the land. They would bring back evidence that the unknown land was indeed as fruitful as God had indicated and also would report on the obstacles they would face in claiming their possession. Their abiding faith in God would enable them to win the victories necessary to possess the land. After a forty-day search the twelve representatives brought evidence that the land was indeed all God had affirmed and was worth any struggle (Ex. 3:8; Num. 13:26). Further, they reported on the strength of the inhabitants who certainly would oppose their occupation of the land (Num. 13:31-33). The obstacles challenged the nation's faith in God's promises. The nation had before it not only the prospect of life in a new land, but also the sure promise of a new kind of life — a life of peace and rest.

Rebellion Based on Unbelief

Unfortunately, the nation was overwhelmed by the negative report of the ten spies (14:1-4). Only Joshua and Caleb focused on the promises of God instead of on the obstacles. These two reminded the Israelites of God's faithfulness as evidenced by the fruit of the land. They exhorted, "rebel not ye against the Lord" (14:9), but the people resisted this admonition. At Kadesh the nation rebelled against God because of their unbelief. Their rebellion resulted in a deliberate act of disobedience to God who had led them to the land by the pillar of cloud and pillar of fire (Ex. 13:21-22). The nation repudiated God's leadership, counting Him unfaithful. The people asked for a new leader to take them back into bondage (Num. 14:4). The seriousness of this decision can be seen in God's response.

Result of Unbelief

God had revealed His presence by the display of His glory in the tabernacle. Because of the rebellion of the nation this appearance was not to bring blessing but judgment (Num. 14:26-34). The door into the land would be closed to that generation. Those over twenty years of age would perish in the wilderness without ever seeing the riches of the Promised Land. The nation would wander in the wilderness for forty years.

Several aspects of this judgment are significant. The unbelief of that generation did not cancel God's eternal, unconditional covenant promises. Their rebellion did not change the relation of the nation to God; they were still His redeemed people (Isa. 43:1-3). What they forfeited by their unbelief was the enjoyment of their blessings as a redeemed covenant people. They surrendered the joys of the land and the life of peace and rest. After forty years a new generation would respond to God's promises in faith and would enter and possess the land (Num. 14:31). Rebellion neither canceled God's promises nor changed the status of the nation before God. However, that generation did lose the blessings that God promised to provide.

When the people heard God's judgment, they realized the enormity of their rebellion and coveted the blessings they had forfeited. They were determined to ignore the judgment and to "go up into the place which the Lord hath promised" (14:40). They concluded that the confession "we have sinned" (14:40b) would erase the results of their rebellion. Moses forbade them to attempt to enter the land (14:41-42), but they persisted, only to be turned back by the Amalakites and Canaanites (14:45). Their one act of unbelief and rebellion permanently excluded them from enjoyment of the promised blessings. The Kadesh experience teaches the necessity of believing God and of obeying God in all circumstances in spite of the obstacles. God is faithful and is to be believed and obeyed at all costs. Disobedience will not bring about loss of position, but certainly will result in the loss of blessings.

The psalmist refers to the essential lesson of Kadesh in Psalm 95. After exalting the Lord because of His great power, the people are exhorted to "worship and bow down" before Him (v. 6). The psalmist sees the possibility that his generation might respond to this revelation of the glory of God as their forefathers had done at Kadesh. He exhorts, "Harden not your heart, as in the provocation, and as in the day of temptation in the wilderness: when your fathers tempted me" (vv. 8-9). The writer suggests that his generation could enter into discipline through disobedience and could forfeit the blessings as their forefathers had done. The principle is an ongoing truth: unbelief that leads to disobedience will bring discipline. The result is not loss of position but loss of blessing.

Prospect Based on Promise

In Hebrews 4 the author has recognized that the Christians to whom he is writing are in a situation parallel to that of Israel at Kadesh. Their intense persecution paralleled the opposition Israel faced from the inhabitants of the land. These Jewish believers had severed their relationship to the established systems by identifying with Christ in baptism (Heb. 10:22-23). Their renunciation of established Judaism had incurred the wrath of the religious community. They were undergoing intense persecution (vv. 32-34), but had not yet been martyred (12:4), even though they faced that possibility.

On the other hand, these believers lived close enough to Jerusalem to attend the appointed feasts that were observed there. This proximity provided a possible solution to their sufferings. If they, without renouncing their faith in Christ, were to mingle with the observers of established rituals in the temple, those persecuting them might forget the fact that they had previously renounced it by their baptism. After all, Paul had observed Jewish rituals as memorials to Christ during his ministry (Acts 20:16; 1 Cor. 5:7). Thus many were not assembling with the believers, but were seeking to reidentify themselves with established Judaism in order to escape persecution (Heb. 10:25).

In the second place, like their ancestors at Kadesh, the recipients of the epistle had a promise from God "of entering into his rest" (Heb. 4:1). This is not the rest of salvation, for they are recognized as believers already (3:1). Nor is it the future millennial rest in which all persecution will cease. Such a future expectation

131

would neither provide a solution to their present problems, nor follow the imagery of the rest laid before Israel at Kadesh, which was a faith/life rest to be entered in their present experience. Thus we conclude that the rest referred to in Hebrews 4:1 is that faith/life rest into which a believer enters by faith, and in which he enjoys the promised blessings that God gives to those who believe and obey Him.

The promises of God cannot fail for they rest on the faithfulness of the God who gave them. But those promises may not be realized unless they are claimed by faith. Quoting Psalm 95, the writer of Hebrews drew from the psalmist's warning (that his generation, like their ancestors, could forfeit God's blessings) to sound a severe warning to his generation that they likewise could forfeit the blessings that belong to the redeemed (Heb. 4:7). Affirming that the blessings of a faith/life rest are available to his suffering recipients (v. 9), the writer sounds an earnest exhortation, "Let us labor therefore to enter into that rest" (v. 11). This rest is promised but must be entered by faith in God. Like their forebears, they may not experience the blessings if they do not walk by faith. "Lest any man fall after the same example of unbelief" (v. 11b) does not discuss falling from salvation, but falling short of the full blessings promised to those who walk by faith. It is the failure to live by faith and thus not enter into or experience the faith/life kind of rest, even in present difficult circumstances.

The writer's promise, "There remaineth therefore a rest to the people of God" (v. 9), is strangely parallel to the words of Caleb and Joshua who encouraged the people in the face of adversity: "The land . . . is an exceeding good land. If the LORD delight in us, then he will bring us into this land and give it to us" (Num. 14:7-8). The exhortation in Hebrews 4:11, "Let us labor therefore to enter into that rest," reflects the exhortation of Caleb, "Let us go up at once, and possess it; for we are well able to overcome it" (Num. 13:30). Even as the exhortation given to Israel was based on the promises of God, so that of the writer of Hebrews to his generation is based on the faithfulness of God to His word, for he goes on to say, "For the word of God is quick, and powerful" (Heb. 4:12).

Before proceeding to apply the lessons of Kadesh to his audience, the author reviews their present state (Heb. 5:11-14). First, they are not now in the spiritual state they once had known. "Ye are dull of hearing" (v. 11) indicates severe retrogression. The statement would better read, "Ye have *become* dull of hearing," showing they are not now where they once had been. Next, he indicates that they have been saved a long time, as "for the time" (v. 12) suggests the length of time involved.

Further, he implies that they had been well taught, saying "ye ought to be teachers." The thought of retrogression is restated in that they "are become such as have need of milk, and not of strong meat" (Heb. 5:12). Here he contrasts spiritual maturity and spiritual infancy. Maturity is the ability to use the Word to determine what is right or wrong, to allow all decisions to be governed by the Word. On the other hand, spiritual immaturity is described as the inability to apply the Word to conduct so that life is lived by the Word (vv. 13-14). These believers, who had been taught the Word and had lived by the Word, had now retrogressed to the point where they no longer allowed the Word to control them. In such a state, unbelief easily could dominate them.

The Exhortation to Faith

Present failure to apply the Word is not necessarily a permanent state as indicated by the exhortation, "let us go on unto perfection" (Heb. 6:1). The word "perfection" here looks back to Hebrews 5:11-14 and has the thought of "maturity" or "adulthood." Hebrews 6:1 is an exhortation similar to Caleb's ("Let us go up at once and possess it," Num. 13:30), and an exhortation to enter into the faith/life rest promised to the author's generation, as well as a repeat of Hebrews 4:11, "Let us labor therefore to enter into that rest." The writer has confidence that his readers will so respond because of the spiritual privileges they have previously enjoyed. These believers have been enlightened (have entered into a knowledge of God's truth), "have tasted of the heavenly gift" (received eternal life as a gift from God), were "made partakers of the Holy Spirit" (were indwelt by the Spirit at the time of their salvation), have "tasted the good word of God" (experienced blessings from God through the Word), and have experienced "the powers of the world [age] to come" (entered into the joys of the faith/life rest which Messiah will introduce when He establishes His kingdom here on earth). These terms are never used of mere profession, but always of reality. In spite of all this, these believers were failing to move ahead in their experience of God's blessing. Christian experience never is a permanent plateau but a path to be followed, a race to be run, a course to be pursued.

Warning of Judgment

In his statement "if they shall fall away" (Heb. 6:6), the writer is not speaking of the termination of their salvation, but rather of their failure to continue on the path toward maturity. In their case, maturity will demonstrate itself through their faith in God in their present trying circumstances. That faith will respond to the exhortation, "let us hold fast our profession [confession]" (4:14). They will find strength as they "come boldly unto the throne of grace" and there "obtain mercy and find grace to help in time of need" (v. 16). Such a failure to avail themselves of the help so readily available would be tantamount to Israel's unbelief at Kadesh. This failure to walk by faith is the "falling away" of Hebrews 6:6.

A serious warning of the consequences of such a failure to walk by faith so as to enjoy the benefits of the faith/life rest follows: "It is impossible . . . to renew them to repentance" (Heb. 6:4, 6). Just as that generation in Israel permanently lost the blessings provided by God to those who demonstrated their faith in Him by their obedience to His command to enter the land, so these (by a definitive decision to return to the outward forms of the Judaism that they had renounced at their baptism) would permanently lose the blessings and privileges promised to those who walk by faith. Just as that generation in Israel was turned back into the wilderness for forty years, so those in the writer's generation who refused to continue to walk by faith would experience loss of blessings and privileges in another "wilderness" experience. Just as Israel rejected the God-given leadership of Caleb and Joshua, they would be rejecting the leadership of the Savior in whom they had trusted. Their identification with those who had crucified Christ would be tantamount to crucifying Him again, "seeing they crucify to themselves the Son of God afresh, and put him to an open shame" (v. 6). Such actions would bring about the forfeiture of blessing and privileges and would prevent them from enjoying the benefits of the faith/life rest.

Encouragement to Faith

The writer does not view his readers' state as a permanent one. He encourages them. He is "persuaded better things" (Heb. 6:9) of them than befell Israel at Kadesh. He sees their retrogression as reversible. Their "work and labor of love" (v. 10) demonstrates that they have not given up their confidence. The exhortation is not to initiate such works as a basis of confidence, but to continue in such works as evidence of their persistent faith (v. 11). His exhortation is to patient endurance (v. 12).

Saints throughout the ages have been called upon to show such patience. The great faith chapter of Hebrews 11 records men and women of faith who first received promises from God and then without exception were called on to patiently endure. Some endured for extended periods of time, until the promise they had claimed was fulfilled. The conclusion is reached in Hebrews 12:1, "Let us run with patience the race that is set before us." To those "forsaking the assembling of themselves together" (Heb. 10:25) the exhortation is given, "Let us hold fast the profession [confession] of our faith without wavering (v. 23). In other words, "Don't be like Israel at Kadesh." The alternative is to walk by faith, "for he is faithful that promised" (v. 23).

Like the Israelites of old, we constantly are tempted to draw back from the startling promises of God. When we view those promises through the lens of human weaknesses and difficulties, we lose sight of God's promises and His power to provide despite human limitations.

The context of the Book of Hebrews itself indicates that the author is writing to believers in the church age. The dangers faced by the people of God in the Old Testament serve as fruitful illustrations for God's people today. Failure to enter into the blessings of the life of faith is a danger confronting every generation of believers. Therefore, today "let us labor . . . to enter into that rest."

"While all sins are sinful,
not all sins are of equal magnitude.
Some sins are truly
more sinful than others."
(*Basic Theology*, p. 215)

CHAPTER FIFTEEN

Willful and Non-Willful Sin

John R. Master

I f some sins really are more sinful than others as Ryrie states,
which of these actions would be the most sinful?

Pam looked across the church pew at Sue. Just last week
Pam had confided in her friend, and now she knew that Sue had
betrayed the confidence. Resentment welled up inside her. How
sinful is Pam's behavior? What about Sue's?

Joe accepted the glass of wine. He knew how his boss felt about
people who didn't fit in, and he really wanted that promotion. Is
Joe sinning?

Sam sped down the road, trying to keep the car under 75 mph.
"I'm going to be late if this traffic doesn't move," he fumed. Is
Sam committing sin?

Sally looked into Peter's eyes with joy. At last the divorce had come through, and they could legalize their relationship. Is Sally doing anything wrong?

Ralph shoved the prisoner, nodding as his head hit the ground. "They're all alike," he thought. "Just as well to be rid of the vermin." How guilty is Ralph?

Bill looked at his watch. "Who cares about these dumb rules anyhow? I can get into the dorm and no one will know." Bill's sin isn't as bad as Ralph's, is it?

If "not all sins are of equal magnitude" (*Basic Theology*, p. 215), which sins are the worst? Some would list those that affect others the most as being more severe. How then should murder be ranked in relationship to adultery, or to gossip? Probably many people would select as the "worst" those sins of which they themselves are not guilty. But what sort of distinction does the Bible make? And how should this distinction affect our decisions and our actions?

"Certainly the chief characteristic of sin is that it is directed against God" (*Basic Theology*, p. 212). All sin and all kinds of sin deserve God's judgment. No sin can be taken lightly. Sin has a profound impact on our relationship to God, to others, and even to ourselves.

Yet the Bible does make a distinction between willful and non-willful sin. Ryrie observes:

> The Old Testament distinguished sins of ignorance from defiant sins. Defiant sins were, literally, sins with a high hand; that is, sins with a raised, clenched fist in defiance of God and His commands. For such sins there was no acceptable offering (Num. 15:30-31). . . . By contrast, the sin offering atoned for sins of ignorance; that is, sins done unintentionally out of weakness or waywardness (Lev. 4:2). Some examples included withholding evidence when called on to testify; accidental ceremonial defilement because of contact with an unclean animal or person; and inability to fulfill a rash vow (Lev. 5:1-4) (*Basic Theology*, p. 228).

This same distinction between willful sins and sins of ignorance seems to be carried over directly into the New Testament by our

Lord. In Jesus' illustration recorded in Luke 12:47-48, both slaves had sinned and therefore deserved judgment. The judgment, however, was related to the willfulness of the sin. All sin deserves divine judgment, but willful sin receives a judgment different from that assigned a sin committed in ignorance.

What is willful sin? Willful sin is that committed by a person who knows what to do and deliberately chooses not to do it. Such a sin is a conscious choice by someone fully aware that the act is wrong. The person knows what is right and decides to do wrong in direct rebellion against God. Willful sin mimics Satan's original sin. Satan knew God's word and his role in God's creation, but he rebelled against it.

Numbers 15 equates willful sin with blasphemy. In committing a willful sin, the individual is, in effect, cursing God by refusing to obey Him. The sinner sees himself as "god," qualified to determine his own actions. Willful sin is so serious that the person committing it "must be cut off; his guilt remains on him" (Num. 15:31, NIV). In the context of this teaching about willful sin, Numbers 15 records an incident in which a man was found gathering sticks on the Sabbath in violation of the sanctity of that day (Ex. 20:8-11). Most people might consider gathering sticks a trivial sin. Yet, after directly consulting the Lord, Moses put the man to death (Num. 15:35-36).

Sins of ignorance, on the other hand, are done with no deliberate intent. They can be committed because of forgetfulness or lack of adequate information. Interestingly, Paul viewed his attitude toward the Lord Jesus Christ and his persecution of early Christians (cf. Acts 7–9) as an example of non-willful sin. Acts 7:58 mentions Saul as a participant in the death of Stephen. As a guardian of the garments of those witnessing against Stephen, Saul would no doubt have heard Stephen's message. Yet "Saul was there, giving approval to his death" (Acts 8:1). Saul then went on to destroy others who believed in Jesus Christ (Acts 8:3). How could such actions be viewed as non-willful sins?

Perhaps Saul should have known better because he had the opportunity to hear the Gospel message, authenticated by the miracles of Christ. However, the New Testament does not say that. In fact, in reflecting on the situation, Paul concludes that "even though I was once a blasphemer and a persecutor and a violent man, I was shown mercy because I acted in ignorance and unbelief" (1 Tim. 1:13). Saul's actions were related to his understanding of the Old Testament and his belief that Jesus Christ was not Messiah as He claimed. The death of Christ on the cross was, for Saul, divine justice for a blasphemer. In other words, Saul's actions were perfectly appropriate in light of his understanding of the Scriptures and his understanding of Jesus' ministry. Though his acts were sinful, they were done in ignorance.

Evidently the actual type of sin is not the critical factor in God's view. An act in ignorance of the will of God is viewed differently from one that deliberately rejects the known will of God. This distinction, biblically based, provides valuable help in our relationships to God, to others, and to self.

Our Relationship to God

God does not view sin in the same way that a human court of law would judge. A human court would consider Saul's acts far more terrible than those of the wood-gatherer. Why does God treat them so differently?

God knows our hearts (1 Sam. 16:7). With God the real issue is not simply how a sin affects others or how others may view it. The important factor is what we are saying to God or about God. A willful sin tells God that we choose to rebel against Him, even though we know exactly what He wants us to do. It is an outright rejection of God's will for our lives. We tell God that we will have our own way rather than His. The issue is clear; we refuse to recognize God as God.

Of course, rarely do we present the decision to ourselves in such an overt way. Rather, like Eve, we rationalize "that the fruit of the tree was good for food and pleasing to the eye, and also desirable for gaining wisdom" (Gen. 3:6). We try to justify our action by reasoning that our own way is better than God's.

For instance, all would agree that the Bible forbids hatred of another believer. So, if I hate another believer, I am wrong, and I know it. Why do I then harbor animosity? I can think of all sorts of reasons to justify my attitude. I may consider it a small matter that does not really affect others in a significant way. God would surely not be angry with me for such a small sin, I reason. After all, the person I hate shows an unloving spirit to me. He may have wronged me. Actually, though, I do not want to love him, even though I know it is God's will.

While this may be, to the world, a small and very common sin or not even a sin at all, it is, for me, a deliberate and willful one. I am telling God that I will do what I please, even though it does not please Him. My pleasure takes precedence over His. Anyone who knows what I am doing (and certainly God knows) would rightly interpret my actions as an outright rejection of God's claim on my life. My secret hatred is no less a rejection of God than an open blasphemy. Both reflect the same mind-set of rebellion against God.

On other issues, biblical teaching may be less clear. Take, for instance, the use of alcoholic beverages. All Christians that I know would agree that drunkenness is wrong. Not all would agree that total abstinence is the biblical position. If a believer understands the Word of God to teach total abstinence, then his use of alcoholic beverages would be wrong. For such a person, drinking any alcoholic beverage would be willful sin.

Other believers would argue that the Bible does not teach total abstinence. For them, the appropriate use of alcoholic beverages is a good gift from a good God. For these people social drinking might be viewed as an individual choice and drunkenness would be the sin.

For the sake of illustration, suppose that the Bible does indeed teach that abstinence is the biblical position for the child of God today. In that case, if either individual mentioned above used an alcoholic beverage, he would be committing sin in the sight of God. The one who believed it was wrong to partake and did so would have committed a willful sin; the second person would have committed a non-willful sin.

Suppose, however, that the Bible actually taught that only drunkenness was sin and that total abstinence was not necessary. Even if the first individual later came to that conclusion, his earlier indulgence would remain a willful sin against God because when he partook he was willfully rejecting what he believed was God's will for his life. The fact that the action was not a sin in God's sight would not change the reality of his willful rejection of what he perceived to be the will of God at the time.

What happens when we do sin willfully? From the very outset, deliberate sin has brought separation from God. When Adam and Eve sinned, they hid from God (Gen. 3:8), causing an alienation that only God could restore. Today, a believer who willfully sins also alienates himself from God. Perfect fellowship requires perfect sharing in the thoughts God has for His creatures. Willful sin separates us from God's thoughts. Willful sin demands repentance, realignment with God's thoughts, abandoning our rebellion to cast ourselves on the mercy and grace of God (cf. Pss. 32; 51).

Non-willful sin does not carry with it the conscious rejection of God's will. The person who commits non-willful sin is sinning but is not knowingly rejecting the will of God. In fact, like Saul, he may be trying to please God. Just as a parent reacts quite differently to a child's actions done in ignorance, so does God.

In the Old Testament, God provided for non-willful sin through an offering to be sacrificed when the sin was discovered (Lev. 4:1–6:7; Num. 15:22-29; Heb. 9:7). The offering provided a public confession of the reality of the sin, though unintentional. These offerings were known as non-sweet savor offerings, because they were required. A person who obeyed the Lord in the offering could once again have confidence in his relationship to a holy God. In the New Testament, 1 John 1:9 describes the same process. A person who discovers he has committed a non-willful sin simply confesses it to the Lord. Based on the promise of this verse, the child of God would have his sins forgiven and be cleansed from all unrighteousness.

God knows whether a sin is willful or non-willful. No one can claim ignorance concerning the will of God in the same way a child might claim ignorance of a parent's command. The child may tell a parent that he forgot, and the parent may have no way of evaluating the child's truthfulness. Unlike a human parent, God always knows what is in our minds and hearts.

The distinction between willful and non-willful sin becomes important in evaluating my relationship to God. I may see myself as free from sins viewed by some as serious. Actually, my more accepted sins may have created a greater obstacle to fellowship with God. Even "small" sins, done willfully, reject God's claim on my life. My fellowship with God and His fellowship with me is directly related not to how the world might view my sins but to how God views them. A critical question is whether my sins were done in ignorance or were done deliberately. As Creator, God deserves total loyalty and perfect submission.

In Relationship to Others

The distinction between willful and non-willful sin also impacts our relationship to others. If God distinguishes between willful and non-willful sins, then we should view them differently as well. Sometimes a person may admit that he knows God's will in a matter but may refuse to obey it. Such a person needs to be confronted with the heinous nature of such outright rebellion. That believer cannot claim to love the Lord, because doing so requires obeying His Word (2 John 6).

In 1 Corinthians 5 Paul addressed a problem in the local church in which a member was having sexual relations with his father's wife. Paul condemned this; even the pagan world rejected such behavior. The Corinthians knew this situation was wrong in the sight of God. The willful nature of the sin and the failure of the church to deal with it prompted Paul to deal swiftly and strongly with the church and with the sinner. He ordered the church to "hand this man over to Satan, so that the sinful nature may be destroyed and his spirit saved on the day of the Lord" (1 Cor. 5:5). Willful sin would destroy the purity and reputation of the church (v. 6). Not dealing with willful sin would cause it to spread and infect others.

In many cases, however, people genuinely differ concerning whether a given activity is sinful. If we judge others based on our understanding of what the Bible teaches rather than on their understanding, we may misjudge their relationship to the Lord. Even if our understanding of God's Word is right and theirs is wrong, are we able to identify their intention? What for us would be willful rebellion, for them may not reflect that heart attitude at all.

Christians may disagree, for instance, about what the Bible

teaches concerning divorce and remarriage. Some would argue that the Bible forbids a second marriage while the first spouse is alive. Others believe that the "innocent party" is free to remarry. In this situation a person's actions could be either a non-willful sin or a willful one, depending not only upon what the Bible actually teaches but also upon his or her understanding of its teaching.

A person who believes the Bible teaches that to marry again while the first spouse is alive is sin would be committing a willful sin if he or she did remarry. In fact, the action would be willful sin even if the Bible were actually to teach that the remarriage was not sinful at all. Willful and knowing rejection of what he or she thought to be the will of God would involve rebellion against God.

Suppose, upon further study of the Word of God, the person were to conclude that, as the "innocent party," he or she had been free to remarry. Would that now change the earlier action into a non-willful sin? Not at all. At the time the action was committed it was deliberate rebellion. The person acted with a "high hand," one stretched out in rebellion against God, refusing to submit to God's will as he or she understood it.

Another person, perhaps even in the same church, might believe that the Bible gives an "innocent party" freedom to remarry. Even if that person later concluded that the Bible gives no grounds for remarriage after divorce, his or her action would have been a non-willful sin. In other words, the same action, even if wrong, could be either willful or non-willful, depending on the understanding of the person at the time.

Unlike the Lord, we cannot read someone else's mind. The critical factor in discerning willful and non-willful sin is not open to us unless the person chooses to reveal it. We should be slow to judge the nature of another's sin. Especially when believers differ concerning the moral teachings of Scripture, we should remember that we are individually accountable to the Lord (Rom. 14:4).

In Relationship to Ourselves

The theology of sin is important to us as individuals as well. Our experiential relationship and fellowship with the Father is directly connected to willful sin. Therefore, we must focus our spiritual attention on doing what we know God wants us to do. Comparing our sins to those of another is pointless. Instead, we must do God's will as we understand it.

What people may not even recognize as sin may be, in God's sight, a much greater sin in my life than something about which they show great concern. The standards of others will not be those for which I must give account. The approval of my church community does not make me pleasing to the Lord. I must evaluate my life in terms of His Word, not on the basis of people who cannot see my heart attitude.

The heart of each of us "is deceitful above all things and beyond cure. Who can understand it?" (Jer. 17:9) We can so easily deceive ourselves. As Paul said, "My conscience is clear, but that does not make me innocent. It is the Lord who judges me" (1 Cor. 4:4). Not only must I refrain from doing what I know is wrong, but I must remember that, in the final analysis, God alone can accurately judge what I do. "All a man's ways seem innocent to him, but motives are weighed by the Lord" (Prov. 16:2).

Where I live there are a number of major highways. The speed limit is posted at 55 miles per hour. Driving at this speed may lead to a major highway accident or at the very least may frustrate other drivers. If I drive above 55 miles per hour and go with the "slow flow" of traffic, how is my relationship to the Lord affected? Am I willfully sinning against the Lord's command to be in submission to the laws of human government? (Rom. 13:5; Titus 3:1)

If I believe that the Word of God mandates my going no faster than 55 miles per hour, then to exceed that speed limit would be willful sin. If I believe that the speed limit that is actually enforced becomes the *de facto* standard and I am not exceeding that limit, then I may not be sinning at all. My driving (in submission to the laws of human government) would be right and proper. In the latter case I would not be sinning willfully.

In situations like this, however, I must be extremely careful. My heart is open before God; I may be deceiving myself. In light of the importance of my relationship to the Lord, I must study the Word of God to know as much as possible what His will is (2 Tim. 2:15).

The supremely important factor for my relationship to the Lord is to avoid willful sin. If I am willfully sinning, I need to recognize exactly what that implies in terms of my relationship to the Lord: I am blaspheming against God by rejecting His will for my life. I need to stop and change my mind (repent). If I want to have an intimate relationship of fellowship with God in this life, I need to obey Him. Indeed, all my sin, willful and non-willful, is deserving of God's wrath. Only God's grace and the wonder of the salvation He has provided in Christ can bridge the chasm to allow me—a willful and non-willful sinner—to have fellowship with a holy God.

Jesus Christ Our Lord

"The Incarnation... truly is
the central fact of history."
(*Basic Theology*, p. 245)

CHAPTER SIXTEEN

Christmas!
So What?

Robert Gromacki

I n *The Lion, the Witch, and the Wardrobe*, C.S. Lewis' master-
piece of children's literature, Mr. Tumnus the faun lamented
to Lucy about the land of Narnia: "Always winter and never
Christmas, think of that!" Narnia, under the thumb of the White
Witch, was cold, lifeless, and apparently with no hope. Winter in
Narnia without Christmas meant bondage without deliverance,
fear with no hope of joy.

The story reflects the plight of humanity under the control of
Satan — dead in trespasses and sins, without God, and without
hope (Eph. 2:1-3, 12). Christmas points to the incarnation of
Jesus Christ, the provision of freedom, new life, and forgiveness.

What does *incarnation* mean, and why is it important to us?

Although the term itself is not found in the Scriptures, the concept is there. Literally, incarnation means "in flesh." The Apostle John wrote: "And the Word [Jesus Christ] became flesh and dwelt among us" (John 1:14, NKJV). Paul added: "And without controversy great is the mystery of godliness: God was manifested in the flesh" (1 Tim. 3:16).

Biblical Christians believe in a trinitarian, monotheistic God. God is one in being, but He eternally exists in three Persons— Father, Son, and Holy Spirit. There is an intrapersonal oneness of the three Persons within the one divine Being.

In the Incarnation, God the Son, a divine Person with the divine nature, obtained a human nature. Thus, after His incarnation (through the virgin conception and birth), Jesus Christ was one Person with two natures. He was very God of very God, and He was very man of very man, yet apart from sin. This doctrinal concept is known as the hypostatic union.

Without the historical incarnation, there would have been no Christmas. Without the first advent of Christ, despair would have overwhelmed humanity. But God the Son became human in order to do something about our predicament. Christ Himself said: "I have come that they may have life, and that they may have it more abundantly" (John 10:10).

What, then, are the biblical reasons for the incarnation of Jesus Christ? Why did the eternal Son come into our time-space universe? Why is Christmas relevant?

The Incarnation Reveals God

What is God like? Is He like a tree? a star? a lion? Is He like us humans? Does God have feelings? Does He care about us? Can He love and forgive us? John wrote: "No one has seen God at any time" (John 1:18). Though God is spirit and everywhere present in His divine being (John 4:24; 1 Tim. 1:17), we cannot see or touch Him. So how can we know God? *We need to know.*

We can know truths about God as we examine His creative works. With David, we can testify: "The heavens declare the glory of God; and the firmament shows His handiwork" (Ps. 19:1). By empirical investigation and rational thinking, we can conclude that

God exists and that He is both powerful and intelligent (see Rom. 1:19-20).

However, we could never know God personally unless He chose to reveal Himself to us. That is the reason Christ became human. He declared: "He who has seen me has seen the Father" (John 14:9). Jesus Christ and the Father are two separate persons. Christ was not the Father, nor was the Father the Son. But all that the Father is in His divine essence, so was and is Jesus Christ. "The only begotten Son, who is in the bosom of the Father, He has declared Him" (1:18).

What is God like? Look at Christ! Is God compassionate? We can know positively that He is because Christ wept and was moved with compassion toward people and their needs (John 11:35-36). Does God care about children? We can know that He does because Christ welcomed children and blessed them (Matt. 18:1-2). Will God forgive our sins? We can know that He will because Christ forgave many, including harlots (Luke 7:40-50). God wanted us to know Him, and we can know Him through His Son, Jesus Christ.

The Incarnation Provides the Promised Messiah

Can God be trusted? Does He always keep His word? Will His promises to us be completely fulfilled? We need someone in whom we can have implicit confidence. *We need to believe.*

God promised a fallen Adam and Eve that He would send one who would destroy Satan. In the Garden in Eden God declared to Satan: "And I will put enmity between you and the woman, and between your seed and her Seed; He shall bruise your head, and you shall bruise His heel" (Gen. 3:15).

The promise of the seed of the woman finds its ultimate fulfillment in the virgin conception and birth of Christ. Paul wrote: "But when the fullness of the time had come, God sent forth His Son, born of a woman" (Gal. 4:4). God preserved the line of the promised Messiah through Seth, Noah, Shem, Abraham, Isaac, Jacob, Judah, David, and Mary, who traced her physical ancestry through these men (Luke 3:23-38). Thousands of years passed before "the fullness of time" occurred, but God kept His word.

The Angel Gabriel announced to Mary the divine message that she would be the mother of the promised Messiah, the one who would rule as the divine-Davidic king over the world (Luke 1:26-33). Paul expounded the Gospel of God "which He promised before through His prophets in the Holy Scriptures, concerning His Son Jesus Christ our Lord, who was born of the seed of David according to the flesh" (Rom. 1:2-3).

Since God kept this promise, we can believe Him for the fulfillment of His other promises to us. Even though we may not live long enough to see the finalization of all of His promises, we can believe that they will come to pass. God is trustworthy; His word of promise is sure. We need to believe Him and we can believe Him.

The Incarnation Provides Redemption for Humankind

As the walls of eastern European communism fell, we saw the insatiable desire of people to be free from totalitarianism, fear, and economic bondage. Freedom is part of what it means to be in the image of God. God is a free being, free to do what expresses His essence. We, however, have become enslaved to sin. Jesus taught that "whoever commits sin is a slave of sin" (John 8:34). Without Christ we are not free to become what we should be because we live in bondage to sin. Christ openly declared, "Therefore if the Son makes you free, you shall be free indeed" (v. 36).

We need to be free. In sin is limitation; in redemption is deliverance. Only through the Incarnation could Christ secure such freedom for us. Christ redeemed us with His "precious blood" (1 Peter 1:19). God has no blood in His spirit being, yet there can be no remission of sins apart from the shedding of blood (Heb. 9:22). God the Son needed to acquire a complete human nature, including a material body with its essential properties, in order to die and to shed blood.

Through the incarnation, God provided a human body for His Son (Heb. 10:5). We then were "sanctified through the offering of the body of Jesus Christ once for all" (v. 10). Death requires a body, and Christ acquired that body through his birth by a virgin.

Paul wrote: "For there is one God and one Mediator between God and men, the Man Christ Jesus" (1 Tim. 2:5). God could not arbitrarily forgive or excuse sin. There had to be a divine-human mediator who could satisfy the righteous demands of God for our sin (2 Cor. 5:21). One day, believers will praise Christ with this anthem of worship: "You are worthy to take the scroll and to open its seals for you were slain, and have redeemed us to God by your blood out of every tribe and tongue and people and nation" (Rev. 5:9). Yes, we need to be delivered from our human bondage to sin. *We need to be free.*

The Incarnation Destroys Satan

All of us have been tempted to sin by our adversary Satan, and all of us have succumbed to his evil solicitations. Satan and his fallen angelic followers have constantly fought against God, the holy angels, and God's redeemed people. We need to be on spiritual alert. We need to win over Satan. *We need to have victory.*

Satan is the father of lies and the author of sin (John 8:44). He encouraged Adam and Eve to rebel against God. As a result, the "whole world lies under the sway of the wicked one" (1 John 5:19). Satan uses "the lust of the flesh, the lust of the eyes, and the pride of life" to tempt us to sin (2:16).

How can we finite humans win against such an experienced enemy? Christ became incarnate in order to destroy Satan, to provide victory for us against the evil one. John wrote: "He who sins is of the devil, for the devil has sinned from the beginning. For this purpose the Son of God was manifested, that He might destroy the works of the devil" (1 John 3:8).

The Book of Hebrews states: "Inasmuch then as the children have partaken of flesh and blood, He [Christ] Himself likewise shared in the same, that through death He might destroy him who had the power of death, that is, the devil, and release those who through fear of death were all their lifetime subject to bondage" (2:14-15).

James wrote: "Therefore submit to God. Resist the devil and he will flee from you" (James 4:7). Peter cautioned: "Be sober, be vigilant; because your adversary the devil walks about like a roaring lion, seeking whom he may devour" (1 Peter 5:8). Paul warned: "Put on the whole armor of God, that you may be able to stand against the wiles of the devil" (Eph. 6:11).

Christ won over Satan through His incarnation, death, and resurrection. Believers can also gain victory over the devil as we submit ourselves to the triumphant Savior. We don't have to sin. We don't need to lose spiritually. We can have victory over the world, the flesh, and the devil.

The Incarnation Makes the Resurrection Possible

I once saw a funeral home covered with Christmas lights. Initially it seemed odd, but was it really? A mortuary is a place where the dead body is treated with respect and the loved ones of the deceased gather in sadness. But perhaps Christmas lights may be most appropriate there, for Christmas reminds us of a reality that offers hope to the questions death raises: Does a cemetery mark the end of human life? Is there life after death? Will there be a resurrection? Will we see our loved ones again in the after life? Surely human existence does not end at physical death. There must be deliverance for disease and death. *We need to have hope.*

In his classic chapter on the Resurrection, Paul wrote: "The first man was of the earth, made of dust; the second Man is the Lord from heaven" (1 Cor. 15:47). Christ is both the heavenly Lord and the earthly man; He is both divine and human. He became man in order to provide victory over death. Christ died and rose again, and His resurrection guarantees the resurrection of all (15:20).

When Christ returns, "the dead will be raised incorruptible, and we shall be changed. For this corruptible must put on incorruption, and this mortal must put on immortality" (1 Cor. 15:52-53).

Christ's birth has made possible the spring of resurrection that follows the winter of death. Today Christ has a resurrected, immortal, incorruptible body. One day we also will have new bodies no longer subject to disease and death. In that day "we shall be like Him for we shall see Him as He is" (1 John 3:2). Because of His victory over death, we can have hope.

The Incarnation Enables Fellowship

God is a social Being. Within the eternal oneness, there is an intrapersonal fellowship of the Father, the Son, and the Holy Spirit.

God likewise created humans to be social. After He made Adam, the Creator said: "It is not good that man should be alone" (Gen. 2:18), and God formed Eve to be Adam's social companion.

As humans made in the image of God, *we need to share life with others.* And we need to relate to both God and man. We were never designed to spend life alone, estranged from other humans or from God. In the Incarnation, God reached out to reconcile us to Him and to bring us into living fellowship with Himself and His people (1 John 1:2-3). To have fellowship is to share in common with others the very life of God—to love Him and to enjoy Him and all that He has abundantly provided through Christ.

The Incarnation Gives Us a Sympathetic High Priest

An old Gospel song says: "I am weak, but you are strong." As Alexander Pope observed, "To err is human; to forgive is divine." We are finite, prone to sin and moral weakness. *We need compassion and mercy—understanding and help.*

How could God ever sympathize with our human frailty? Through the Incarnation, God the Son acquired our human essence apart from sin. He does understand what we are going through. He experienced rejection, disappointment, and betrayal. He felt hatred, ridicule, and scorn. "For we do not have a High Priest who cannot sympathize with our weaknesses, but was in all points tempted as we are, yet without sin. Let us therefore come boldly to the throne of grace, that we may obtain mercy and find grace to help in time of need" (Heb. 4:15-16).

Christ can comfort and encourage us. He has walked in our shoes. We can go to Him at all times to receive His gracious support.

The Incarnation Provides the Ultimate Example

Role models are all around us, but unfortunately, they often disappoint us. Athletes succumb to drugs, politicians deceive their public, and parents cheat on each other. We soon find out that all of our heroes have feet of clay. They are imperfect just like we are.

But there is one perfect human example—Jesus Christ. *We*

should walk "just as He walked" (1 John 2:6). Christ left us "an example, that [we] should follow His steps" (1 Peter 2:21). Whenever we have to make a moral decision, we should ask: "What would Christ do if He were in our situation?" We must remember that we are in Christ and that Christ is in us. Paul expressed the essence of the Christian life: "For to me, to live is Christ" (Phil. 1:21). As the life of the vine flows through its branches, so Christ wants to live His life through us.

Paul admonished: "Let this mind be in you which was also in Christ Jesus" (Phil. 2:5). We must have His mind-set. We must live in obedience to the will of God, as He did. We must serve others in humility, as Jesus did (John 13:13-15; Phil. 2:5-8).We must give in love as He did (John 15:13; 2 Cor. 8:9). Ralph Waldo Emerson wrote: "Rings and jewels are not gifts, but apologies for gifts. The only gift is a portion of thyself." In the Incarnation, we can see the very essence of the gift and the giver (John 3:16).

Christmas did happen 2,000 years ago. Because it happened, the ice of winter is thawing. The eternal spring of new life has broken through. "Thanks be to God for His indescribable gift!" (2 Cor. 9:15)

"Some do not present [the Gospel]
purely; some do not present it clearly;
some do not present it sincerely.
But because God is gracious,
He often gives light and faith
in spite of our imprecise witness."
(*Basic Theology*, p. 335)

CHAPTER SEVENTEEN

What Is the
Gospel?

Thomas R. Edgar

Although it is commonly thought that all of the main theological issues have been resolved, after almost 2,000 years the most fundamental issue of all is still debated: What is the Gospel? Bible-believing Christians, even evangelists whose very ministry is to proclaim the Gospel, disagree on this issue. This is not a debate over some minute detail of theology, but concerns that most basic of eternal issues,"How can I become a Christian? How can I go to heaven? How can I be right with God?"

One of the main purposes for the church's continued existence on earth is to proclaim the Gospel. But how can I proclaim the Gospel if I don't know what to say? If I, as a professing Christian, cannot clearly tell someone how to become a Christian, then how can they rely on anything else I say about spiritual things? If I cannot clearly tell someone else how to be saved, then how can I be sure that I am saved?

The Gospel Is . . .

The biblical message of the Gospel is stated in many passages (such as John 20:31; Acts 10:43; 13:39; Rom. 1:16-17; 3:22-24; 4:3-5; 10:4; 1 Cor. 15:3-7), but is summed up well in Acts 16:31. In answer to the Philippian jailer's question, "What must I do to be saved?" Paul and Silas answered, "Believe on the Lord Jesus Christ and you will be saved." People must hear that Jesus is the Son of God; that is, He is deity, He is Lord. They must also hear that He died for our sins; thus, we can be forgiven. They must hear that He rose from the dead and is living now. The Gospel includes this content to specify that Jesus Christ is the object of our belief. The Gospel also includes what we must do in order to receive this salvation: we must believe on Jesus Christ, the Living Lord.

Distinctives of the Gospel

There are at least two major distinctions between the Gospel of Jesus Christ and other religions. First, the Gospel focuses on Jesus, God's Son, as the only way to be right with God. Jesus Himself made this very clear when He said, "I am the way, the truth, and the life. No one comes to the Father except by Me" (John 14:6). The Apostle Peter also said, "There is no salvation in any other, for there is no other name under heaven given to men, by which we must be saved" (Acts 4:12, author's trans.). According to the Bible, Jesus Christ is the only way. No other religious or secular system, or method, or deeds, or sincerity, or zeal can make people right with God. Any other approach will leave them facing God in the final judgment, still accountable for their sins.

God has not left us alone to sort through the bewildering array of religions, philosophies, and methodologies present in this world. Such a task would be like standing at an intersection with no way to determine which of the roads leads to our destination. We would have no way to know which way is correct, or whether we made the right choice. Life's most important decision would be left to chance. But God has made the way clear and definite, so we can have hope. We can know the way. We know that when we belong to Jesus Christ we have eternal life.

Not only does this fact give assurance of eternal life to us who believe, but it also means that all unbelievers lack eternal life, no matter how good or sincere they may be. Apart from this Gospel there is no hope. We are bearers of a message which all must hear and believe to be right with God. Thus, we have a serious responsibility to understand and to accurately proclaim the Gospel, backing up our words with our lives.

The Gospel also differs from all other religious systems in how we personally appropriate its benefits. The salvation offered in the Gospel is received through faith and given entirely by God's grace. It is a free gift to everyone who believes. It does not depend on ability or effort. We know that Jesus' death on the cross was sufficient. Because we contribute nothing, and it all depends on Jesus' death on the cross, we can have assurance of eternal life. This is an assurance which we could never have if any part of our salvation depended on us.

Faith Alone: No Additions

All professing Christians claim that faith in Christ is necessary for salvation. However, some add the requirements of baptism, or repentance in the sense of sorrowing or turning from sin, or confession before others to that faith. Every one of these is a work, and is thus contrary to the statements of Scripture. All of the passages discussing salvation and baptism conclude that baptism is not necessary to or part of salvation, although it should follow salvation. The repentance mentioned in the Scripture is neither sorrow nor turning away from sin, but a "change of mind" involved in turning from sin to the Lord Jesus Christ by faith for salvation. The word "confession" in connection with salvation only occurs in Romans 10:9-10. The structure of this passage and argument reveals that this confession corresponds to the "calling on the name of the Lord" in Romans 10:13-14, and is the natural response of faith when someone responds to the Gospel (v. 14). It is the confession, "Lord, I believe."

Any addition to faith in the Lord Jesus Christ clouds the issue and removes the Gospel's focus on Jesus Christ as the specific object of faith. Such additions have at least two very serious practical ramifications: (1) If the person trusts in Christ plus something else, can he really be trusting completely in Christ? (2) If one responds to a proclamation that Christ plus something is necessary for salvation, can one really understand that Jesus Christ has completely accomplished all that is necessary for salvation? Experience shows that sooner or later such a gospel results in stressing the "something else," and faith in Jesus Christ is taken for granted and deemphasized.

Faith Alone: What Does It Mean?

Faith alone is the biblical view of the proper response to the Gospel, and this response itself is also part of the Gospel. As straightforward as this seems to be, there are two opposing camps among those who claim that faith alone is necessary for salvation. The "Free-Grace" position not only believes that salvation is only by faith alone in Christ, it defines faith in the customary way as belief or trust.

The opposing view, "Lordship-Salvation," claims to believe in faith alone, but defines faith as belief that includes a commitment to let Christ rule (be Lord) over one's life. This commitment involves doing whatever Christ requires and living as a Christian should (see John R.W. Stott, *Basic Christianity* [Downers Grove, Ill.: InterVarsity, 1964], 107–15, for example).

We gain real insight into what this means when we ask the obvious question, "Suppose someone genuinely commits himself to let Christ be Lord over his life and thus is saved. However, later that person does not follow through on this commitment and does not live in submission to Christ—what then?" "Lordship" proponents do not directly address this problem, but their overall position reveals what their answer must be. Any person who claims to be a Christian but is not letting Christ be "Lord" over his life (that is, who is not living up to a certain level of Christianity), is not really saved. No matter what the person thought when he or she responded to the Gospel, that individual's faith was not real, "saving faith" because it did not include a commitment which actually resulted in the required Christian works. From the "Lordship" perspective, the original question presents a situation which cannot occur, since genuine commitment includes the fact that the actions must follow. Not only have the "Lordship" proponents added commitment to the definition of faith as belief, but they have added the required performance of the commitment to the definition of commitment as a promise or dedication. Thus, seemingly straightforward statements conceal important implications.

No matter what standard of Christianity is set as a minimum acceptable level, some borderline cases will still arise. So who defines the minimum acceptable spiritual level Christians must maintain, or how properly they must live? If zero spirituality seems to be unacceptable, then is 5 percent acceptable, or 90 percent, or somewhere in between? In fact, there is no reliable way to set a minimum acceptable standard, since Scripture gives no such specifics. But until someone gives reliable and specific standards of minimum acceptable conduct, there can still be no definite way from the "Lordship" perspective to determine whether I or someone else is truly a Christian. My faith was only saving faith if it included a commitment to let Christ rule as Lord over my life, a commitment which must produce the appropriate works. I can only know I am saved by my actions. But since I cannot know what I might do in the future, then I can never have assurance that I am really saved. For example, suppose I live at 95 percent effectiveness most of my Christian life, but when I reach the age of sixty-five I become completely "carnal." By the "Lordship" definition, I wasn't really saved at all.

Although "Lordship-Salvation" proponents deny it, their view seems works-oriented, not only with respect to assurance but regarding salvation itself. In effect, the person works out a "deal" with God, "If You save me, I will live according to a certain standard and do what You ask." God knows that this promise is either genuine, and so saves him; or that it is not genuine, and so does not save him.

If I contract to buy a house and commit myself to make payments (works), and on that basis move into the house and make the payments, is a gift by the owner's grace, or am I paying (working) for it? If I make payments in order to move into the house and must maintain these payments in order to stay in the house (standard works-salvation), is this any less a gift by the owner's grace? Ownership is based on works in both cases. "Lordship-Salvation" provides no more assurance than any works-oriented gospel.

"Lordship" proponents often argue that, according to Scripture, all believers will produce fruit. However, even if all believers do produce fruit, this does not argue for their position. Since the Spirit of God is resident in every believer, the fact that a believer produces fruit can depend entirely on the post-conversion action of the indwelling Spirit. Therefore, we cannot assume that any fruit in a believer's life is due to any type of commitment prior to or involved in the act of salvation. Thus, fruit in a believer's life is no evidence for including "commitment" as part of genuine faith.

"Lordship-Salvation," since it provides no specifics by which to measure the validity of someone's profession, is not a helpful point of view. It is basically an anti-"Free-Grace" position. This is revealed, not only in the content of the arguments, but by the frequent use of negative and emotional terms such as "cheap grace" and "easy believism" to refer to the "Free-Grace" position.

Since both groups make it clear that our salvation was very costly to God in giving His Son, "Lordship" proponents cannot be using "cheap grace" to refer to what it cost God. Rather, they are referring to what salvation costs the recipient. If "free" is called cheap, then "cheap grace" in this sense can only mean that it should cost something to the recipient; that he should earn or pay (work) for it. In other words, the term "cheap grace" can logically be used to refer to salvation as a free gift only by those oriented to a works-perspective on salvation.

From the "Lordship" perspective, the term "easy believism" can only mean that believing in Jesus should instead be difficult in that it must include more than just believing. But when anything is added to "free" it means that it is not free, and implies that it must be paid for or earned in some manner. In actuality, the fact that salvation is received by belief alone does not mean it is easy. A person stranded on the third floor of a burning building may be asked to jump into a net. All he needs to do is believe the firemen and jump. Jumping is still hard.

Faith Is Believing

The verb "to believe, to exercise faith," occurs 243 times in the New Testament. Most occurrences are in contexts where one or the other of these opposing views cannot be proved. However, out of these 243 occurrences there is not one instance where the idea of commitment to do something or to be in submission to someone is clear. There are numerous instances where the idea of believing something or believing in (trusting in) someone is both clear and required in the context.

Romans 4:5 specifically differentiates faith from works, which seems particularly inappropriate if faith is a commitment which must also actually produce the works. The noun "faith" also occurs 243 times and gives the same evidence. In every instance where a definition is possible, it means to believe something, or to believe or trust in someone. Passages such as 2 Corinthians 5:7, 2 Thessalonians 2:13, and Hebrews 11:6 seem to make this point clear. The most specific statement of all is Hebrews 11:1, which states that faith is the conviction or certainty regarding things hoped for, but not seen. This demands the idea of belief, but does not even hint at a commitment to do certain things.

"Lordship" proponents sometimes argue that the "Free-Grace" position encourages "mere intellectual assent." What does this term really mean, and who preaches that mere intellectual assent saves? If we deny that faith includes commitment as well as belief, is mere intellectual assent the only other option? Why not define faith as the Bible uses the term, that is, a genuine and trusting belief. To believe the Gospel is not merely to believe facts. The hearer must believe in or on Jesus Christ in order to be saved; that is, believe (trust) in a person. How can there be "mere intellectual assent" in or on a person? This expression is not accurate or helpful, and only serves to obscure the fact that "Lordship" proponents are arguing against the concept that believing in the Lord Jesus Christ is sufficient to save.

The Gospel

The Gospel requires belief in the Lord Jesus Christ, and belief alone, in order for us to be saved. Salvation is by grace (a gift) through faith. Jesus paid it all. I am not required to add anything to His gift, nor can I. It costs me nothing, although it cost God very much. When I believe in the Lord Jesus Christ, I am saved and can have the assurance of my salvation. This assurance gives me hope and a basis for my testimony. I do not need to wonder if someday I might discover that my faith was not a "saving faith." Rather than focusing on the kind of faith in the hearer, this "Free-Grace" Gospel focuses on Jesus Christ, who is the Lord, as the object of our faith and the finisher of our salvation. I receive salvation as a free gift by God's grace based solely on the finished work of Christ.

> "Romans 12 begins with that
> great call to dedication of life."
> (*Basic Theology*, p. 372)

CHAPTER EIGHTEEN

The Lordship
of Christ
in Romans 12:1-2

Zane C. Hodges

I beseech you therefore, brethren, by the mercies of God, that you present your bodies a living sacrifice, holy, acceptable to God, which is your reasonable service. And do not be conformed to this world, but be transformed by the renewing of your mind, that you may prove what is that good and acceptable and perfect will of God (Romans 12:1-2, NKJV).

This vibrant passage from the writings of the Apostle Paul forms one of the greatest biblical summaries of Christian experience. It is also a text that is relevant to our lives every day, describing principles that make up the very essence of a truly Christian lifestyle.

The Audience

The audience of Romans 12:1-2 is the same audience that Paul addressed in the entire Epistle to the Romans: Christians, "the called of Jesus Christ" (Rom. 1:6), "beloved of God, called to be saints" (v. 7), those whose "faith is spoken of throughout the whole world" (v. 8). The Apostle Paul regarded his readers as believers destined for heaven. The audience should be kept in mind when Paul opens chapter 12 with "I beseech you therefore, brethren." He considers them brothers, with no doubt of their eternal destiny, even if they failed to live up to his admonition. Nowhere in Paul's writings does he suggest that a true believer can be discerned by the degree of his dedication to Christ. On the contrary, Paul's approach in Romans 12:1-2 is consistent with his other teachings. His readers should follow through on this command precisely because he and they can be assured of their Christian calling.

The Exhortation

Paul exhorts these believers to "present [their] bodies a living sacrifice" (Rom. 12:1). Though these words are well known in most Christian circles, they deserve a second look.

The Motivation for the Command

Paul prefaces his command with an important phrase, "I beseech you by the mercies of God" (v. 1). This phrase provides the motivation that Paul believes should lead to fulfilling his exhortation. "The mercies of God" refers to his discussion of God's dealings with Jews and Gentiles earlier in Romans 11. There Paul writes:

> Concerning the gospel they [the Jews] are enemies for your [the Gentiles'] sake, but concerning the election they are beloved for the sake of the fathers. For the gifts and the calling of God are irrevocable. For as you were once disobedient to God, yet have now obtained *mercy* through their dis-

obedience, even so these also have now been disobedient, that through the *mercy* shown you they also may obtain *mercy*. For God has committed them all to disobedience, that He might have mercy on all (Rom. 11:28-32, emphasis added).

These words conclude the discussion begun in Romans 9. In light of God's promises to Israel, how can Paul explain the fact that so many Jews rejected the Gospel and so many Gentiles accepted it? Paul's answer is because of the mercy of God.

The Jewish people have indeed been temporarily set aside as the focus of the divine purpose, Paul argues. But this will only last until "the fullness of the Gentiles has come in" (Rom. 11:25). Once the full complement of Gentile conversions has been reached, Israel will experience national salvation (vv. 26-27). Thus the setting aside of Israel is an impressive act of mercy on God's part toward the Gentile world.

No one could claim that the Gentiles were worthy of this mercy. Paul's indictment of the pagan world in Romans 1:18-32 demonstrates that, like the Jews themselves, the Gentiles were shut up to the grace of God. Paul explains that the Mosaic Law, which had been given to the Jews, indicts all humankind. "Now we know that whatever the law says, it says to those who are under the law, that every mouth may be stopped, and all *the world* may become guilty before God. Therefore by the deeds of the law no flesh will be justified in His sight, for by the law is the knowledge of sin" (Rom. 3:19-20, emphasis added).

God leveled the playing field so that all people would have no recourse other than His grace. This applied equally to Jews and Gentiles. So Paul writes: "Is He the God of the Jews only? Is He not the God of the Gentiles? Yes, of the Gentiles also, since there is one God who will justify the circumcised by faith and the uncircumcised through faith" (Rom. 3:29-30).

By chapter 12 Paul's readers would have felt the full weight of his argument. The justifying grace that had reached them was itself a special extension of God's mercies. They had been reached precisely because the Jews had rejected the same grace. In this light, the Roman Christians had a powerful motivation for offering to God the living sacrifice of their bodies. And so should we! There is no more powerful motivation to yield ourselves to the Lordship of Christ than the realization that we have been fully accepted before God—justified by faith—due to His immense mercy to the Gentile world.

The Content of the Command

What does it mean to present your bodies as a living sacrifice to God? Many have said it is an invitation to a once-for-all dedication to God on the part of a Christian. This view has sometimes been presented as though it were a step only slightly less important than conversion itself. The proof for such an approach is often said to lie in the fact that the Greek word for "present" (*paristano*) is in the aorist tense, implying a one-time dedication.

This approach is very doubtful. Sophisticated students of New Testament Greek know that the aorist tense is not a tense that in itself signals once-for-all action. Of course, if an action *is* once-for-all, the aorist could express it. But very few actions are actually done only once, and there would not be much use for a tense that only expressed such actions. Anyone with access to a Greek New Testament can easily discover how often the aorist tense is used of ordinary actions that are fully repeatable.

The aorist tense used in Romans 12:1 does not tell us what kind of an action is involved. It simply looks at the action as a whole without reference to any issue of process or repetition. It is crucial to note that this word for "present" (*paristano*) is used no less than five times in Romans 6:13-19. In these verses "present" indicates both what we *have done* before our conversion, and also what we *should do* as Christians. Paul writes in Romans 6:19, "For just as you *presented* your [body's] members as slaves of uncleanness, and of lawlessness leading to more lawlessness, so now *present* your [body's] members as slaves of righteousness for holiness" (emphasis added). The meaning of "present" here must certainly be virtually equivalent to the word "used." The text most naturally means: "As you have used the members of your bodies for sin, now use them for righteousness." The idea of a once-for-all pre-conversion dedication to sin is obviously out of place in Romans 6:19.

Another way of paraphrasing the idea would be: "As you handed over your bodies as actual instruments of sin, now hand them over as actual instruments of righteousness." This understanding is confirmed by Romans 6:16 where Paul asks, "Do you not know that to whom you present yourselves slaves to obey, you are that one's slaves whom you obey, whether of sin leading to death, or of obedience leading to righteousness?" Here the expression "present yourselves slaves to obey" in verse 16a is the equivalent of "obey" in 16b.

This principle is stated by the Lord Jesus Himself in John 8:34, "Most assuredly, I say to you, whoever commits sin is a slave of sin." To the extent that we use the physical members of our bodies for the purpose of sin, to that extent we are acting as bondslaves of sin. But Paul calls his readers to serve a new master—that is, to use the members of their bodies as bondslaves to "obedience" (Rom. 6:16).

In light of Romans 6:13-19, it seems likely that "present" in Romans 12:1 is used the same way, since both passages refer to the same subject matter of Christian living. Presenting our bodies as a sacrifice to God means using them in obedience to Him. We conclude that Romans 12:1 does not refer to a once-for-all dedication to God. It is not suitably used as an appeal to a one-time commitment to God's will. Instead, Romans 12:1 refers to an on-going commitment to God that is expressed in on-going acts of obedience to God's will. It is when I am *actually obeying God* that I am presenting the sacrifice of which Paul speaks. Romans 12:1 summarizes the Christian life. Christian living is nothing less than a continuous act of sacrifice in which we use our bodies to carry out God's will.

The Qualities Connected with the Command

The spiritual sacrifice which Paul is urging has three important qualities associated with it, expressed in the words "living," "holy," and "acceptable." Unlike the English translation of Romans 12:1, in the Greek text the word "living" actually follows the word "sacrifice." An accurate translation could read: "present your bodies a sacrifice—living, holy, and acceptable." "Living" is thus one of the three characteristics of this sacrifice. As before, Romans 6 can shed some light on the aspects of these qualities.

The verb meaning "to live" *(zao)* occurs six times in Romans 6, but the most pertinent occurrences are found in 6:11 and 6:13. Paul says in verse 11 that his readers should consider themselves "to be dead indeed to sin, but *alive to God*," and in verse 13 he tells them to "present [themselves] to God as *being alive from the dead*, and [their] members as instruments of righteousness to God" (emphasis added).

The Christian is to think of oneself as a person who has died to sin (in Christ) and now possesses a resurrection life which can express itself through his physical body as he uses the members of his body for God. In offering one's body as a sacrifice to God, he or she offers it as a vessel for the expression of the very life of Christ which is within him as a born-again believer. The behavior involved in such a presentation will be "holy" and "acceptable to God." This does not mean, of course, that we are ever fully free from sin (see 1 John 1:8). It does mean, however, that any sinful act is not at all a part of this sacrifice. Only those acts of obedience to God's will, which we use the members of our body to perform, are truly a part of such a sacrifice.

A sacrifice with the qualities Paul has enumerated can be summarized as "your reasonable service" (Rom. 12:1). The Greek term for "service" here is *latreia*, which carries overtones of religious or priestly activity. The word rendered "reasonable" *(logikos)* might better be translated by some word like "spiritual" (NASB and NIV), but even that is not quite on target. The Greek word signifies something that is related to man's rational or reasoning abilities, and is clearly related to the Greek verb *logizomai*.

The verb *logizomai* is used in the same cluster of verses in Romans 6:11-19 which we have looked at already. Its one use there is pivotal. Paul writes in 6:11, "Likewise you also, *reckon [logizomai]* yourselves to be dead indeed to sin, but alive to God in Christ Jesus our Lord" (emphasis added). In order to carry out the command of Romans 6:11 the readers would need to employ their mental faculties. They must adopt the mind-set of one who considers himself "divorced" from sin but very much alive in his relationship to God. The old relationship to sin is dead; living to God is all that matters.

The *act* of sacrifice presented in Romans 12:1 is quite inseparable from what we *think*. If we regard our obedience to God as a mere requirement to which we respond legalistically, we have missed the point of Romans 12:1. Instead we must consciously and rationally take the stance Paul has urged on his readers in Romans 6:11-19. To borrow Peter's phrase (1 Peter 1:13), we need to "gird up the loins of [our] mind" by consciously acting as believer-priests who recognize their own deadness to sin and who deliberately offer their obedience to God as an act of religious service to Him.

The Call to Change

If we grasp the nature of Paul's admonition in Romans 12:1, we will be prepared to relate it to his call for change in 12:2. While it is true that the youngest believer in Christ can begin the sacrificial service of verse 1, there is still much room for him to improve his priestly performance. Paul has no concept in these verses of some static or fixed plateau which we attain when we obey Romans 12:1. It is not a question of carnal believers and spiritual believers being distinguished by some act of dedication which carnal believers have not yet taken. On the contrary, the sacrificial activity of verse 1 represents a kind of continuum which involves increasing perception of God's will. We can learn this important lesson from Romans 12:2.

The Warning against Conformity

The first command of Romans 12:2 begins with "and." Paul writes "And do not be conformed to this world." In view of the activity of sacrifice he has urged in verse 1, this sequence might strike us as strange. If *we* were writing we might have reversed the order: "Do not be conformed to this world; instead, offer your bodies in obedience to God." But Paul's sequence reminds us that conformity to the world is an ongoing danger, even if we have been yielding our bodies to God for years. The subtleties of the world's allurements (1 John 2:15-16) are no less powerful in their own way with Christians of long-standing obedience to God than they are with young and immature believers. Did not Solomon himself turn toward idolatry after building God's temple and actually writing books of Scripture? (1 Kings 11:1-8)

Strictly speaking, of course, the words "this world" are more literally "this age." But the sense is very much the same. Yet the word "age" suggests that there is a time limit to the world as we now know it. The believer-priest must always be <u>mindful of the transience of his everyday life</u>. Only his obedience to God will outlast this fast-expiring age in which we live (1 John 2:17).

The Invitation to Transformation

In contrast to allowing ourselves to be conformed to the present age, we should be "transformed." So Paul writes, "but be transformed by the renewing of your mind" (Rom. 12:2). Paul has described this kind of transformation elsewhere. In 2 Corinthians 3:18, Paul states, "But we all, with unveiled face, beholding in a <u>mirror</u> the glory of the Lord, are being transformed [same word as in Rom. 12:2] into the same image from glory to glory, just as by the Spirit of the Lord." The preceding context in 2 Corinthians suggests that the "mirror" of verse 18 is the Word of God in which we can see the glory of Christ. The Holy Spirit takes what we see and uses it for our transformation into the Savior's likeness.

Romans 12:2 and 2 Corinthians 3:18 are the only two places where Paul uses the Greek word <u>*metamorphoumai*</u> to express his concept of Christian transformation. The two texts complement one another. From them we learn that the Holy Spirit, working in and through the mind of the believer by means of the Word, can effect ongoing change in the direction of Christlikeness. Thus "the renewing of your mind" turns out to be a process in which both the Spirit and God's Word are active. But the believer also has a responsibility to open himself to this process by setting his mind on the things of the Spirit so that the Spirit can minister Christ to him through the Scriptures.

There are many applications of this. But one simply is this: if the TV screen means more to me than the Scriptures, I have clearly chosen the mind-set of the world, and my thought life and conduct will be affected accordingly. On the other hand, if the

Spirit is working in the renewal of my mind, the result will be that I will "prove what is that good and acceptable and perfect will of God" (Rom. 12:2b). The word translated "prove" (*dokimazo*) seems to combine the sense of "discover" with that of "approve." We might translate Paul's words like this: "that you may *discern with approval*" the will of God. The transforming work of the Spirit not only discloses God's will to us, but gives us the insight and disposition to approve of it—to desire it to be realized in our lives. The same principle is found in Philippians 2:13, "For it is God who works in you both to will and to do for His good pleasure."

It follows that, when the Spirit is giving us this approving perception of God's will, we can discern the excellent qualities in that will. We are able to perceive it as something inherently worthwhile—we can see it as "good." We are also able to see it as something in which God can properly take delight—"acceptable," or "pleasing" to God (*euarestos* includes overtones of being "delightful"). Finally, we are able to see God's will as "perfect" (*teleios*, "complete").

Sadly, in our rebellious ignorance we often think that God's will is not really beneficial, but is deeply flawed. This was precisely what Satan persuaded Eve was true of God's prohibition of the fruit of one of Eden's trees. But the transforming work of the Spirit delivers us from such deceptions and makes the will of God so desirable that our obedience to it can come directly from our hearts.

So Great a Salvation

"Man needs to see his state of sin,
have proof of the righteousness
which the Savior provides,
and be reminded that if he refuses
to receive that Savior he
faces certain condemnation."
(*Basic Theology*, p. 325)

CHAPTER NINETEEN

A Biblical Paradigm for World Missions

Ron Blue

I n earlier years only a select group of sociological futurists used the word *paradigm*. Most people hearing "paradigms" pictured two thin coins, "a pair of dimes." Not anymore. "Paradigm" has become a buzzword. Taken from the Greek *paradeigma*, the term means "model or pattern."

Today, leaders frequently refer to "paradigm shifts in many different fields." Not only in our country, but in many parts of the world, the standards, the frame of reference, the rules of the game are changing. To meet the challenges of a changing world, missions need to change. The standard approach is breaking down. Three significant shifts are affecting the advance of world outreach.

① First, a growing tolerance for religious differences is taking its toll on the sense of need for missions. Many Christians have traveled around the world and now see distant heathen as friendly neighbors. "These foreigners may be a bit confused about God, but they could hardly be eternally lost. They seem too nice to be condemned."

② Second, churches are preoccupied with worship style and attendance figures. Many church leaders view world missions as a drain on the budget and a distraction from their own programs. "We have a mission field right here," they argue.

③ Third, a consumer society has produced a generation with low commitment. Young men and women seek self-satisfaction and material success. They shun sacrifice and spiritual discipline. They have been taught to get all they can, can all they get, and sit on the can. The can is not filled with savings, however. It is filled with purchases. This is a debt-driven society with little disposable cash and little desire to give.

With these obstacles, missions is in a crisis. A new paradigm is needed. Sometimes a new paradigm can be found in old parchments. The old becomes new, especially when it relates to eternal truth. There is no better source than the Bible.

The World

Paul's letter to the Romans reveals a key to world outreach in his opening statement in chapter 10, "My heart's desire and my prayer to God for them is for their salvation" (Rom. 10:1, NASB). Paul had a passion for lost people.

One of the primary reasons for the decline in missions interest is the erosion of the fundamental truth that every person without Christ is lost. The doctrine of total depravity is seen as too harsh. Surely people are not the sinners the Bible makes them out to be. However, depravity is not some invention of an over-zealous seminarian. Depravity is real. The Bible says so. Experience proves it. The network news announces the depravity of the world on a daily basis.

A new paradigm for missions must include an old view of sin. The idea that well-dressed, properly educated, good-natured, and actively religious people are somehow spiritually all right is all wrong. The Bible makes it clear that people without Christ are as lost as Little Red Riding Hood. "There is none righteous, not even one" (Rom. 3:10).

In contrast to clear biblical teaching, tolerance is the mood today. Soft theology has produced fuzzy thinking and mushy love. The Roman Catholic Church, for example, now welcomes Muslims, Hindus, and Bhuddists into the family of God. Even well-meaning agnostics and atheists are included, according to Vatican II documents.

This new openness is prevalent even among evangelicals. Evangelical and Roman Catholic leaders rece :ly pledged to cease seeking converts from each other's flocks. The evangelicals who endorsed this document are well known: Chuck Colson, Bill Bright, Os Guinness, and J.I. Packer, as well as representatives from leading church groups and schools ("Evangelicals & Catholics Together," *First Things*, 1994).

Paul was not easily swayed by religious appearances. He had a passion for people because he had an understanding of their spiritual condition. "For not knowing about God's righteousness, and seeking to establish their own, they did not subject themselves to the righteousness of God" (Rom. 10:3).

Even those who sense the spiritual need in the world unwittingly contribute to some confusion. The present focus on "unreached peoples" and the "10/40 window" has caused many to turn their attention from the reachable lost. The masses of Asia, the Middle East, and Central Europe merit full attention, but never to the neglect of the responsive people of Latin America and Africa. This is no time to fixate on a window and miss the open doors.

The point is clear. Apart from Christ, every person is lost. In the new paradigm this truth is foundational. Theology affects action. Until God's people grasp the lostness of humankind, world missions will stagnate and decline. "How shall we escape if we neglect so great a salvation?" (Heb. 2:3) This is addressed to believers. Perhaps the greatest neglect is the failure to reach out with God's message of life.

The new paradigm must have a sense of urgency. It must reflect a wartime model of emergency preparedness, costly involvement, and a cause of great consequence. The holocaust continues to haunt the world. Should not the horror of hell and eternal damnation of those without Christ haunt the believer? A renewed emphasis on the lost will prompt action. The need is urgent. Missions is not optional. People need the Lord.

The Word

God's Word is the only effective answer to the needs of the world. Society is corrupt because humankind is corrupt. Sin lies at the heart of all problems.

One of the great megatrends of this century has been the fall of Communism. The Marxist experiment has failed. What was once conceived to be the answer for the ills of society lies like a broken toy on a heap of discarded philosophies. Karl Marx held high ideals, but provided shallow analysis. He concluded that social structures were the problem. If he could change the structures, he could change the world.

Marx failed to realize that the flaws in society were flaws within humanity. Society does not murder, rape, and steal; people do. Not only did Marx fail to probe the human heart, he threw out the only force that could touch the heart. He rejected God. His atheistic analysis was bankrupt from the start.

By contrast, Paul was fully aware of the answer for a lost world. People need the Lord, and they can only know the Lord through His Word. "The Word is near . . . the word of faith we are preaching" (Rom. 10:8).

The new paradigm for missions must return to the centrality of the Word of God. It is little wonder that God's people are spiritually weak. Churches have become entertainment centers designed to attract crowds. Shallow praise songs, dramatic performances, and "pop-psych" sermonettes have replaced biblical teaching.

Is the church winning the world or is the world winning the church? Increasingly, the church is conforming to the world by being "seeker sensitive." There is a fine line between adapting to meet the needs of the world and adopting the ways of the world.

Effective preaching and teaching of God's Word is of highest

180

priority in the new paradigm. Until pastors get back to solid exposition of God's Word, missions will suffer. World outreach is anemic because Christians are anemic. Oh, that they would feast from God's Word!

The Witness

How does the Word get to the world? God has chosen people who know Him to reach those who do not know Him. The entire missions endeavor revolves around people, those taking the message and those needing the message.

Christians must see their essential role in world evangelism. Most believers leave missions to missionaries and mission agencies. "Missions means 'go.' I am not going, so don't bother me." The paradigm is wrong, therefore the response is wrong.

Four key questions in Romans 10:14-15 prove that the key concept in missions is not "go":

1. "How shall they call upon Him in whom they have not believed?" People who have not believed are lost, dead, condemned. Paul starts with the target, a lost world.

2. "How shall they believe in Him of whom they have not heard?" It is logical. They cannot believe in a vacuum. They must hear. Paul stresses the truth of God's Word.

3. "How shall they hear without a preacher?" It makes sense. Somebody who knows the Lord has to tell those who have not heard. Paul focuses on the testimony of God's people.

4. "How shall they preach unless they are sent?" There can be no "goers" unless there are "senders." All of God's people must work together to reach the world. Paul recognized the importance of the team.

Paul's final question reveals the essential element in missions. Believers who send others must be challenged to make the same kind of commitment expected of those who go as missionaries. Where are the men and women who will rise above the trends of society and demonstrate sacrifice, commitment, and spiritual devotion? The day of detached missions giving is over. Personal involvement and mutual partnership are the order of the day. Senders and missionaries must join in a bonded team.

A Simple Six-Step Adoption Plan

Here is a model that will revolutionize missions. Every believer who does not go into missionary service must be enlisted as a sender. Instead of being asked to support a missionary as a detached giver, the sender is asked to adopt a missionary. The adoption gives opportunity to get involved in six specific ways:

1. Daily—pray. Each sender uses the adopted missionary's prayer card to prompt daily prayer. There is constant contact through the miracle of intercession.

2. Weekly—give. Money is needed. But giving takes on new significance when it is personalized. Generosity brings abundant blessings to the sender. "He who sows sparingly shall also reap sparingly; he who sows bountifully shall also reap bountifully" (2 Cor. 9:6).

3. Monthly—write. Personal contact provides added encouragement. The use of aerograms, FAX machines, and E-mail can make this step easy and enjoyable.

4. Quarterly—send a package. It is fun to be able to supply items that are unavailable to the adopted missionary. Senders' children can help shop for the toy or book that will bring joy to the missionary kid. It can be a family project.

5. Annually—send greeting cards. Birthdays and anniversaries provide special opportunities to send a card. This personal touch gives a great lift to the missionary and deep satisfaction to the sender.

6. Every five years—visit on site. A growing, close relationship finds ultimate fulfillment in a visit to the missionary's place of ministry. No resort vacation can compare with the blessing of a short-term trip like this.

The adoption plan fits the new generation. Tangible returns and personal benefits appeal to those who find it hard to accept the traditional "establishment." Involvement with personal friends and world-changing projects is attractive and fulfilling.

Theology is made practical. "Total depravity" presents the challenge. Humanity is lost. "Biblical authority" provides the cure. The world needs the Word. "Ecclesiastical community" promotes a cooperative effort. Every child of God has a vital part in getting the Word to the world. A new paradigm offers new opportunities for involvement with rewards that are out of this world!

"Simply stated the question is:
does the lack of commitment
to the lordship of Christ
over the years of one's life
mean a lack of saving faith?"
(*Basic Theology*, p. 338)

CHAPTER TWENTY

The Rich
Young Ruler

Keita Takagi

(Translated from Japanese into English by Roger Hederstedt)

Now a man came up to Jesus and asked, 'Teacher, what good thing must I do to get eternal life?' . . .
Jesus answered, 'If you want to be perfect, go, sell your possessions and give to the poor, and you will have treasure in heaven. Then come, follow me'" (Matt. 19:16-21, NIV).

Some people teach that in order to be saved one must not merely believe in Christ, but also surrender all and obediently follow Him. Walter J. Chantry, in his book *Today's Gospel: Authentic or Synthetic?* (Carlisle, Pa.: Banner of Truth, 1970), develops a doctrine of salvation based on the passage about the rich young ruler. He attacks "free grace" evangelistic methodology, which he views as typical of modern evangelicalism. Among other things, he charges that today's evangelicals fail in preaching the Law of God and preaching repentance toward God.

A Japanese writer, Hisashi Ariga, inspired by Chantry's work, wrote a book entitled *Kagono Torito Miruna* (Shugu Shobo, Tokyo, 1975) that received broad support among evangelicals and profoundly influenced Japanese pastors. He wrote:

Today's youth are not told that, if they will forsake all their wealth, they can receive eternal life; thus they take a lazy, carefree attitude towards life. Because preachers do not proclaim this critical step, we never get the chance to see the sorrowful faces of those who, like the rich young ruler, must walk away from the Lord in deep anguish because they have refused to forsake all. We are told people will stop coming to Christ if we insist that they cast aside their wealth. I respond by saying that, precisely because such thinking prevails, today's church overflows with people who profess faith yet remain ignorant of Jesus' demand for repentance (p. 105).

Some readers will undoubtedly nod in agreement with this statement and will feel a sort of righteous indignation toward preachers who fail to demand rigorous self-sacrifice when proclaiming the message of salvation. But this version of the Gospel can be distorted and can make a powerful appeal to the sin nature.

Why Does It Sound So Appealing?

While we tend to associate the "sin nature" with acts of atrocity and licentious behavior, we do well to recall another aspect of the sin nature: the yearning for religious and legalistic control. All non-Christian religions have evolved from this part of the sin nature which longs for a legalistic guide. Consequently, the human mind instinctively tends to assume the correctness of the idea, "To be saved, faith alone is insufficient; I have to do something." This attitude, however, quickly becomes a tool in the hand of Satan, who employs methods that appear spiritual and sound acceptable in order to fulfill his primary objective of drawing men and women away from God. In detouring people from the path of salvation, Satan expends every effort to blind "the minds of unbelievers, so that they cannot see the light of the gospel of the glory of Christ, who is the image of God" (2 Cor. 4:4).

At the mention of "salvation by faith alone," some retort, "God doesn't let people off so easily. If He did, it wouldn't be fair. After all, when we came before God we sought Him in earnest; we weren't just looking for a free ride." How interesting that this reaction should so closely parallel the indignant response of the prodigal son's elder brother when the father unconditionally welcomed the return of his wayward son!

Likewise, the scribes and Pharisees devoted themselves to religious activity. But upon seeing Jesus forgive and fellowship with tax collectors and prostitutes, they became incensed that such horrendous sinners could so easily receive forgiveness; it simply was not fair! How ironic but true that these very religious devotees ended up opposing the Lord most bitterly.

The Narrow Gate

Matthew 7:13-14 is often quoted to support the idea that the gateway to salvation is indeed a narrow one: "Enter through the narrow gate. . . . Small is the gate and narrow the road that leads to life, and only a few find it."

Granted, in proportion to the total world population the number of recipients of Christ's salvation is low. But that definitely is not because the conditions for salvation are restrictive. The gate leading to salvation is as broad as "whoever believes in Him." Moreover, the following verses reinforce the point that the "gate" and "road" of which Jesus spoke refer to nothing other than Christ Himself: "I am the gate; whoever enters through me will be saved" (John 10:9); "I am the way; no one comes to the Father except through me" (John 14:6).

The narrow gate and road do not refer to rigorous conditions to receive salvation. Rather, out of all the world's religions and philosophies, those who actually end up choosing the path of salvation through Christ are few. Naturally, this means that the resulting number of people who believe and are saved is low. Herein lies the true meaning of Jesus' words in Matthew 7:13-14.

Once again we return to the fundamental question: Must one give away all that he has and follow Christ in order to be saved? Did we who are saved attain our salvation by fulfilling such a condition? No! Scripture consistently and repeatedly emphasizes that salvation is a gift from God, not the result of works. Over 150 New Testament passages teach that "believing" or having "faith" stands as the sole condition. This notwithstanding, Jesus' words to the rich young ruler found in Matthew 19:16-26 still demand explanation.

Awareness of the Need for Salvation

The young man in this account sought eternal life. He erred, however, in thinking that he could attain it by doing something, as evidenced by his query, "What good thing must I do to get eternal life?" (Matt. 19:16) This man's basic premise was all wrong. Nonetheless, Jesus did not reply, "You have totally missed the point! Eternal life is not obtained by doing something." Instead the Lord answered the man as though his assumptions were correct.

Hence we see Jesus open with, "If you want to enter life, obey the commandments" (Matt. 19:17). In reality, people are not saved by obeying commandments. But Jesus, who sees the inner heart of people, said this because He knew the young man took great pride in his complete obedience to the law. Brimming with confidence, the man promptly blurted out, "Which commandments?" To this Jesus replied, "Do not murder, do not commit adultery, do not steal, do not give false testimony, honor your father and mother, and love your neighbor as yourself" (vv. 18-19).

We would do well to keep in mind that it was still during the age of the law that Christ spoke these words to the rich young ruler. Since Christ lived under the law and abided by the law throughout His lifetime, it was natural that He should deal with the young man on the basis of the law. Jesus enumerated the demands of the law to help the young man recognize that he really was not fully obedient to the law. Christ applied the law so that the young man might see his own needs and thus be drawn to salvation. As Lawrence says: "In commanding him to sell all his possessions and give to the poor, Christ is telling him to love his neighbors as he loves himself; in the command to give up all and follow Him, Christ is telling him to love God with all of his being" (William Lawrence, *The New Testament Doctrine of the Lordship of Christ,* Dallas, Texas: Dallas Theological Seminary, 1968, 109).

Applying the Ten Commandments

The man, again bursting with self-confidence, replied, "All these I have kept . . . what do I still lack?" At this point, Jesus, in order to make him understand the hopeless inadequacy of his "obedience," said, "If you want to be perfect, go, sell your possessions and give to the poor."

In effect Jesus was saying, "If, as you claim, you really love your neighbor as yourself, you should be able to sell all your possessions and give to the poor. So then, go do it." Jesus then added, "Then come, follow me." In other words, show me with your life that you "love the Lord your God with all your heart, soul and mind."

The Lord's command to "sell your possessions and give to the poor . . . then come, follow me" was given to a specific young man who took pride in having obeyed the whole law. Through Jesus' specific application of the law the young man was tested. Would he indeed despair over his helpless, sinful condition? Jesus boldly demanded the very thing which the young man could not bring himself to carry out. It was, in effect, an exaggerated demand meant to awaken the man to his pride and self-proclaimed orthodoxy. This awakening, and not the persuading of the young man to cast aside his wealth, was Jesus' primary objective. Hal Haller, Jr. writes: "The advocates of discipleship salvation fail to recognize the commands of Christ as a test. They see them, rather, as conditions for discipleship, which if followed, will issue in salvation. The terms of discipleship and the terms of salvation cannot be equated as such" (*The Interpretative Problems in the Account of the Rich Young Ruler,* Dallas, Texas: Dallas Theological Seminary, 1968, 41).

If forsaking all of one's possessions is a condition for salvation, one may ask "To what extent must one forsake his possessions?"

If taken literally, one would have to become a penniless pauper. It is obvious that God does not demand that.

Since the idea that "you must give away all your wealth in order to be saved" sounds less than scriptural, some try to make the concept more palatable by teaching that, in order to be saved, one must *be willing* to sacrifice everything to the Lord. In other words, they interpret this passage to mean that the rich young ruler would have proven himself worthy if only he had the will to give it all away and to follow Christ unreservedly.

Dr. Ryrie replies to this interpretation by noting that "the characteristics of discipleship require action, not merely willingness to act. . . . If Matthew 19:21 explains how to be saved, the Lord did not tell the young man merely to be willing to sell all; He told him to do it" (*Balancing the Christian Life*, Chicago: Moody, 1970, 179).

If willingness is the condition, matters become even more complicated, since we are then confronted with the issue of how willing one must be. Debate over that question would never end! Moreover, no one would be able to lay out the exact terms of salvation. Neither would anyone be able to have assurance of salvation, because no truly humble person would be able to say, "I have surrendered enough to meet God's standard."

Trusting in Wealth

The young ruler not only prided himself in his strict adherence to the law, he also depended on his riches to save him. As Hodges points out, it is likely that when he asked what he might do to inherit eternal life, he suspected that his wealth might be tapped for some act of benevolence which would surely qualify him for eternal life (see Zane C. Hodges, *Grace in Eclipse*, Dallas, Texas: Redencion Viva, 1985, 41). Furthermore, the Jews of Jesus' time assumed that the wealthy elite were already recipients of God's unique blessing and thus more likely than the common man to enter into eternal life.

Yet after the man "went away sad" (Matt. 19:22), Jesus told His disciples, "It is hard for a rich man to enter the kingdom of heaven" (v. 23). Jesus thus turned common thinking upside down by informing His followers that wealth is not a pathway to heaven, but an obstacle to be overcome if one is trusting in it for entrance into the kingdom. To emphasize the point, Jesus continued, "It is easier for a camel to enter the eye of a needle than for a rich man to enter the kingdom of God" (v. 24). Taken aback, the disciples exclaimed, "Who then can be saved?" They reasoned, "If entering heaven is extremely difficult for the wealthy, who have received God's grace in greater measure than others, then how can anyone hope to be saved?"

The Supernatural Work of God

In response to the disciples' question of bewilderment, Jesus said, "With man this is impossible, but with God all things are possible" (Matt. 19:26). Herein lies the weightiest point of Jesus' instruction. Salvation requires a miracle, a supernatural intervention on the part of God in the heart of each one who believes. Jesus' primary emphasis was not on how difficult it is for rich people to be saved. He frequently told people to give up whatever kept them from accepting God. But in the case of the rich young ruler, the decisive obstacles were his pride, stemming from his rigid obedience of the law, and his trust in riches. Michael Cocoris has observed that in order to be saved, the rich young ruler would have had to stop trusting in his own works and wealth so that he could transfer his trust to Christ; he would have been better off giving his riches away. Therefore, the issue in the passage is not the giving up of material possessions. Rather, the issue here is faith (Cocoris, *Lordship Salvation — Is It Biblical?* [Dallas: Redencion Viva, 1983], 17). Salvation is not brought about through human endeavor but is a miraculous work performed by God at the moment one believes.

Jesus' words, "Sell your possessions and give to the poor," were not aimed at everyone who walks the face of the earth. They constituted a private lesson spoken to a young man bearing the specific problem of self-righteousness. Hence, anyone who uses the story of the rich young ruler as a basis for urging unbelievers to cast away all they own in order to be saved has completely missed the point of the message.

The Obligatory Work of Christians

Countless people face eternal destruction despite the fact that on the cross Jesus Christ became the atoning sacrifice for each one. God desires that all people be saved, and He has entrusted us with the Gospel of reconciliation. Unbelievers have the right to hear about God's finished work. However, they have no idea of the tremendous work of atonement Christ has performed on their behalf through His death and resurrection. Christians bear the responsibility of communicating the crystal clear message of salvation exactly as God has intended it, without adding humanly fabricated elements. The Good News has to be presented as good news. If by unwarranted human intervention we distort the Good News, then we forfeit the battle to Satan who seeks to deter people from knowing the salvation of our Lord.

Meeting Non-Christians at Their Level

When proclaiming the Gospel, we should make our message clearly understandable to unbelievers: "Believe on the Lord Jesus Christ and be saved." Why? Because our listeners already instinctively hold to the idea that they have to do something in order to be saved. If we offer them a salvation package that includes both believing and reforming one's life, they will automatically focus their attention on the latter. As a result, the essence of the message shifts from believing to changing. Satan gains a tool by which to confuse unbelievers into thinking that such "shoulds" and "should nots" are actually prerequisites to salvation. When unbelievers are confronted with a "muddy gospel" of faith plus works, some will despair and totally give up. Others will put forth every effort to get their act together in preparation for becoming a Christian, thus postponing (often indefinitely) their decision for Christ.

Many Japanese people consider a Christian to be someone who doesn't smoke, drink, or do anything sinful. This mistaken image traces back not only to the rigorous Confucian spirit of ancient Japan, but also to the modern use of the "muddy gospel" by Japanese Christians.

The Universal Gospel

In the Japanese Christian community, some argue that the message of "saved by faith alone" may suffice for a Western audience, but not for a culture like Japan's where non-Christian religious traditions dominate. In such contexts, it is asserted that, in addition to "belief," we must preach separation from sin and total commitment. But we must reject this notion. The prerequisites for salvation remain the same for all people around the globe. It is unfathomable that the basic nature and method of obtaining salvation would change according to geographic and cultural variables.

Usage of this "muddy gospel" leaves people today thinking that they have to turn over a new leaf before they can ever become Christians. Once someone is programmed to think in this way, it later becomes extremely difficult to accept the truth that a Christian is simply one who is bound to Christ through faith, and that living a lifestyle pleasing to God is a process of growth that takes place after one is saved. Demanding that a non-Christian be rid of his sins and give up his evil ways becomes nothing more than an exercise in futility, since he has not yet received the power of the Holy Spirit to make possible such changes. Likewise, it is unreasonable to demand one who has not yet experienced the goodness of Christ to surrender to Him complete control of his life.

At any rate, the best way to avoid such confusion is simple: when presenting the Gospel, do not mention any "do's" or "don'ts" required of a person after he is saved. Something that only can be done with the help of the Holy Spirit after salvation should not be demanded of one who has no such help. The communicator of the Gospel should emphasize, "After you believe in Christ, you enter into a new relationship with God; you will receive a new power from God that will enable you to live for His glory. Don't worry about the things that are ahead, only believe in Christ now, for you must first be born again."

> "Premillennialism insists that
> all the provisions of the
> Abrahamic Covenant must be fulfilled
> since the covenant was made
> without conditions."
> (*Basic Theology*, p. 457)

CHAPTER TWENTY-ONE

The Application of the Abrahamic Covenant to Jewish and Gentile Believers Today

Arnold G. Fruchtenbaum

An understanding of the Abrahamic Covenant is crucial to integrating all subsequent biblical revelation. Traditionally important to theologians, the Abrahamic Covenant also has a major impact on the everyday practical experience of all believers. In this chapter we shall take a close look at the Abrahamic Covenant and its relationship to believers today.

The Theology of the Abrahamic Covenant

Six primary passages of Scripture pertain to the Abrahamic Covenant: Genesis 12:1-3, 6-7; 13:14-17; 15:1-21; 17:1-21; and 22:15-18.

The Provisions of the Covenant

God makes His covenant known to Abraham, who is the representative head of the Jewish people. These Genesis passages reveal a total of fourteen provisions in God's covenant:

(1) A great nation was to come out of Abraham, namely, the nation of Israel (12:2; 13:16; 15:5; 17:1-2, 7; 22:17b);

(2) Abraham was promised a land, specifically the land of Canaan (12:1, 7; 13:14-15, 17; 15:17-21; 17:8);

(3) Abraham himself was to be greatly blessed (12:2b; 15:6; 22:15-17a);

(4) Abraham's name would be great (12:2c);

(5) Abraham would be a blessing to others (12:2d);

(6) Those who blessed Abraham would be blessed (12:3a);

(7) Those who cursed him would be cursed (12:3b);

(8) In Abraham, all would ultimately be blessed, including the Gentiles (12:3c; 22:18);

(9) Abraham would receive a son through his wife, Sarah (15:1-4; 17:15-21);

(10) His descendants would undergo the Egyptian bondage (15:13-14);

(11) Nations other than Israel would also come forth from Abraham (17:3-4, 6);

(12) His name would be changed from Abram to Abraham (17:5);

(13) Sarai's name would be changed to Sarah (17:15); and,

(14) Circumcision would be a token of the covenant, distinguishing Abraham's covenant descendants (17:9-14).

These provisions of the Abrahamic Covenant can be categorized in three areas: promises to Abraham, to his seed (Israel), and to the Gentiles.

Concerning Abraham: Certain promises were directed to Abraham individually. Abraham was to be the father of a great nation (Israel); he was to possess all of the Promised Land; other nations (including the Arab states) were to descend from him; many of his descendants would become kings (both Jewish and non-Jewish); he would receive personal blessings; he would be a blessing to others; and his name would become great—and so it is even today among Jews, Muslims, and Christians. Some of these promises were fulfilled in his lifetime, but some (such as ownership of the land) still await fulfillment.

Concerning the Seed (Israel): The term "seed" as a collective singular refers to Israel. Several promises were made to the nation: It was to become great; it was ultimately to become innumerable; it was to possess all of the Promised Land; and it was to receive victory over its enemies. The fact that the promises were made to both Abraham and his seed shows that these blessings have not yet been completely fulfilled, but await the messianic kingdom.

Concerning the Gentiles: Promises made to the Gentiles included blessings for blessing Israel, cursings for cursing Israel, and spiritual blessings ultimately to come through one specific Seed of Abraham—the Messiah. When the term "seed" was used as an absolute singular, it refers to the Messiah. Note that the Abrahamic Covenant contained both physical and spiritual promises. While the physical promises were limited to Israel, the spiritual blessings were to extend to the Gentiles, as stated early in the covenant (Gen. 12:3).

The Reconfirmations of the Covenant

Abraham had eight sons by three different women. Through which of those sons would the Abrahamic Covenant be confirmed? God revealed that the promise was through Sarah's son Isaac (Gen. 26:2-5, 24). The confirmation of the covenant to Isaac stated five specific provisions: Isaac was to be blessed (26:3a, 24a); Isaac was to stay in the land, for the land was promised to both him and his seed (26:2-3b, 4b); his seed would be multiplied (26:4a, 24b); Gentiles would someday be blessed through the Seed (26:4c); and the basis of the confirmation was God's covenant with Abraham (26:3c, 5, 24c). It was to Isaac and not to Ishmael that the Abrahamic Covenant was reconfirmed (26:6).

Of Isaac's two sons, God confirmed the covenant with Jacob only (Gen. 28:13-15). In the confirmation of the covenant to Jacob, three specific provisions were made: Jacob and Jacob's seed would inherit the land (28:13, 15); his seed would be multiplied (28:14a); and Gentiles would someday be blessed through his seed (28:14b). God also promised to bring Jacob (who was at this point departing from the land) back to his inheritance (28:15). God subsequently confirmed the covenant through all of Jacob's twelve sons, who fathered the twelve tribes of Israel (Gen. 49).

The Token of the Covenant

The sign of the Abrahamic Covenant was circumcision, to be performed only on males and only on the eighth day of birth. Circumcision on the eighth day distinguished Jewish circumcision from others practiced at that time. It served as a reminder that this was a blood covenant. Circumcision marked out the Jews. Failure to circumcise a son would "cut off" a father "from among his people" (Gen. 17:14). Even Moses nearly died for failing to circumcise his second son; only when the act was done was his life spared (Ex. 4:24-26).

The Timing of the Provisions of the Covenant

While a covenant may be signed and sealed at a specific point in time, every provision may not become effective immediately. Some aspects, like circumcision and the changing of Abram's and Sarai's names, were immediately implemented; some, such as the birth of Isaac twenty-five years later, and the Egyptian sojourn, enslavement, and Exodus 400 years later, went into effect in the same historical era; and others, such as the possession of all of the Promised Land by the patriarchs and their descendants, are still to be fulfilled in the future.

The Application of the Abrahamic Covenant Today

The Application to Jews and Jewish Believers

Among the many provisions of the Abrahamic Covenant were three main facets: a seed, land, and blessings. The visible seal and symbol of the covenant was circumcision.

The Seed. Abraham's seed was to develop into a nation, and so it did at Mount Sinai. Today, Israel is a scattered nation but a nation nonetheless. Just as Israel remained distinct in ancient Egypt, so the Jewish people have remained distinct throughout the Church Age. Other scattered nations eventually intermarried and disappeared into a melting pot. Not so the Jews. Their continued survival, in spite of many attempts to destroy them, shows that this covenant has continued to operate. It is the basis for Jewish survival today.

Furthermore, this covenant provides a biblical definition of Jewish identity in the repeated statement that a nation will come through the line of Abraham, Isaac, and Jacob. This nationality is not confined to the State of Israel alone, but includes all Jewish people, no matter where they are. Biblically speaking, the Jewish people are a nation because the Jews are descendants of Abraham, Isaac, and Jacob. This definition implies that, no matter what a Jew does, he can never become a non-Jew; no matter what he may believe or disbelieve, he remains a Jew. He may be Orthodox, Reform, atheist, or communist. He may believe that Jesus is his Messiah. Nothing, absolutely nothing, can change the fact that he is a descendant of Abraham, Isaac, and Jacob. While no Jew can become a Gentile, regardless of what he believes, the converse is also true: no Gentile can become a Jew or a "spiritual Jew." Believing Gentiles are never called "Jews" or "Israel" in the New Testament.

The Land. Since A.D. 70 the land has been overrun many times and ruled by many people. It has been controlled by Romans, Byzantines, Arabs, and the Turks. Most recently, before Israel became a nation, the land was ruled by the British. Even under Arab control, no independent government has ever been established on the land, but Israel has been ruled from Baghdad, Cairo, Damascus, Amman, and so on. Though renamed "Palestine" by Hadrian, the land never contained a Palestinian state with a Palestinian government or a Palestinian flag. The first independent government formed in the land since A.D. 70 was the State of Israel (1948). So the history of the land also shows the fulfillment of the Abrahamic Covenant. The Jewish believer also views Israel as his homeland, though believers today are legally barred from immigrating by Israeli law.

The Blessings. History shows that those who blessed the Jews were blessed, just as those who cursed them were cursed. Furthermore, the spiritual blessings have now been extended to the Gentiles.

The Seal. The seal of the Abrahamic Covenant was circumcision, still mandatory upon all Jews, both believers and unbelievers. In Galatians the Apostle Paul condemns circumcision as a means for justification and sanctification. Circumcision is equally invalid when based on the Law of Moses, since the Law of Moses ended with Messiah's death. But Galatians does state that the Abrahamic Covenant is still very much in effect (Gal. 3:15-18) with all of its features, including circumcision.

Paul did not rule out circumcision *per se*, but rather circumcision on the basis of the Mosaic Law. Because Jewish believers today still fall under the physical and spiritual provisions of the Abrahamic Covenant, they also fall under the rule of circumcision as a sign and seal of this same covenant. Circumcision on the basis of the Abrahamic Covenant, therefore, is still appropriate for Jewish believers. While some may insist on the continuity of the Abrahamic Covenant but deny the continuity of circumcision, their inconsistency fails to distinguish circumcision under the Abrahamic Covenant from circumcision under the Law of Moses.

The Application to Gentiles and Gentile Believers

The Blessings

The application of the covenant to Gentiles in general focuses on the Genesis 12:3 statement that those who curse the Jews will be cursed, and those who bless the Jews will be blessed. This principle is applicable both on a national level and on an individual level. History bears witness to the fall of those nations that have persecuted the Jews and the prosperity of those who have blessed them. The same is true in the lives of many Gentile individuals.

But the greatest application of the Abrahamic Covenant to Gentiles today is their share in the spiritual blessings of this and other Jewish covenants. The fact that Gentile believers do share in the spiritual blessings has led many theologians to teach a theology of replacement or transference, believing that the church has taken over the Jewish covenants. A better explanation lies in understanding that this covenant contained two types of promises: physical and spiritual. The physical promises were, and still are, limited to Israel and will be fulfilled only to, in, by, or through Israel. However, the first passage on the Abrahamic Covenant (Gen. 12:3), promises that the *spiritual* blessings would extend to the Gentiles.

A further explanation of these two types of promises is found in Ephesians 2:11–3:6. God made four unconditional covenants with Israel: the Abrahamic, the Palestinian, the Davidic, and the New Covenant. All of God's blessings, both physical and spiritual, are mediated by means of these four covenants. A fifth covenant, the conditional Mosaic Covenant, became the middle wall of partition that kept the Gentiles from enjoying the spiritual blessings of the four unconditional covenants. For a Gentile to receive the blessings of the unconditional covenants, he had to submit to the Mosaic Law, take upon himself its obligations and, for all practical purposes, live as a son of Abraham. Only as proselytes to Mosaic Judaism could Gentiles enjoy its spiritual blessings. Gentiles as Gentiles were not able to enjoy the spiritual blessings of the Jewish covenants and hence were *strangers from the Commonwealth of Israel.* When Messiah died and rose again, however, the Mosaic Law—the middle wall of partition—was demolished. Now Gentiles can, by faith, enjoy the spiritual blessings of the four unconditional covenants. That is why Gentiles today are partakers of Jewish spiritual blessings.

The relationship of the Gentile believer to the Abrahamic Covenant is the same as his relationship to the other Jewish covenants. The physical promises of the Abrahamic Covenant were promised exclusively to and will be fulfilled exclusively with Israel. However, Gentile believers are enjoying the spiritual blessings of these covenants: salvation through faith in the Messiah, forgiveness of sin, the permanent indwelling of the Spirit, and others.

The Abrahamic Covenant is not now being fulfilled with Israel. This does not mean it is, therefore, being fulfilled with the church. Again, not all provisions go into effect immediately. The church is related to the Abrahamic Covenant only in receiving the spiritual benefits of the covenant; but the church is not fulfilling it. The church has become a *partaker* of Jewish spiritual blessings, but the church is not a *taker-over* of the Jewish covenants.

The Gentile Obligation

Becoming *partakers* of Jewish spiritual blessings has placed an obligation on Gentile believers. Paul discussed this indebtedness near the end of his letter to the Roman Christians. In Romans 15:25-27 he explained why he could not come to them immediately. While he had a long-term desire to go to Rome (expressed in Romans 1), his desire was subject to his duty to collect an offering and take it to Jewish believers in Jerusalem (cf. 1 Cor. 16:1-4 and 2 Cor. 8–9). The Gentiles of Macedonia and Achaia had given the money specifically for the poor Jewish believers of Jerusalem (Rom. 15:26). In verse 27, Paul taught the theological basis for Gentile indebtedness to the Jews: Gentiles have become *partakers* of Jewish spiritual blessings, mediated through the *Jewish* covenants (cf. Rom. 11). According to Romans 15:27, Gentiles repay their indebtedness by ministering to Jewish believers in material things. One practical means of carrying out this obligation today is for every Gentile believer to consider supporting a Jewish ministry.

The Purposes of Gentile Salvation

The major spiritual blessing of the Abrahamic Covenant is salvation, and numerically Gentiles are the primary recipients of this salvation today. But it was not always so. During the first decade of church history, the church was Jewish and Christianity was Hebrew only. The few Gentiles in the early church were proselytes to Judaism before they became believers in Messiah Jesus. Gentiles were not to be found in the church until Acts 10. It took a special revelation from God to show Peter the necessity of witnessing to Gentiles as Gentiles, rather than limiting his witness to Gentiles who were proselytes to Judaism (Acts 10:9-16, 44-48). Even then, Peter had to defend his actions to the Jewish believers in Jerusalem (Acts 11:1-18). At about the same time, Paul was saved for the purpose of being the apostle to the Gentiles (Acts 9:15, 20-21; 26:16-18). With the gospel of grace now open to all, Gentiles by the multitudes were saved and in a very short period of time greatly outnumbered Jews in the church. A natural question occurs here: Why has God turned to the Gentiles? The Scriptures give two reasons for the salvation of the Gentiles.

First, God is gathering from among the Gentiles a people for His name (Acts 15:13-18). As God had a select group of Jews known as the "faithful remnant" — the Remnant of Israel — He is now also developing a select group of Gentiles so that among them God will have a people for His name.

While the calling of the Gentiles began with the Book of Acts in the New Testament, it was not unforeseen in the Old Testament. The great Gentile response actually fulfills the Old Testament and further proves the Messiahship of Jesus. One such Old Testament prophecy is found in Amos 9:11-12, and another is recorded in Isaiah 49:5-6. Indeed, the Messiah was not only to bring about the future regeneration, regathering, and restoration of Israel, but also to be the light to the Gentiles. "Behold, my servant, whom I uphold; my chosen, in whom my soul delighteth: I have put my Spirit upon him; he will bring forth justice to the Gentiles" (Isa. 42:1). The calling of the Gentiles is temporary until the full number of Gentiles is completed; then God will again turn to Israel as a nation and begin dealing with her (Rom. 11:25-27).

The second reason God is saving Gentiles today is found in Romans 11:11-14: so believing Gentiles can provoke the Jews to jealousy in order that many of them will come to Messiah. The Greek word translated "to provoke to jealousy" is *parazelao*. It is a combination of two Greek words: *para*, meaning "to come alongside of," and *zelos*, meaning "to cause to burn, to seethe, to make red hot, to flame, to envy." The picture is one of the Gentile believer coming alongside a Jew with daily contact, living such a life and being such a witness that the Jew will begin to burn with red-hot envy and will want what the Gentile believer has: the Jewish Messiah. God still has a remnant among the Jews today (Rom. 11:1-10), and the remnant will come to saving faith by being provoked to jealousy by Gentile believers. Accordingly, Gentile believers today have the evangelistic opportunity and responsibility to be positive witnesses to Jewish unbelievers by their demonstration of godly, Spirit-controlled living.

The Holy Spirit

> "The word for spiritual gifts (charisma),
> obviously related to the word for grace,
> means something that is due to the
> grace of God."
> (*Basic Theology*, p. 367)

CHAPTER TWENTY-TWO

A Fruitful Life
That Counts

Joel T. Andrus

Believers in Jesus Christ often live day after day in spiritual defeat and do not know what to do about it. They may have tried diligently, yet completely failed to achieve the Christlike character they desire for themselves. How encouraging it ought to be for them to discover verses like Galatians 5:22-23, "But the fruit of the Spirit is love, joy, peace, patience, kindness, goodness, faithfulness, gentleness, self-control; against such things there is no law" (NASB). Here are the character qualities they have been looking for but have been unable to produce. Paul calls these qualities the "fruit of the Spirit." In other words, they are the product of the Holy Spirit's working within us, not the result of our own efforts. Our responsibility is to be "walking by the Spirit"

(5:16); that is, cooperating with Him in all He wants to accomplish in our lives. Through Him we can be what we want to be.

Also very common among Christians is a heavy sense of uselessness, a sense of not being able to make any difference in the lives of other people. Christians want to have a significant impact, but they have no hope that it will ever happen. They see fellow believers who are effective in many ways, but they don't see themselves as having similar potential. How encouraging it ought to be for them to discover a chapter like 1 Corinthians 12, which explains that the Holy Spirit has given to every believer one or more "spiritual gifts" (1 Cor. 12:7). These gifts (or manifestations of the Spirit) are special abilities for contributing in a significant way to the spiritual welfare of other believers. There are approximately twenty gifts mentioned in the New Testament including teaching, giving, hospitality, helps, administration, showing mercy, evangelism, and exhortation. Each believer's ministry is necessary to everyone else. There is no believer whom we can say we do not need, and none who does not need us.

The fruit of the Spirit and the gifts of the Spirit are distinct provisions for every Christian. Though both are ministries of the Spirit to believers, they differ in several ways.

First, gifts are rooted in the Spirit's work of baptizing. They are apparently given to believers at the moment of conversion when the Spirit places them into the body of Christ. Fruit, though, is rooted in the Spirit's work of filling. Only as He is allowed to control us will His fruit be made apparent.

Second, gifts vary from one believer to another. No believer has them all. However, every believer should exhibit all the fruit of the Spirit. It will not be present to the same degree in all because of different maturity levels, but these qualities should be present to some degree.

Third, gifts are temporary, given for the welfare of the church on earth. Fruit, however, is eternal. It begins to be developed now and reaches perfection when we go to be with Christ and are made fully and forever like Him.

Finally, gifts have to do with what a Christian does, his ministry to the body of Christ. Fruit has to do with what a Christian *is*, the inner qualities of character.

Texts on Spiritual Gifts

Although these two provisions of the Holy Spirit are definitely distinct, they are still clearly related. That relationship can be demonstrated by looking at the four major texts dealing with spiritual gifts. In each of these passages the discussion concerning gifts is either immediately preceded or followed by a discussion of the qualities of character that comprise the fruit of the Spirit.

In Romans 12:3-8 Paul discusses spiritual gifts and their use. The very next verse moves into an extended explanation of those traits of character that are the fruit of the Spirit. Ephesians 4, another important passage concerning spiritual gifts (4:7-16), begins with a strong appeal to manifest those qualities that make up the fruit of the Spirit (4:1-6). In 1 Peter 4:10-11, the Apostle Peter names several gifts and discusses the goal and manner with which they should be exercised. But just preceding this appeal he urges believers to exhibit the fruit of the Spirit: "keep fervent in love for one another, because love covers a multitude of sins" (1 Peter 4:8).

The relationship between gifts and fruit is quite explicit in a fourth text. First Corinthians 12–13 gives the most detailed discussion in Scripture of spiritual gifts, their purpose, and their importance. Then, by way of transition, the Apostle Paul says, "I show you a still more excellent way" (1 Cor. 12:31). He moves immediately into a discussion of the quality of love in a believer's life, the supreme fruit of the Spirit.

His point is that, apart from the fruit of love, gifts are going to be without effect. For example, the most highly developed gift of tongues possible would be meaningless without love (1 Cor. 13:1). The same is true with the gifts of prophecy, knowledge, faith, and giving (13:2-3). Gifts are important. But they are totally dependent for their effectiveness upon the presence of the fruit of the Spirit within a believer.

Illustrations of this interconnectedness between fruit and gifts abound in Scripture. One negative example can be seen in 1 Timothy 1:2-7, where Paul reminds his "true child in the faith" why he wanted him to stay behind in Ephesus. Certain men were exercising their spiritual gifts in a manner that did not further "the administration of God which is by faith" (1:4), but was "fruitless"

(1:6). The reason was not lack of skill. They may well have been the most polished speakers, the most creative communicators, or the most energetic teachers. These Ephesians were fruitless because they had "strayed" from the kind of pursuits that are foundational to producing the spiritual fruit of love in a person's life.

Paul explains that "the goal of our instruction is love from a pure heart and a good conscience, and a sincere faith" (1 Tim. 1:5). These men had not cared about the purity of their heart, the goodness of their conscience, or the sincerity of their faith. They were not walking in the Spirit. As a result, they had none of the spiritual fruit of love. And in turn they were fruitless in the exercise of their gifts. The same pattern is evident today. We may not pursue "myths and endless genealogies" as they did. But if we have no fruit, we won't be any more effective than they were in furthering the purposes of God in the lives of those we seek to help.

A positive example of the connection between fruit and gifts is found in 1 Thessalonians. In chapter 1 Paul declares that "our gospel did not come to you in word only" (1 Thes. 1:5). That is, it was not just an empty exhibition of gifts that these people had observed. Rather, Paul and the team had exercised their gifts "in power and in the Holy Spirit and with full conviction." The explanation he offers has to do with the "kind of men we proved to be among you." In other words, their gifts were effective because their lives were consistent. The fruit of the Spirit was so apparent that "our coming to you was not in vain" (1 Thes. 2:1). He and those with him had not wasted their time. Their ministry was not fruitless, and the verses that follow are basically a recounting of the fruit of the Spirit in their lives. In 1 Thessalonians 2:2 Paul infers the fruit of patience and self-control. Even though they had just experienced much abuse in Philippi, they hadn't quit or responded in kind.

In 1 Thessalonians 2:3-6a Paul talks about the fruit of faithfulness. There was no "error or impurity or deceit" in their message. Neither was there any attempt to choose words according to what would please men. They never resorted to flattery as a pretext for getting fortune or fame for themselves. Their sole desire was to please God and to be faithful to the Gospel He had entrusted to them.

Beginning with 1 Thessalonians 2:6b, the apostle reflects upon the fruit of gentleness and love. As apostles, they could have acted with "authority." Instead, they acted with all the gentleness of a nursing mother. They demonstrated this parental concern by supporting themselves financially rather than depending upon these new believers. Finally, they were careful to behave "devoutly, uprightly and blamelessly" (1 Thes. 2:10). In every way, they sought to exhibit in their lives those qualities that would support the message they proclaimed. They knew that gifts without fruit would produce nothing.

The grand result of this concern by Paul is that the Thessalonians accepted their message "not as the word of men but for what it really is, the word of God" (1 Thes. 2:13) and were forever changed. Not only did they come to believe, but they themselves began to manifest the fruit of the Spirit as they exercised their own gifts (1 Thes. 1:6-10; 2:14-16; 3:6-8; 4:9-10).

That is always the goal of the exercise of gifts, and that is the heart of the explanation as to why there is such a close connection between gifts and fruit in our lives. It would be impossible to be effective in someone else's life to encourage them to produce fruit if we ourselves were not exhibiting the fruit of the Spirit. We do not have to do so perfectly, but we do have to do so consistently and increasingly. To try to exercise the gifts of the Spirit without the fruit of the Spirit is futile.

Life in the Spirit: Fruit and Gifts

What should this relationship of fruit and gifts mean to us? What do we need to do about it? First, we must consciously seek to discover and develop the gifts which the Holy Spirit has entrusted to us. The key to that discovery is involvement in different kinds of ministry. Over a period of time the Holy Spirit will make clear what our precise gifts are and will work with us to refine them.

But it is especially important that we commit ourselves to having the fruit of the Spirit developed within us. The key for doing this, according to Galatians 5:16, is to "walk by the Spirit," to cooperate with Him in all that He is present in our lives to accomplish. For example, since He is present to teach us (1 John 2:27), we need to cooperate with Him by exposing ourselves to the truth of God's Word, reading it, meditating on it, memorizing it, listening to it being taught.

Since He is present to help us in our prayer life (Rom. 8:26), we need to cooperate with Him by praying, both in abbreviated times throughout the course of a day and in more extended times.

Since He is present to guide us (Rom. 8:14), we need to cooperate with Him by a daily surrendering of ourselves to His will for us, consciously allowing Him to be in control.

Since He is present to build unity between ourselves and others in the church, the body of Christ (Eph. 4:3), we need to cooperate with Him by maintaining a serious involvement with a local fellowship of believers, being faithful not to forsake "our own assembling together" (Heb. 10:25).

And since He is present to work through us in the fruitful exercise of our spiritual gifts (1 Cor. 12:4-11), we need to cooperate with Him by making ourselves available to serve in any way He sees fit. As we pursue those disciplines with diligence, He will produce His fruit in us. That is His promise. And in turn His gifts will be made effective through us.

Now that is a wonderful prospect, but diligence in these pursuits never comes automatically or easily. Consequently, many passages challenge us very pointedly to give the diligence required. One good example is 2 Peter 1:3-7, "Now for this very reason also, applying all diligence, in your faith supply moral excellence, and in your moral excellence, knowledge; and in your knowledge, self-control, and in your self-control, perseverance, and in your perseverance, godliness; and in your godliness, brotherly kindness, and in your brotherly kindness, love." We do not produce these qualities ourselves. The Holy Spirit does it as we cooperate with Him. But that cooperation requires effort, hard work, determined purpose.

For example, spending significant time studying the Word or praying does not come easily. But we must do it. No matter how attractive other activities may be, we must set our hearts to do that which is essential. Our great encouragement is that it will result in being "neither useless nor unfruitful in the true knowledge of our

Lord Jesus Christ" (2 Peter 1:8). Our gifts will count. Besides, "entrance into the eternal kingdom of our Lord and Savior Jesus Christ will be abundantly supplied to you" (2 Peter 1:11).

A believer may have the gift of faith, but if he does not have the fruit of love, he is nothing (1 Cor. 13:2). By the same token, he may have the gift of exhortation, but if he does not have the fruit of joy, there will be little spiritual result. He may have the gift of encouragement, but if he does not have the fruit of peace, he won't make much difference. He may have the gift of evangelism, but if he does not have the fruit of patience, he won't get far. He may have the gift of helps, but if he does not have the fruit of kindness, his efforts will be futile. He may have the gift of teaching, but if he does not have the fruit of goodness, he will meet constant frustration. He may have the gift of giving, but if he does not have the fruit of faithfulness, he will accomplish little. He may have the gift of wisdom, but if he does not have the fruit of gentleness, he is not going to be much help. He may have the gift of mercy, but if he does not have the fruit of self-control, he's going to sabotage his own efforts. Gifts without fruit will always render us weak and ineffective in whatever we seek to do for Christ.

The conclusion of the matter is that we must "walk by the Spirit." We must diligently cooperate with the Holy Spirit in all that He is present in our lives to accomplish. As we do so, He will produce the fruit within us that will work with the gifts He has given us to produce an eternal impact through us. Our lives will count.

"No believer can afford not
to be filled [with the Spirit]
at every stage of his or her
spiritual growth."
(*Basic Theology*, p. 378)

CHAPTER TWENTY-THREE

The Filling
of the Spirit

Stanley D. Toussaint

T oday's generation is living under extreme pressure. People
who outlived the depression of the '30s worried about
physical and financial survival. "Will I have a job next
month?" "Can we afford to buy Johnny a new pair of shoes?"
"Will we have enough money to pay the rent or to buy groceries?"
Their pressures were basically external.

In addition to those stresses people living today struggle with
severe emotional, mental, and spiritual tensions. The breakup of
the home, the high number of suicides and attempted suicides,
alcoholism and drug addiction, teenage pregnancies, violent domestic relationships, single parents—the tragic list seems endless.

The sad reality is that *the sins of the culture always become the sins of the church.* If immorality permeates a culture, invariably it becomes a problem in the church. This is true of divorce, domestic violence, lying, or any other sin. The church in today's society is confronted with tremendous problems from which Christians are not exempt.

If this is so, how do believers live a so-called "victorious life"? How do believers in Christ stand firm in the midst of pressures and temptation? How does the church manifest Christlikeness in the circumstances surrounding it?

Obviously there are no simple solutions. But one essential ingredient in any answer to questions like these is the power of God the Holy Spirit. Believers must be filled with the Holy Spirit, a condition simultaneous with and almost synonymous with walking by means of the Holy Spirit (Gal. 5:16).

This study will consider the filling of the Holy Spirit under three headings: (1) a definition of the filling of the Holy Spirit, or the meaning of the term; (2) how to be filled with the Holy Spirit, or a method to follow to be filled with the Spirit; and (3) evidences or manifestations of the filling of the Spirit.

The Meaning of the Filling of the Holy Spirit

When a person is filled with the Holy Spirit, he or she is controlled by the Third Person of the Trinity. To be filled by Him is to be brought under His influence and control.

Two factors support this idea of control. One is the contrast of drinking and drunkenness with the filling of the Spirit. On more than one occasion the New Testament makes this contraposition. When Zecharias, the father of John the Baptist, was told by the Angel Gabriel that John would be born, Gabriel also announced, "He will drink no wine or liquor; and he will be filled with the Holy Spirit while yet in his mother's womb" (Luke 1:15, NASB). When the apostles were filled with the Holy Spirit on the Day of Pentecost (Acts 2:4), the people accused them of being full of wine (v. 13). However, Peter denied the allegation, saying it was too early in the morning for all of them to be inebriated. Instead Peter pointed to Joel's prophecy as an explanation (Acts 2:14-16). In Ephesians 5:18 Paul commanded the church not to be "drunk with wine, for that is dissipation," but instead to "be filled with the Spirit." Even today when someone is drunk, he is said to be under the influence of alcohol. In a similar sense a person filled with the Holy Spirit is controlled by Him.

The vocabulary used of the filling of the Holy Spirit leads to the same conclusion. Three Greek words in the New Testament describe this spiritual condition—two verbs and an adjective. The first is *pimplemi*. Although this verb may be used with other meanings, such as the fulfilling of prophecy (Luke 1:20; 21:22) or the filling of something such as a sponge or a boat (Matt. 27:48; Luke 5:7)), when it is employed of a person's inner life, it has the meaning of control or influence. For instance, *pimplemi* is used of being filled with wrath (Luke 4:28, KJV), with fear (Luke 5:26), with foolishness or rage (Luke 6:11), with wonder and amazement (Acts 3:10), and with jealousy (Acts 5:17; 13:45). In each of these occurrences the word does not mean *fill* in the sense of filling up a bottle or jug; rather it has the idea of being controlled by or influenced by. This is the significance of the verb in connection with the filling by the Holy Spirit (cf. Luke 1:15, 41, 67; Acts 2:4; 4:8, 31; 9:17; 13:9).

The second word used for "filling" is the verb *pleroo*. Like *pimplemi*, it has a number of meanings and nuances: to fulfill prophecy (Matt. 1:22), to bring to a full number (Rev. 6:11), or to fill something (Acts 5:28). However, it also may refer to a person's inner life being influenced or controlled by something as in John 16:6, "But because I have said these things to you, sorrow has filled your heart." Certainly the verb refers to control in Ephesians 4:10 where it anticipates Christ's ultimate rule over all things (cf. Eph. 1:23). This is its significance in Ephesians 5:18 where Paul commanded his readers to be filled with the Holy Spirit. In other words, they were to so live that the Spirit would be the dominant force in their lives.

The third word is the adjective *pleres*. Although it may refer to literal fullness, as in the full baskets of Matthew 14:20 and 15:37, it usually is used in a metaphorical sense to describe an influence or power controlling a person. Elymas the sorcerer was full of deceit and fraud (Acts 13:10), and the Ephesian mob was filled with rage (Acts 19:28). It clearly signifies control in these instances. The same is true when a person is described as being filled with the Holy Spirit (Luke 4:1; Acts 6:3; 7:55; 11:24). All three words, when used of some force or power, refer to *control or influence in a person's inner life.*

This definition is important because the filling of the Holy Spirit is very confusing to many Christians. A believer is not filled as a jug or bottle is filled with a liquid. If this were the idea then one would pray for more of the Holy Spirit. The fact is, the Spirit is a person, the Third Person of the Trinity. When a sinner trusts in Christ, he or she is immediately indwelled by the Holy Spirit (Rom. 8:9). At that point the believer possesses all of the Spirit he or she will ever have. The issue then is not how much of the Spirit a Christian possesses, but how much of the Christian's life the Spirit controls. In other words, the Spirit-filled life is a Spirit-controlled life.

A Method for Being Filled with the Spirit

Sincere Christians will always respond, "I would like to be filled with the Spirit. But how?" The New Testament gives no specific instructions on this subject. Evidently, any heart that is open toward God and is in submission to the Scriptures will be filled with the Spirit. However, Scripture does hint at how to be filled. John 7:37-39 pictures the process.

> Now on the last day, the great day of the feast, Jesus stood and cried out, saying, "If any man is thirsty, let him come to me and drink. He who believes in Me, as the Scripture said, 'From his innermost being shall flow rivers of living water.'" But this He spoke of the Spirit, whom those who believed in Him were to receive; for the Spirit was not yet given, because Jesus was not yet glorified.

According to this passage, the first step for anyone thirsting for this fullness of life is to come to Christ and drink. The meaning of this figure of speech is found in verse 38: coming and drinking means to believe in Christ. A lost person believes for salvation and finds fullness of life as he continues to walk in faith (John 10:10).

In time he will fail and will need to come back to Christ in contrition and faith. When he does, he will know the fullness of the Spirit once again. It should be noted that the verbs "come," "drink," and "believe," are all present tense, implying a continual life of faith.

Of particular import is the object of faith—it is the Lord Jesus. Christians are not told to trust in the Holy Spirit or even to pray to Him. The Holy Spirit is at home when Christ is glorified (John 16:14). When a believer turns to Christ Jesus and says, "This is beyond me to accomplish, I'm trusting You, Lord Jesus, to do this," the Holy Spirit then influences or controls that person to do His will.

This may be illustrated by an automobile with a powerful engine. The driver may start the engine and rev it up until the tachometer is redlined. Yet that automobile will move only when it is in gear. The Holy Spirit is like that engine. All of His potent resources become influential only when a Christian shifts into gear by trusting Christ.

The second passage which implies a method for the filling of the Spirit is Colossians 3:16-17.

Let the word of Christ richly dwell within you, with all wisdom teaching and admonishing one another with psalms and hymns and spiritual songs, singing with thankfulness in your hearts to God. And whatever you do in word or deed, do all in the name of the Lord Jesus, giving thanks through Him to God the Father.

Although these verses say nothing directly about the filling of the Spirit, they parallel and illustrate Ephesians 5:18-21.

And do not get drunk with wine, for this is dissipation, but be filled with the Spirit, speaking to one another in psalms and hymns and spiritual songs, singing and making melody with your heart to the Lord; always giving thanks for all things in the name of our Lord Jesus Christ to God, even the Father; and be subject to one another in the fear of Christ.

Ephesians and Colossians are sister epistles, written at the same time and carried by the same courier to destinations only 100 miles apart. While their themes are different (Ephesians emphasizes unity in Christ; Colossians accents His supremacy and sufficiency), both follow a similar pattern. Therefore, one epistle helps to explain the other.

In this section both Ephesians and Colossians describe the same basic qualities of life. In Colossians the results come from letting the word of Christ dwell in them; in Ephesians the filling of the Spirit produces the fruits. In other words, humble submission to Christ's words is the same as being filled with the Spirit. One of the prerequisites to filling is obedience to Scripture. Letting the word of Christ richly dwell within a person means the Bible is at home as it resides in the human heart. No rebelling, no compromising with its meaning and intention, no debating with what it says is to be characteristic of the Christian's life, only quiet submission. When that is the case, the Holy Spirit is at work impacting a person's life for Christ.

It seems then that two main thrusts are present in any method for the filling of the Spirit—trusting and obeying. But both must be present. *If either is absent, no work of the Spirit to accomplish His will is present.* Many illustrations in life portray this truth—an airplane needs two wings, a rowboat needs two oars, an engine needs both fuel and spark. Continual trust in Christ and obedience to His word will result in a believer's being controlled or influenced by the Holy Spirit. While this has many implications, it is a simple truth.

Some Manifestations of the Filling of the Spirit

The filling of the Holy Spirit manifests itself in a number of ways, several of which are found in Ephesians 5:19-21. Three participles used here—speaking in song (v. 19), giving thanks (v. 20), and submitting (v. 21)—all point to actions that accompany the influence of the Holy Spirit in the Christian's life. The three participles indicate actions occurring simultaneously with the filling. When a believer is controlled by God the Spirit, he or she will sing, be thankful, and submit his or her will to others.

The first manifestation of a God-controlled life is singing. Very early church history attests to the practice of congregational singing, as does the New Testament (cf. 1 Cor. 14:26). That this is corporate singing is seen in the words "to one another." This is significant. A unified, loving, Spirit-filled church will express itself in congregational singing that is uplifting and enthusiastic. Dead churches are marked by lethargic and listless singing. Congregations whose people are walking by the Spirit sing with their hearts to the Lord (Col. 3:16). Although corporate worship is in view, the emphasis here seems to be on encouragement and exhortation since the singing is to one another.

The "psalms and hymns and spiritual songs" describe all kinds of Christian songs, including hymns of praise. Such a hortatory Christian song probably is illustrated in Ephesians 5:14. Other hymns and spiritual songs are reflected in the New Testament (cf. 1 Tim. 3:16; 2 Tim. 2:11-13), and certainly singing is described as taking place in heaven (Rev. 5:9-10; 15:3-4). Singing has always been the occupation of the redeemed (cf. Ex. 15:1-21; Deut. 31:30–32:43). Singing is the spontaneous result of being filled with the Spirit, even if the believer is a monotone!

A second result of being filled with the Spirit is "always giving thanks for all things" (Eph. 5:20). This injunction goes beyond that of 1 Thessalonians 5:18, "In everything give thanks." Giving thanks *in* everything is much easier than giving thanks *for* all things. No matter what the circumstances, one can give thanks *in* them for they could be worse. If one is in an automobile collision, thanks may be given that the car was not totaled. If it was totaled, one may be thankful there were no injuries. If someone was hurt, one can be thankful that nobody was killed. If someone was killed, one may be thankful more people were not killed. No matter what the circumstances, one can be thankful *in* them!

Ephesians commands being thankful always *for all* things. That is much more difficult. It means one gives thanks for financial reverses, for sickness in the family or in one's own life, and even for the death of a loved one. A Spirit-filled believer does this because he or she sees things from God's perspective. Even when that believer does not understand why something happens, he or she knows God is sovereign and ultimately will work all things for the believer's eternal good (cf. Rom. 8:28-30). One of the first steps away from God is not giving thanks to Him (Rom. 1:21); on the other hand, one of the highest acts of worship for a human is to be thankful for all things continually. A Christian controlled by the Third Person of the Trinity is always thankful.

A third evidence of the Spirit's filling is found in Ephesians 5:21, "being in submission to one another in the fear of Christ." The Greek verb translated "being in submission" has the idea of subordination to a higher authority. Here the sense seems to be to submit one's own well-being to another. In this context one would love another as he loves himself; this then is a subordination of self to others in the kingdom of love. The following verses (Eph. 5:22–6:9) describe how the principle of submitting works out in everyday home and work life. In practical terms, Spirit-filled Christians help others in the fear of Christ, acknowledging His lordship over all of them.

Any discussion of the manifestations of the filling of the Spirit would be incomplete without referring to Galatians 5:22-23: "But the fruit of the Spirit is love, joy, peace, patience, kindness, goodness, faithfulness, gentleness, self-control; against such things there is no law." This fruit is the result of walking by the Spirit as commanded in Galatians 5:16. Walking by the Spirit emphasizes enablement but is the same as being controlled by the Spirit. When the various aspects of the fruit of Galatians 5:22-23 are analyzed and then synthesized they spell J-E-S-U-S C-H-R-I-S-T. In other words, one becomes like Christ as he or she walks by means of the Spirit. This is to be the goal of every child of God and is a preeminent result of being filled with the Spirit.

Conclusion

What does it mean to be filled with the Spirit? It means to be controlled by Him or influenced by Him. How is this accomplished? One is filled by the Spirit when he simply trusts Christ in a moment by moment walk of faith and of obedience to the Scriptures. What are the results? They are singing, giving thanks, mutual submission, and Christlikeness, to name a few.

Several other particulars need to be mentioned. First, Ephesians

5:18 *commands* the readers to be Spirit-filled. This is not simply good advice; it is an imperative. The Spirit-filled life is not optional for the Christian, like chrome trim on an automobile; it is critically essential like the chassis is to a car. Significantly, the church has correctly taken the preceding command "not to be drunk with wine" very seriously. If Christians are so conscientious about the command not to be drunk, they should be just as scrupulous about obeying the imperative to be filled with the Spirit.

Furthermore, the injunction to be controlled by the Spirit is in the present tense. Past experience is not a valid test for the reality of a present walk with the Lord. The Spirit-filled life is very literally a moment by moment experience of trusting Christ for His sufficiency by means of the Holy Spirit.

In addition, the verb for "be filled" is normally taken to be passive here. The believer is filled by the Spirit when he or she fulfills the conditions for being filled, namely, trusting Christ and obeying His Word. When this is done the Christian is filled, that is, impacted by God the Spirit.

In discussing the fullness of the Spirit, H.C.G. Moule writes: "It is a state of man wholly unattainable by training, by reasoning, by human wish and will. It is nothing less than . . . God in command and control of man's whole life, flowing everywhere into it, that He may flow fully and freely out of it in effects around" (H.C.G. Moule, *Ephesian Studies* [London: Pickering & Inglis, n.d.], 275–76). May this be the blessed portion of all who read these words.

"To believers God has given
His Holy Spirit to reveal
the things of God."
(Basic Theology, p. 27)

CHAPTER TWENTY-FOUR

The Holy Spirit,
Our Teacher

Stephen J. Nichols

We are living in the age of the specialist. My grandfather had only one doctor who did everything from treating common colds to performing surgery; he even made house calls. Today a visit to our doctor may result in a referral to a specialist. With the advances in the medical field, generalists may feel less than fully prepared to offer technical and specialized services.

Unfortunately, this reverence for specialists has also affected our views of studying the Bible. Even the term *hermeneutics* and its definition (the art and *science* of interpretation) can be quite intimidating. Some may wonder if only professionals or specialists should interpret Scripture. And some may ask if they are even able to understand the Bible at all. Understanding the Holy Spirit's role in the inspiration and the interpretation of Scripture can help answer this question.

The Role of the Holy Spirit in Inspiration

Peter describes the process of the inspiration of Scripture when he writes, "For no prophecy was ever made by an act of human will, but men moved by the Holy Spirit spoke from God" (2 Peter 1:21). This description, as Dr. Ryrie points out in the note in his study Bible, "shows the dual authorship of God's Word—the Holy Spirit guiding and guarding the men involved in the actual writing." Both the concept of the Holy Spirit as God and His unique role in the giving of Scripture remind us that the Spirit is the Author.

In some of my college and seminary classes the textbooks were written by the professor of the class. This offered a distinct advantage. If I had any questions about the reading, I could simply go to the source and ask the author. As Christians indwelt by the Holy Spirit, we have a distinct advantage. When we have questions as we read the Bible, we can go to the source and ask the Author who knows the Bible completely and perfectly. And we can rest assured in the confidence that He wants us to understand it too.

The Role of the Holy Spirit in Interpretation

Wouldn't it be great if every morning God came and sat across from you at the breakfast table and gave you your instructions for the day? Then you could know how He would want you to relate to people and respond to the various situations that you face. J.N. Darby observed: "One might say, 'Ah, if I had the Lord here to direct me, how well should I do and bear! But if we know redemption-deliverance through the death and resurrection of Christ, we have Him still with us, and in the best and nearest way. For the Holy Ghost dwells in us to unfold Him to our souls, to teach us the glory of Him who has loved us and shed His blood for us" (*Collected Writings*, vol. 21 [Sunbury, Pa.: Believer's Bookshelf, 1972], 156–57).

Darby penned these comments in his exposition of John 16. In the larger context of John 14–16, Christ gives the promise of the coming of the Spirit and of His rich and vital ministry. Within this section of John, two passages relate specifically to the ministry of the Holy Spirit as our teacher. Christ tells His disciples in John 14:25-26, "These things I have spoken to you, while abiding with you. But the Helper, the Holy Spirit, whom the Father will send in My name, He will teach you all things, and bring to your remembrance all that I said to you" (NASB). He adds in John 16:13, "But when He, the Spirit of truth comes, He will guide you into all the truth; for He will not speak on His own initiative, but whatever He hears, He will speak; and He will disclose to you what is to come."

Some have suggested that this promise of Christ was specifically related to the apostles and to their future activity of writing Scripture. Christ assured the apostles that as they wrote about Christ and about His teachings, the Holy Spirit would guide them into recording the truth. This provides us with a great comfort that we can rely on their writing and that we know that the Holy Spirit disclosed to the apostles exactly what they were to write. Dr. Ryrie notes, "He (the Spirit) *takes of mine* (Christ's), *and will disclose it to you* (the apostles). These truths were then recorded in the New Testament" (*Ryrie Study Bible*, John 16:15).

There is also an extent to which these verses have a broader application. After discussing the meaning of John 14:25-26 in terms of its relationship to the apostles, D.A. Carson observes, "Yet there is a legitimate secondary application which concerns Christians today. The Holy Spirit comes to live with us and be in us (John 14:17), too; and He helps us to call to mind, as we need them, the words of Scripture we have first learned" (*The Farewell Discourse and Final Prayer of Jesus* [Grand Rapids: Baker, 1980], 74).

The Spirit's ministry of teaching began with the giving of Scripture itself and continues in the life of the church and the lives of believers. He assures us that Scripture is truth and brings that truth to our minds as we go our way throughout the day.

Another crucial passage in understanding the ministry of the Holy Spirit as our teacher is 1 Corinthians 2:6-16. Here Paul writes that the Spirit searches the depths of God and also reveals and teaches them to us, in order that "we might know the things freely given to us by God" (1 Cor. 2:12b). This passage further teaches that only those who have received the Spirit can understand the things of the Spirit, for the natural (unsaved) person does not accept or welcome them (v. 14).

When I was enrolled in an astronomy course, our class went outside one evening to use a telescope. It was a beautiful, clear night, and with the aid of the telescope we were able to see Saturn and its rings. When I looked without the telescope, all I could see were stars against the darkness of the night. The telescope did not add anything to the picture; it simply enabled me to *see what was there*. In a similar way, the Spirit enables us to see into the depths of God. Without the Spirit, the things of God are foolishness to us (1 Cor. 1:18-25).

Paul also speaks of this ministry of the Spirit in his letter to the Ephesians. Paul prays that God would grant them the Spirit of wisdom and revelation in order that they may know God better (Eph. 1:17, see NIV). He goes on to pray that their hearts may be enlightened so that they may know the hope of their calling, the riches of God's inheritance for them and the greatness of His power (Eph. 1:18-19).

The Holy Spirit's role in interpretation is not to impart new revelation to us; nowhere do we find such a promise in Holy Scripture. However, as we faithfully read Scripture, the Spirit enlightens our hearts and enables our minds to receive the myriad riches of God's revelation found in the Bible and the blessings of our relationship to Him.

Implications

The Bible teaches that the Holy Spirit plays a significant role in our understanding of Scripture. This leads to some obvious questions: How is He our teacher? In what way am I involved in the process of interpreting and understanding Scripture? Should I use the insights of others, or can I simply rely on the Holy Spirit? These questions will be considered by looking at what having the Holy Spirit as our teacher involves.

What Having the Holy Spirit as Our Teacher Does Not Mean

1. *It does not mean that we do not need human teachers.* In a lecture to his students on the importance of commentaries, the great preacher C.H. Spurgeon said, "It seems odd, that certain men who talk so much of what the Holy Spirit reveals to them, should think so little of what he has revealed to others." Because the Holy Spirit is our teacher, it does not follow that we have no need for the work of others in commentaries, reference works, or other books. As Spurgeon's comment implies, if it is true that the Holy Spirit works in us to help us understand Scripture, then surely He has worked in others throughout the history of the church.

Sometimes an appeal is made to 1 John 2:27 to argue that we do not have a need to use the knowledge of others or consult works like commentaries. Here John writes, "And as for you, the anointing which you have received from Him abides in you, and you have no need for anyone to teach you." It is helpful, however, to understand the context of John's exhortations. He is writing against false teachers who were denying that Jesus was the Messiah, the Christ (1 John 2:18-19, 22), and simply reminds his readers that they know the truth. They had been taught the truth from the beginning (1 John 2:24), and His anointing (which can be taken as the anointing of the Holy Spirit) would confirm the truth to them (1 John 2:27). For this particular situation they had no need for a teacher. However, John is not saying that we do not need human teachers altogether.

Scripture teaches that we do in fact need teachers and that one of the gifts of the Spirit to the church is that of teacher (Rom. 12:7; Eph. 4:11). As we take confidence in the fact that the Holy Spirit is our teacher, we need to remember that He may teach us through what He has taught others.

2. *It does not mean that we make infallible interpretations.* "Even the devil can use Scripture for his purposes," claims the old adage. While this is a bit extreme, we all know examples of how people have used (or rather *abused*) Scripture either by misunderstanding or misapplying it. Sometimes, those who do so even claim that the Spirit gave them their interpretations. Because the Holy Spirit is our teacher, it does not follow that all of our interpretations are

infallible. Roy Zuck aptly observes, "To elevate one's interpretations to the level of infallibility would blur the distinctions between inspiration (a past, now completed work of the Spirit in the recording of Scripture) and interpretation (a present, ongoing work of the Spirit in helping interpreters in the comprehending of Scripture)" ("The Role of the Holy Spirit in Hermeneutics," *Bibliotheca Sacra* [April–June 1984]: 122).

We also need to keep this point in mind as we use the work of others. Commentaries are not infallible; neither are all of the teachers whom we hear. Like the Bereans (Acts 17:11), we need to examine what we hear and read from others, comparing it with God's Word as our final authority.

What Having the Holy Spirit as Our Teacher Does Mean

1. *It means we can understand Scripture.* While the promise of the Holy Spirit as our teacher does not mean that we will automatically have a perfect understanding of Scripture, it does mean that we can have confidence and security that we can interpret and know Scripture. God's purpose in giving His revelation was so we could know it, and know Him through it. He has also given us His Spirit as a guarantee that our efforts in trying to understand and apply Scripture to the situations we face will not be fruitless.

2. *It means we need to diligently study the Word.* The Spirit does not work through osmosis. He does not bring Scripture to mind when we need it, unless we have learned it in the first place. Similarly, He does not guide us in our understanding of Scripture, unless we have invested time and effort in doing so. Because the Holy Spirit is our teacher, we should be diligent in our study of the Word (2 Tim. 2:15).

Consistently reading the Bible is probably one of the most difficult things for us to do. A friend of mine once asked Dr. Ryrie for some advice on how he could get the teens in his youth group to regularly read and study the Bible. Ryrie recommended that they start slowly, reading enough to do some good but not so much that it becomes a burden. That is good advice for us as well.

3. *It means we need to study the work of others.* Just as we may be thankful for a specialist in medicine who provides the right

treatment, or for a mechanic who is able to pinpoint the exact problem, so too we can be thankful for the specialist or the biblical scholar whom the Spirit has given to the church. There is a balance then in acknowledging, on the one hand, that we are able to understand Scripture and on the other acknowledging the need for biblical scholarship to enhance our understanding of the Bible. Roy Zuck expresses the balance this way, "The Bible was given to be understood by all; hence its interpretation is not in the hands of an elite few (cf. 1 John 2:20, 27). And yet believers ought not neglect the interpretive helps that can be afforded by biblical scholars" ("The Role of the Holy Spirit in Hermeneutics," 125).

We are living in an age when there are tremendous resources available to aid us in our study of the Bible. Commentaries, reference works, and even a good study Bible can help point out the nuances of the original language, draw attention to cultural practices, or bring out the historical background. All of this information can illuminate our understanding and keep us from overlooking a crucial factor in correctly interpreting Scripture.

4. *It means we need to approach Scripture in humble dependence upon the Spirit.* In the reformer's classic work, *The Bondage of the Will*, Martin Luther observes, "The Spirit is needed for the understanding of all of Scripture and every part of Scripture." This underlines our need to approach Scripture in humble dependence upon Him. As we read the Bible and listen to teachers, we can pray and ask the Spirit to illuminate our minds and to help us understand God's Word.

5. *It means we need to be obedient to the Spirit's conviction.* The Spirit's ministry as teacher does not simply mean that He helps us understand and interpret Scripture. It also means that He convicts us in those areas where we need to change. James reminds us that hearing the Word is not enough; we also need to be doers of the Word (James 1:22). Because the Spirit is our teacher we need to be obedient to that which He teaches us.

Conclusion

Dr. Ryrie observes, "Perhaps in no doctrine is this wedding of truth and life more important than in the doctrine concerning the

Holy Spirit" (*Basic Theology*, 390). This is true because the Holy Spirit dwells in us and is intimately involved in our lives. Through His enablement, we are able to grow as Christians. That growth involves reading, understanding, and applying God's Word. The ministry of the Holy Spirit offers us a great source of comfort in knowing that as we study the Bible, He will teach us. The promise of the Spirit's ministry also challenges us to be diligent in our study, knowing that our efforts will be fruitful.

"I Will Build My Church"

> "No one can deny that leadership
> was considered necessary in
> New Testament churches."
> (*Basic Theology*, p. 412)

CHAPTER TWENTY-FIVE

Who Is Qualified to Lead the Church?

Jeffrey L. Townsend

Everyone in the church admires Dick's consistent walk with the Lord, but he is reluctant to serve as an elder because he doesn't feel qualified. Should he serve?

Mike committed adultery but later submitted to discipline, reconciled with his wife, and matured enormously through the process. Could he run for the deacon board?

Ron grew up in the church, went away to college, and returned to set up a business in the community. He knows the church and the people love him, but he just turned 28. Is he old enough to be an elder?

Ralph has served as an elder for years. But his teenage son was arrested for drug possession. Should he step down from the board?

Bill speaks with authority, knows the Bible inside out, loves the Lord with all his heart, but thinks the church is headed in the wrong direction. Should he be added to the elder board?

With all the changing situations in churches today, who is qualified to lead? Thankfully, God has given us His qualifications for elders and deacons in 1 Timothy 3 and Titus 1. The challenge comes in applying the scriptural qualifications to real life. But we must accept the challenge. Many significant problems in the local church stem from unqualified leadership.

The Qualification of Blamelessness

Many a person has considered the office of elder or deacon, looked at the list of qualifications and immediately felt disqualified. Why? The first qualification in 1 Timothy 3 and Titus 1 seems to require that an elder or deacon live a "blameless" (KJV) life (1 Tim. 3:2; Titus 1:6). No one can meet that standard! But such a restrictive interpretation of the qualifications for church leadership misses Paul's point.

In these passages Paul prescribes these qualifications so Timothy and Titus may seek the right individuals for leadership of the churches in Asia Minor and Crete. It makes no sense to understand Paul as requiring sinless perfection, for then no one would qualify. Paul must have had something else in mind.

He did not mean blameless in God's sight, but blameless in the estimation of those choosing leaders for the local church. "Blameless" should not stand as a separate qualification, but as the standard of measure for all of the other qualifications. For example, consider the qualification, "husband of one wife" (literally, "a one-woman man," 1 Tim. 3:2, 12; Titus 1:6). A man qualified to serve as an elder or deacon must demonstrate a high level of faithfulness to his wife as judged by those responsible for choosing church leaders *using God's standards*. Obviously, perfect husbands and perfect wives do not exist. Thus the qualification is not so high as to require virtual perfection. But it does require that those choosing church leaders observe a significant record of marital faithfulness.

Some people advocate overly restrictive (going beyond the biblical intent) standards for church leaders that highly qualified men perceive as unreachable. This is not a scriptural perspective. We must never set the standard too high or too low. At the same time, we need to recognize that Paul stressed securing the best possible leaders.

The Qualification of Marital Faithfulness

Increasingly churches face the difficult question of whether or not to accept a former adulterer as a church leader. Some would say that moral failure of that magnitude constitutes grounds for permanent disqualification. Certainly sexual immorality on the part of a presently serving elder or deacon constitutes grounds for his removal from office. But what about the man who has repented, submitted to church discipline, been reconciled to his wife, and done everything possible to grow in Christ? Can he serve?

Clearly the qualification, "husband of one wife," in the sense of marital faithfulness, was violated. But the man remained the husband of one wife throughout the ordeal. Hence the real issue concerns whether or not this qualification should be applied in a life-long manner. By comparison, consider a man who is an alcoholic but who has abstained throughout his Christian life of some twenty-plus years. Though he had a drunken past, he has proven his sobriety over a long course of time. Normally such a man would not be excluded from church leadership since the qualification, "not given to much wine" (1 Tim. 3:3, 8; Titus 1:7), is not applied in a life-long sense.

Similarly, just because a man routinely solved his problems with his fists when he was a teenager, the qualification to not be a fighter (1 Tim. 3:3; Titus 1:7) does not disqualify him from serving as a deacon or elder if he has long since changed his ways. In the same way, sexual infidelity by itself ought not permanently disqualify a man from church leadership.

But another issue presents itself. The man in question must appear above reproach as the husband of one wife in the eyes of those choosing local church leaders. Here the issue hangs on whether the infidelity is sufficiently remediated to regain the confidence of the people the man will serve as elder or deacon.

231

Consider an illustration from civic life. If a police officer is convicted on a shoplifting charge, he will no doubt lose his job. If repentant, could he ever serve again on the same police force? Probably not, even with a lengthy clean record. Why? Because the citizens would always have doubts about the man's integrity. He never would appear "above reproach" in their minds. At a later time could he serve elsewhere in law enforcement? Though still problematic, it is more likely that the man will find employment as a police officer in a community where his past record is not a public issue.

Likewise, though not automatically disqualified by adultery, a man might have difficulty regaining confidence of the church in which the adultery took place. More likely he would be able to serve in church leadership in another congregation.

The Issue of Age

Scripture does not delineate a specific age one must reach before serving as an elder or deacon. Nevertheless, age remains an important factor in selecting church leaders. The wisdom that time and life experience bring constitutes a valuable asset for potential church leaders. One well-known pastor has confided that "most of the major problems in the churches I've helped start were caused by the appointment of men to leadership who were too young" (Gene A. Getz, *Sharpening the Focus of the Church*, revised [Wheaton, Ill.: Victor, 1984], 170). On the other hand, age does not guarantee wisdom, and some men have attained maturity beyond their years.

The scriptural term "elder" means an older person, but how much older? Timothy occupied a position of significant leadership in the early church, yet Paul refers to Timothy's "youthfulness" in 1 Timothy 4:12. However, a comparison of Acts and Paul's epistles reveals that Timothy may have been over thirty years old when he began his ministry in Asia Minor.

We must avoid invoking standards that are unwarranted by Scripture. No hard and fast rules can be made for the age of elders and deacons. Still, it seems wise in most cases to choose church leaders who have had the time and experience to gain the wisdom necessary to function well in leading and serving the local church. The middle years of thirty-five to forty serve well as a minimum age range for church leaders in most cases.

But what about a young church that does not have qualified middle-aged or older leaders? As Charles Ryrie has aptly stated, "Paul not only commanded that things be done decently and in order but also that they be done" (*The Role of Women in the Church* [Chicago: Moody, 1958], 80). The New Testament presents church leadership as a necessity. Therefore young congregations should appoint the best qualified men available and seek to work in more experienced men as time goes on.

The Qualification of Home Management

My wife and I live daily with the challenge of parenting two sons with attention deficit-hyperactivity disorder (ADHD). Typically children with ADHD experience more behavioral problems than the average child. That, coupled with the fact that most church members have high expectations for their pastor's children, has made us ripe for criticism over the qualification, "manages his own household well, keeping his children under control with all dignity" (1 Tim. 3:4, 12, NASB; cf. Titus 1:6).

Does Paul require here that an elder or deacon have exceptionally well-behaved children, or that he manage well the potentially difficult children he does have? Management ability, not child behavior per se, surfaces as the main issue in 1 Timothy 3:5 where Paul asks, "But if a man does not know how to manage his own household, how will he take care of the church of God?" Paul does not require that an elder have a perfect family but that he manages well the family he has. Qualification for church leadership must not ride on the degree of difficulty that comes with each child born to a man. He can serve depending on how well he manages what God has given him.

For example, if a man's children misbehave in church, is he disqualified? It depends on whether the children's misbehavior relates to the man's mismanagement of his household. If the man ignores the misbehavior, takes no steps to correct the problem, and generally neglects his family, then his lack of family management disqualifies him from church leadership. But if the man is aware of the behavior problems, has taken steps to minimize them, and handles well the discipline of difficult children, then the church has found a wonderful asset. Frequently a man who manages well in a dysfunctional family will manage well the family of God which is composed of imperfect saints. An elder or deacon need not have a perfect family, but he must take good care of the imperfect people with whom he lives. This will prepare him well for the imperfect people he will deal with in church leadership.

But what about a man, already serving as an elder or deacon, whose son commits a crime or whose unmarried daughter becomes pregnant? Can he continue to serve? Again the issue is not whether the man has perfect children, but whether their indiscretion is traceable to the man's mismanagement of the home. If those who know the man well are convinced that well-trained children made wrong choices, then the man should not step down. However, the man himself may ask for a leave of absence to focus attention on the crisis at home. A wise church honors such a request.

Other Qualifications?

Are there other areas to consider for choosing leaders? Bill knows his Bible, loves the Lord with all his heart, seems to meet all the scriptural qualifications, but just doesn't fit with the existing board. Should he serve in church leadership? This brings up the question of whether or not other issues besides scriptural qualifications merit consideration. Seasoned pastor Larry Osborne shares this advice:

> As important as spiritual maturity is, to build a harmonious and effective leadership team there are other qualifications to look for as well. We've learned to ask two more questions: 1) Is this person in basic agreement with our current philosophy of ministry? 2) Will this person fit the leadership team we've already assembled? If the answer to either is no, we've found it is a mistake to add the person to the board, no matter how spiritually mature he might be (*The Unity Factor*, The Leadership Library, vol. 20 [Waco, Texas: Word Publishing, 1989], 40–41).

For instance, if Bill agrees that the local church exists to make disciples, but thinks the current board is going about it in the wrong way, to add him to the board will only cause debilitating conflict. Likewise, if Bill meets all the other qualifications but has a personality conflict with the current board chairman, putting Bill on the board invites trouble. Addressing such philosophical and relational differences *before* a man is added to the elders or deacons greatly enhances board harmony and effectiveness.

This is not to say that candidates for church leadership must be in complete agreement with every decision existing church leaders have made. Potential leaders with differing perspectives and backgrounds bring fresh insights and ideas to share with existing leaders. This should be encouraged. However, churches should realize that unless a man agrees with the basic direction of the church's ministry and relates well to existing leaders, trouble looms ahead.

Conclusion

As in any area of the Christian walk, appointing qualified leadership for the local church requires balance. On one hand, too stringent a view of the qualifications in 1 Timothy 3 and Titus 1 deprives the church of desperately needed leadership experience. Paul was not telling Timothy and Titus to look for perfect men, but for men whose spiritual maturity was held in high esteem by the churches.

On the other hand, if the qualifications are diluted or discarded for a set of human criteria (such as wealth, business success, natural talents, or simply a willingness to serve), the church will suffer under spiritually inept leadership. The scriptural qualifications do not demand perfection, but they do demand significant spiritual maturity.

Who is qualified to lead the church? Effective, qualified leaders for the local church will exhibit the scriptural qualities of maturity, the wisdom that comes with age and experience, and a compatibility with existing leaders and the ministry direction of the church.

CHAPTER TWENTY-SIX

Keeping the Church Clean: A Matter of Discipline

Paul Benware

Though church discipline has sometimes been misused and often misunderstood, done properly it is essential to the health and well-being of the church. The church is like a body. Each member in the body builds up other members. This is the ministry of edification. But the body must also keep itself clean from the infectious spiritual disease of sin. This is the ministry of purification and involves church discipline.

Defining Discipline

The word *discipline* simply means "to train" in both a positive and negative sense. Practicing good discipline is much like practicing good medicine. Both preventative and corrective medicine are vital to good health. A church that properly disciplines its members will be involved in regular preventative discipline (training). As the Word of God is taught and applied, believers will be strengthened and will become healthier. However, the need for corrective church discipline will sometimes arise. Those in church leadership positions are then responsible to deal with a believer whose sins have a clear, harmful effect upon the entire church body. These leaders will attempt to bring that believer back into a lifestyle that conforms to the standards of godly living as set forth in the New Testament.

The Foundation for Church Discipline

A church must administer corrective church discipline for two fundamental reasons. The first is the holiness of God. The Lord Jesus desires that His church be holy and blameless (Eph. 5:27, NASB) because He is holy (1 Peter 1:16). Church discipline helps a sinning believer turn from sin and pursue righteousness. Second, a church is to be involved in corrective discipline because God commands it (1 Cor. 5:12-13).

These reasons ought to be sufficient, but many churches do not exercise corrective discipline. Some are ignorant of the church's responsibility to discipline or of the procedures to follow. They assume that the Lord will deal with a sinning believer much as He dealt with Ananias and Sapphira (Acts 5:1-11). But the Lord has given the church responsibility to function in this realm. If the church fails to do so, discipline will not take place. A careful study of a number of key New Testament Scriptures will give clear guidance on how to discipline church members correctly (cf. Matt. 18:15-17; 1 Cor. 5:1-13; 2 Thes. 3:6-15; Titus 3:10-11).

Another reason for failure to discipline is fear of negative consequences. Sometimes believers will wrongly rally behind the individual being disciplined, dividing the church. Attendance and budgets sometimes are affected. But a church must never forget that obedience and purity are of primary importance and that the Lord blesses a church that takes His Word seriously.

Another reason that a church may fail to discipline its members relates to the leaders of the church. If a leader's own life is sinful, he may be reluctant to discipline another's sinfulness. Such a leader may appear gracious in emphasizing the need to love and not condemn. But this approach is like putting cosmetics on skin cancer. It covers the problem while the disease continues to damage the body.

Whatever the reason for avoiding corrective church discipline, it is really an issue of obedience. In 1 Corinthians 5:12-13 the Apostle Paul declares, "Do you not judge those who are within the church? But those who are outside, God judges. Remove the wicked man from among yourselves" (NASB). (Also note Matt. 18:15-18; 2 Thes. 3:6, 14; 1 Tim. 5:20; Titus 3:10.)

Those Involved in Church Discipline

Who is to do the disciplining? In one sense, any believer can deal with sin, just as almost anyone can put first aid cream on a cut or give an aspirin for a headache.

Sometimes, however, serious afflictions may require help from someone with knowledge and discernment. The spiritually mature believer must handle more difficult and complex situations in the church. Paul states, "Brethren, even if a man is caught in any trespass, you who are spiritual (mature), restore such a one" (Gal. 6:1). In Acts 20:28-30 the elders of the Ephesian church were exhorted to keep sin from the flock (church). Ordinarily, spiritually mature leaders will deal with those sins that affect the church body. God gives authority to these leaders, not only to build up His church, but also to deal with sin within it (2 Cor. 13:10).

The Purposes of Church Discipline

Church discipline often has unpleasant side effects which cause many to question its value. Leaders must focus on the reasons for discipline. First of all, church discipline is needed to *purify the church*. Sin is a spiritual cancer which cannot be allowed to grow. Sin that is not dealt with can corrupt the entire church (1 Cor. 5:6). The health of the church requires its removal through repentance or excommunication.

A second purpose of discipline is *to restore the sinning believer*. Discipline by church leaders should focus on restoration, not judgment and condemnation (Matt. 18:15; 2 Thes. 3:15; 1 Tim. 1:20; 2 Tim. 2:25; Heb. 12:10). Correction and discipline are designed to alert the sinning member to the sure consequences of sin. This process is intended to bring about godly sorrow, to encourage restoration, and to return one's joy of salvation.

A third purpose is *to deter sin in the church*. The discipline of an individual reminds everyone that sin and righteousness are serious matters. Discipline instills godly fear (Acts 5:11) which is a significant deterrent to sin (Ex. 20:20; Prov. 16:6).

A fourth purpose for discipline is *to maintain a credible witness before the world*. Known sin that is not challenged brings shame to the church. The refusal of the Corinthians to deal with known sin discredited them before the unsaved world. If Christ could not give victory over sin, then the church was not only hypocritical, but also had nothing to offer the unsaved world (1 Peter 2:11-12). Perhaps more people would be impressed with their own sin and need of a Savior if churches were more serious about sin.

Disciplinary Offenses

Church discipline is not God's method of making the church sinless. He uses the Word and the Holy Spirit in the daily lives of believers to bring about their sanctification. Corrective discipline focuses on those sins that clearly affect the whole body. Mature, knowledgeable leaders need to determine whether a sin is doing damage to the church, weakening its testimony, or promoting disunity. The New Testament mentions some guidelines and specific areas of sin in the church that call for discipline:

1. *Doctrinal deviation* (Acts 20:28-30; Gal. 1:6-8; cf. 1 Tim. 1:18-20 with 2 Tim. 2:17-18). When an individual departs from a fundamental truth of the faith, such as the deity of Christ or justification by faith, leaders must deal with this deviation. The Lord Jesus commended the elders at Ephesus for doing this (Rev. 2:1-7). Believers may differ on the interpretation of certain passages of Scripture or about what Christians may or may not do in their Christian lives, but they must agree on fundamental doctrines.

2. *Divisiveness* (Rom. 16:17-20; 2 Thes. 3:11; Titus 3:10). A self-centered individual who brings division within the church is to be warned twice and then removed. He or she is turning aside from the command to strive for unity in the body. Divisiveness can come from many sources, including misuse of the tongue and propagating wrong doctrine in nonessential areas.

3. *Undisciplined living* (1 Thes. 5:14; 2 Thes. 3:6, 11, 14). Scripture does not focus on Christians who happen to procrastinate or who have a tough time getting up in the morning, but on those who are dramatically out of step with the scriptural standards of righteous living. In the church at Thessalonica undisciplined living was manifested in idleness, gossiping, and taking resources from the church.

4. *Conflict between believers* (Matt. 18:15-18; 1 Cor. 6:5; Phil. 4:2-3). When two believers do not settle a dispute privately and it spills over into the church, then the leadership must become involved.

5. *Sins of the flesh* (1 Cor. 5:11). Most Christians probably think of sexual immorality as the sin deserving of corrective discipline. But Paul also mentions reviling (abusive speech), drunkenness, and swindling as the sort of external sins of the flesh that bring shame and weakness to the body of Christ.

6. *Sins of the spirit* (1 Cor. 5:11). Such sins as covetousness and idolatry manifest themselves in a pattern of life dominated by wrong desires, greed, self-promotion, or materialism. While almost all believers at one time or another may grapple with these attitudes, Paul is referring to one whose life is consistently dominated by such behavior.

The Process of Church Discipline

Discipline is necessary in maintaining the purity of the church, but it must be done with a proper approach and attitude. The New Testament teaches a basic process in church discipline that seems to allow for some flexibility. Perhaps other Christians have already approached the sinning believer in an attempt to bring about repentance. Church discipline officially begins when the leadership of the church recognizes the presence of sin that threatens (or already has hurt) the purity of the church. Once the matter has come to the attention of the leaders, they must ensure the accuracy of the report.

Assuming that the evidence of sin is relatively clear, one mature, knowledgeable individual should confront the sinning believer with the Word of God. If he repents, the discipline process stops. The leaders must remember that the purpose is to restore the individual as well as to keep the church pure.

If these efforts fail, then the leader should return to the sinning believer with two or three other spiritually mature believers to encourage repentance and also act as witnesses. If there is no repentance, then action is taken against the individual. The leaders might wisely allow a few days to pass before proceeding so that the sinning believer can contemplate the truth of God.

If no repentance occurs, the leaders should explain the next disciplinary step. Paul's injunction to "reject a factious man after a first and second warning" (Titus 3:10) suggests that the private process is not to go on indefinitely. Jesus said that "if he refuses to listen to them, tell it to the church" (Matt. 18:17). The entire church should now be informed that "brother or sister X" has been dealt with regarding his or her sin and has not repented. The person is now "under church discipline." In this situation, other believers are not to have any fellowship with the person, avoiding the individual as much as possible (2 Thes. 3:6, 14). The person is still viewed as a brother or sister in Christ, but now is being publicly shamed for his or her sin. Perhaps the person can still attend church services, but no real fellowship should be encouraged.

If after a short period of time there is still no repentance, then the final step of excommunication is taken — a formal, public removal from the membership and life of the church. At this point the person no longer should be viewed as a brother or sister in Christ (Matt. 18:17). This individual is now in Satan's realm and, after defying God-given authority, is facing the "destruction of the flesh" by Satan (1 Cor. 5:5; 11:30-32; 1 Tim. 1:20). Matthew 18:18 reaffirms the authority of God's leaders in such situations.

Church discipline is the action of a local church against one of its members. Since that local church is part of the greater universal church, other local churches should respect and support proper actions of corrective discipline. It lessens the impact of discipline if the unrepentant believer simply goes off to another local church where he is happily received.

Attitudes in Church Discipline

Anger, pride, and a condemning spirit can arise in the sinning believer during the discipline process. But proper attitudes must be maintained (1 Cor. 5:2; 2 Cor. 2:2-11; Gal. 6:1; 2 Thes. 3:15). Those involved in discipline must remain ready to love and forgive the sinning believer, genuinely desiring what is best for the person as well as what is best for the church. There ought to be real grief over the sin of the person and the victory won by Satan. These attitudes, produced by the Holy Spirit through much time in prayer and the Word, will insure the power and favor of God in the process.

Mature believers need to lead in corrective discipline not only because of their wisdom, but also because of their awareness of their own frailty and the power of the flesh in their own lives. They have learned that they have been victorious because of the Spirit's power, not because of their own righteousness and energy.

When Repentance Occurs

Whenever the sinning believer repents, the discipline process stops, and the leaders are responsible to determine if genuine repentance really has occurred. Real repentance will produce objective evidence beyond the mere presence of tears. John the Baptist told the people of his day to bring forth evidences of their repentance. It is valid to look for external indicators. For example, a person who is genuinely repentant will not blame others or circumstances for his sin. He will not expect or demand that he be treated in a certain way. In some cases, restitution may be significant in demonstrating genuine repentance.

When the leaders determine that godly sorrow is present, they must then provide the repentant believer with special care and encouragement to keep the person from being "swallowed up with overmuch sorrow" (2 Cor. 2:7, KJV). Under these circumstances the individual must be forgiven and immediately restored to full fellowship. He needs the sense of acceptance and the reality of restoration back into the caring body of Christ. Repentance, of course, does not mean that a believer is immediately restored to ministry. Restoration to a position in the church may have to come later as determined by the leaders.

Church Discipline in a Litigious Society

Church leaders sometimes are frightened by the idea of being sued by a disciplined member, and rightly so. Going to court to settle matters is certainly the mind-set of our culture, and some churches have been forced to pay large sums of money. Given the prevailing attitude of litigation, there is no guarantee that a church discipline case might not end up in court. However, there are several things that a church can do to protect itself.

First, a church must have a clearly written discipline policy as part of the church constitution. This statement should be required reading for those who join the church and periodically called to the attention of those who attend. Second, the church must follow its own written policy carefully, applying it without discrimination. Any history of favoritism or inconsistency will weaken the church's defense in a court of law. Third, when making any public statements about the sinning believer, the church should avoid language that could be seen as vindictive or derogatory. While these three factors cannot guarantee that a church will avoid a lawsuit, they do reduce the chances of its success.

Corrective church discipline is commanded by the Lord. In situations where the purity and reputation of the church is at stake, sin must be dealt with. Exercising corrective church discipline often is a painful process. But obedience to the Lord overshadows any pain and brings His favor, blessing, and power. God's holiness demands that His children practice holiness; church discipline is an expression of the very holiness of God.

> "We should attempt to follow
> as many details as possible
> of the patterns for church life as
> they are revealed in the
> New Testament."
> (*Basic Theology*, p. 404)

CHAPTER TWENTY-SEVEN

Church Missions:
The Antioch Model

Albert T. Platt

Antioch, "Sin City, East," was not exactly a promising springboard from which to reach the world with the Gospel. Though we ordinarily consider Corinth the sin capital during early church times, actually almost any city of New Testament fame could claim that dubious title. Rome ruled a pagan world full of sinful practices. And Antioch, "Queen of the East" (the euphemistic title for this city on the Orontes River in Syria), though beautiful and cultured, was a soiled queen.

In fact, some historic wag wrote that the pollutions of the Orontes River had contaminated the Tiber River, implying that the entire empire suffered from Antioch's sinful extravagances. Strange indeed that this city should provide the backdrop for a world missions outreach; the place sounds more like a mission field! Indeed the "backdrop" for the first missions outreach may have been Antioch, but the "nest" for the birth of world missions was something else. Closer attention to Scripture clarifies our understanding.

Foundation (Acts 13:1): Church

Someone has observed, "Never did the Orontes flow with fouler mud than when God put a lighthouse on her shores." The "lighthouse" on her shores was a local, New Testament church in Antioch. God was certainly not planning to export Antiochan culture to the world. Neither did He intend to concentrate all the missionary manpower in this recognizably evil and unreached area. He had another plan, one that would eventually bring the Gospel even to our distant shores.

Acts 11:19-30 gives a fairly detailed description of this assembly. It was not really apostolic in origin and seems to have been predominately Gentile (v. 20). It was definitely a growing church, well taught, and generous (vv. 21, 26, 29).

However, a most revealing fact is its being called "the *church* that was in Antioch" (Acts 13:1, KJV). Though this term has several other biblical usages, this assembly refers to a specific group in a specific place—a local church. Charles Ryrie states that the meaning of *church* in the local sense is "a group of professing believers in Christ who have been baptized and who have organized themselves for the purpose of doing God's will" (*Ryrie Study Bible*, 1,843).

Obviously not every religious group or gathering meets the qualifications for the name church. Many of today's "arms of the church" would not qualify. Children's work, vital as it is, does not meet the requirements. Young people's ministries, work with university students, or mission boards can be most fruitful, but these are not to be confused with the church. Standing alone, they simply do not meet the standard. Though these may be significant ministries, God chose to begin the worldwide outreach of the Gospel using a local church.

God's choice of the local church should focus our attention on

the final element in Dr. Ryrie's lists of characteristics: "organized
. . . *for the purpose of doing God's will.*" Obviously, the controlling
factor is the revealed will of God. In Acts 13:1 this was revealed
through prophets and teachers; for us today, God's will is revealed
through the Scriptures. We can glorify God only by giving total
assent to what God has said and by demonstrating that agreement
in our words and deeds. God does not call upon the individual or
the church to be creative, inventive, or innovative, but rather to be
obedient to His revealed will.

We need to make sure that relational theology, applicational
emphases, "meeting needs," and growing mega-churches (sometimes called creating or maintaining "a strong base") do not replace the plain teaching of Scripture — obedience to the revealed
will of God.

Preparation (Acts 13:1): Prophets and Teachers

God provided for this local assembly in Antioch by giving them
gifted men, in this case prophets and teachers (Eph. 4:11-12).
Under the tutelage of the Spirit of God and through the instru-
mentality of these men, the church in Antioch received God's
message and plan. These qualified men were committed to giving
God's authoritative message and divine perspective.

Perhaps the order in which these five men are named represents
something of their maturity, Barnabas having seniority in the
things of the Lord and Saul having the least. But Saul still was no
neophyte. On the contrary, he already had grown spiritually during his time in Arabia, in Tarsus, and his time at Antioch, probably
fourteen years of ministry all together. Little is known of the
other three men.

Ministration (Acts 13:2): As They ~~Ministered~~ *Served*

God spoke through these men "as they ministered to the Lord"
(Acts 13:2). While at times translated "worship," the word *minister*
here embraces the concept of service. In the Old Testament it was
used for priestly functions; in the New Testament it was used for
any sacred official service. The events recorded in the following

verses of Acts 13 may well have occurred in the course of the regular public ministry of these five prophets and teachers. That this ministering might be characterized as "worship" is totally understandable since true worship *is* a proper response to God's truth, precisely the ministry to which these men were committed.

Furthermore, God's truth demands service. Conversely, biblically based, Spirit-directed service *is* worship. Admittedly this concept presents a somewhat different picture of worship than is being pursued in some centers today. But the local assembly in Antioch was functioning exactly as it should have. Responsible men were *teaching* the divine point of view with authority and *serving* the group in the light of the message.

Direction (Acts 13:2): Holy Spirit, Separate, the Work, Called

Acts 13 speaks of the direct action of the Holy Spirit but does not state how He intervened. Significantly, His work was recognized by those present and was not contested. There was no dissenting vote. Apparently the group was well-taught and sufficiently committed to the truth (and to the God of the truth) that they gave an immediate and positive response.

The Spirit's message in Acts 13:2, which was the revealed will of God, was a definitive assignment in three steps:

(1) "*Separate* me Barnabas and Saul." "Separate" is the same term used to mark out the field of play in an athletic event. "Draw a line, and put two men on this side and three men on the other." God made plain His choices from the five competent, recognized, experienced, and functioning leaders of the local church.

(2) ". . . for the *work*." The verse does not mention a specific work. It might have been supposed to be a ministry in another part of Antioch. Such an assumption, however, is not borne out by the verses that follow. The appointed men left both that local church and the environs of Antioch, bringing to fruition the prophetic word of Acts 9:15, "he [Saul] is a chosen vessel unto me, to bear my name before the Gentiles, and kings, and the children of Israel." Saul no doubt had treasured this message and referred to it in public more than once.

(3) ". . . whereunto I have *called* them." This assignment had a

specific appointment. The Spirit left no doubt in His direction. The next move was not just a whim of some adventurous leaders nor even the corporate "vision" of the assembly. God had something explicit in mind, and He was the originator and communicator of this assignment.

All five of these prophets and teachers were communicating God's truth. All were ministering. All were fasting. Yet from the five he "called" these two. Scripture does not explain why God chose who He did, but it is of more than passing interest that He selected already functioning leaders in the church. He did not recruit neophytes.

Over the years I have been involved in hundreds of missionary conferences. Invariably someone asks me to "pray for the young people in our church." I do pray, because I know how important it is for young people to hear God's call to missions. However, rarely am I asked to pray for the leaders, for the elders, the deacons, the Sunday School teachers, or the pastors. The pattern in Acts 13 is to send out the knowledgeable, the experienced, the approved believers.

Unfortunately, today's approach often suggests, "Send so-and-so. Maybe he can hack it over there," clearly implying that "He isn't what we want here. After all, we need a strong base!" I wonder what went through the minds of the other believers in Antioch when such high caliber, dependable, important men were commissioned to leave them. I recall vividly a Honduran pastor who requested help commenting, "But please do not send us anyone we must baby-sit."

Implementation (Acts 13:3-4):
The Church Fasted, Prayed, Laid on Hands, Sent Away

The Antiochan church thought this whole matter serious enough to warrant suspending their regular eating habits. A period of self-denial demonstrated that they were in earnest and allowed for special concentration on prayer. Prayer is a spiritual exercise and discipline that God expects of His people. It is the expression of the believer's conformity to God's will. The text does not really indicate the content of their prayers.

Next, the church publicly recognized the whole matter through a laying on of hands by the elders of the assembly, probably right then and there. Then they released the chosen men from their responsibilities in the local assembly and sent them off. These folks had received the divine message, and they knew the credentials of the men God had chosen. The church was not really ordaining Barnabas and Saul to ministry, since they were already involved and recognized leaders. The assembly was merely agreeing with what God had said. Apparently this church had learned that its mission was to respond to the revealed will of God by expressing agreement and demonstrating that agreement in their behavior.

The Holy Spirit's Role: Sent Forth by the Holy Spirit

In this model, who sends whom is perfectly clear: God made His will known. The well-taught church responded in a mature and spiritual fashion. Some of their very best men were thus separated from them. The end result was that these men were "sent forth by the Holy Spirit."

More often than not, mission organizations and ministries do recruiting in places other than the local church. They go to colleges and embrace seniors, shake hands with juniors, speak to sophomores, and nod at freshmen. Talented they are; good students most of them. There is little question about their potential. But in this early church model God entrusted His worldwide message to prepared, experienced men already involved in significant ministry. These were men upon whom the local church could definitely put its stamp of approval.

Observations and Conclusions

Some current church or mission concepts of appointing leadership are notably absent in the Antiochan model. Even if one acknowledges an element of transition at this time in the early church period, it is still significant to note that the church had no choice in the matter of these missionary appointees, except to comply with or reject God's direction. The men chosen were not really homegrown members. They were less a "product" of the local church and more of an imported element to help the church in process. That is, the assembly in Antioch did little in the formation of these men except to provide the venue for maturing their ministry and the use of their spiritual gifts. There is no clear indication that the church "supported" the men in the sense that we understand the term today.

The special character of the nascent church may explain the silence on these matters. The issues faced by the twentieth-century church and mission agencies are probably as colored by culture as were the events of Acts 13. However, the model does present several important trans-cultural, pan-temporal concepts.

God established the instruments He had chosen to be the "nest" of world missions. God used capable, knowledgeable, committed, functioning, mature communicators of His message — men known to be producers; men with the seal of approval of the local church. The church needed and responded to God's direction.

Earlier divinely appointed circumstances caused a Christian diaspora which ignited the spread of the Gospel. Undoubtedly some of the expatriate Jews present on the Day of Pentecost (Acts 2:9-11) believed and took the message home. Acts 8 mentions persecution that forced believing Jews from the city of Jerusalem. It is both normal and commendable that they took their life-transforming message with them and faithfully proclaimed it. However, these instances of the spread of the Gospel lack the special "sending" character of the Antiochan model.

The missions endeavor today should look to the Antiochan model when seeking personnel. The local church can provide mature, capable communicators of the revealed will of God, with the seal of approval of their local body, a seal that indicates, "We know these men and women to have a working knowledge of God's Word. They know how to lead a soul to Christ and how to help new believers grow to maturity." Such an approval is different from and more important than a diploma or a degree. Any assembly of believers which fulfills all the requirements to be called a local church possesses the elements necessary to produce a modern Barnabas or Saul. Should not the pattern of God's Word, rather than popular, culturally developed models, be the guide for missions today?

Things
to Come

"For the believer, the knowledge of prophecy (a) provides joy in the midst of affliction (2 Cor. 4:17), (b) cleanses and encourages holy living (1 John 3:3), (c) is profitable, like all Scripture, for a number of important needs in the Christian's life (2 Tim. 3:16-17), (d) gives facts about life after death (2 Cor. 5:8), (e) gives truth about the end of history, (f) gives proof of the reliability of all Scripture, for the number of prophecies that have come to pass precisely as predicted cannot be accounted for by chance but only by God, (g) draws our hearts out in worship to the God who is in complete control and who will accomplish His will in history. To slight prophecy is to miss these benefits."

(*Basic Theology*, p. 440)

CHAPTER TWENTY-EIGHT

Knowing Tomorrow Helps Living Today (The Practicality of Prophecy)

Charles H. Dyer

Our society fixates on relevance. The "information superhighway" will add to the glut of data already assaulting our senses. We cannot possibly absorb all the data, so we selectively focus on those items that most directly affect our lives. For instance, every thirty minutes "Headline News" broadcasts the important events of the hour. During the day stock quotations flash across the bottom of the screen, while in the evening late-breaking sports scores replace the stock quotes. For those interested in the Dow Jones Industrial Average, the electronic ticker tape is the most relevant information on the screen. But sports fans may barely notice the numbers sliding across the screen and only monitor the sports scores. In other words, viewers perceive and process information based on its relevance to them.

This tendency is a danger in interpreting prophecy as well. One charge made against those of us who call ourselves dispensationalists is that we place undue emphasis on predictive prophecy to the exclusion of what the Bible has to say about the "here and now." Does an emphasis on predictive prophecy automatically result in a lack of relevance for practical living? No. Understood properly, predictive prophecy actively promotes practical Christian living.

Those who take a different approach to specific passages describing future events often become so intent in arguing the meaning of the individual prophecies that they miss the overall point. To avoid this danger, I have chosen one specific set of prophecies that all conservative believers — whatever their millennial conviction — agree are still future ones. By studying these specific predictions we can try to reach some consensus on the relevance of God's prophetic Word.

In at least four specific passages God predicted the still-future resurrection of the dead. No one alive when the prophecies were given ever saw them fulfilled. These passages predict events that seem to have lacked *immediate* relevance for their audience, and yet most believers accept the literalness of their future fulfillment. What practical value could such prophecies have for their original audience — or for us today?

Specific Prophecies on Resurrection

Daniel 12:2, 13

The Prophet Daniel spent most of his life as a royal adviser to a foreign government. After being taken into captivity from Jerusalem as a young man, he rose to prominence in the court of Nebuchadnezzar because of his faithfulness and God-given wisdom. The entire Book of Daniel focuses on the "times of the Gentiles" when the people of Israel would be controlled by foreign governments. Daniel's book stresses the two themes of prophecy and piety. His prophetic sections point to the succession of Gentile governments that would control Jerusalem and the people of Israel. The parade of international powers reaches its climactic end when God's messianic kingdom comes to assume control over all. Between these prophetic visions Daniel focuses on personal piety by urging his readers to remain faithful in spite of persecution.

Chapter 1 introduces both the times of the Gentiles and Daniel's rise to prominence because of his faithfulness to God. Chapters 2–7 form a separate unit with Daniel switching languages from Hebrew to Aramaic. Chapters 2 and 7 focus on the succession of four Gentile powers that will rule over Jerusalem and the Jews until God replaces them with His coming kingdom. Chapters 3 and 6 highlight the persecution God's followers will experience while they await the coming of God's kingdom. Chapters 4 and 5 encourage God's people by revealing that even Gentile leaders will be forced to admit that God is ruling over the affairs of the world.

Beginning in chapter 8 Daniel resumes writing in Hebrew. Chapters 8–12 contain three separate visions (Dan. 8; 9; 10–12). The first and last visions are parallel as God reveals key rulers who will influence events in Israel. Both chapters begin with the kings of Medo-Persia (8:20; 11:2), move to Alexander the Great of Greece (8:21; 11:3), detail the division of his empire among four of his generals (8:22; 11:4), and feature the rise of Antiochus Epiphanes (8:9-13, 23-25; 11:21-35). Chapter 11 continues the drama by jumping from Antiochus to an individual that many identify as the future Antichrist (11:36-45). Between these two visions is Daniel's "vision of the 70 weeks" (chap. 9), focusing on the time element of Daniel's predictions.

Many disagree over the interpretation of various aspects of these prophecies. But after describing all the above, Daniel makes a prophetic utterance that all understand: "Multitudes who sleep in the dust of the earth will awake: some to everlasting life, others to shame and everlasting contempt. Those who are wise will shine like the brightness of the heavens, and those who lead many to righteousness, like the stars for ever and ever" (Dan. 12:2-3, NIV). While believers argue over the specifics of when this resurrection occurs in the general program of God, most agree that the passage is predicting a future resurrection of those who have died.

But *why* include this prediction of resurrection? What practical benefit would such a prediction have for Daniel or for his audience? How relevant was this prophecy to Daniel or to his readers? The immediate context and the larger context of Daniel provide the answers.

Just before announcing this resurrection, Daniel predicted a time of unparalleled persecution that would overtake his people. "There will be a time of distress such as has not happened from the beginning of nations until then" (Dan. 12:1). Many would be forced to choose between staying true to God or staying alive. Much like Shadrach, Meshach, and Abednego in chapter 3, these future readers would be faced with a choice of denial or death.

Daniel's three friends had exhibited remarkable faith in the power of God. "If we are thrown into the blazing furnace, the God we serve is able to save us from it, and he will rescue us from your hand, O king. But even if he does not, we want you to know, O king, that we will not serve your gods or worship the image of gold you have set up" (Dan. 3:17-18). Though facing death, these friends refused to waver in their commitment to God. God spared their lives, but not all believers in the future can expect such miraculous deliverance. (Even these friends allowed for the possibility that God might not physically deliver them.) What hope can future believers have when facing death?

After describing the future persecution for believers, Daniel offers hope to the people of Israel. "But at that time your people — everyone whose name is found written in the book — will be delivered" (Dan. 12:1b). Some will be delivered *from* physical death (like Daniel and his friends in their times of persecution), while others will be delivered *through* physical death (by being resurrected). The announcement of the resurrection is not just added as some theological treatise on future things. God added it to provide encouragement to those facing tremendous persecution and possible martyrdom, and to motivate them to faithfulness. Those who stayed faithful to God would be delivered through God's resurrection power.

The Book of Daniel ends with God's promise to Daniel of future reward at the resurrection. "As for you, go your way till the end. You will rest, and then at the end of the days you will rise to receive your allotted inheritance" (Dan. 12:13). Daniel was torn from his home early in life and he died in a foreign land. Yet Daniel's faithfulness will be rewarded at the resurrection. Daniel could postpone personal reward in his earthly life because God would provide his "allotted inheritance" at the resurrection. The promise of resurrection gave Daniel an eternal perspective on life.

1 Corinthians 15:20-34

Six hundred years after Daniel, Messiah had come, died, risen from the dead, and ascended to heaven. God's new program with the church had begun, and God had chosen Paul as His apostle to the Gentiles (Gal. 2:8). Paul had helped start the church in the largely Gentile city of Corinth (Acts 18) and was writing to this immature church to correct sinful practices and to answer several questions.

One question concerned resurrection: "But if it is preached that Christ has been raised from the dead, how can some of you say that there is no resurrection of the dead?" (1 Cor. 15:12) In defense of the fact of resurrection, Paul reminded the Corinthians of the objective fact of Christ's resurrection, verified by eyewitnesses, some of whom were still alive (15:5-8). He explained that Christ's resurrection was an essential part of God's redemptive program. "And if Christ has not been raised, your faith is futile; you are still in your sins" (15:17).

At the end of the chapter Paul moved from the past resurrection of Christ to the future resurrection of believers. "Listen, I tell you a mystery: We will not all sleep, but we will all be changed—in a flash, in the twinkling of an eye, at the last trumpet. For the trumpet will sound, the dead will be raised imperishable, and we will be changed" (15:51-52). Christians may disagree about when this resurrection occurs or whom this resurrection includes, but those who take the Bible as God's Word do agree that Paul is describing a literal, future resurrection.

257

But what practical benefit did such a prophecy have to the Corinthians? These believers were still struggling in spiritual infancy. Factions, sexual immorality, quarrels, lawsuits, and misuse of spiritual gifts were among some of their more pressing difficulties. How relevant was a theological discourse on future resurrection to a church Paul himself described as "mere infants in Christ"? (1 Cor. 3:1)

Paul did not include the doctrine merely to fill space in his letter. Its first importance was to the believer's salvation. "And if Christ has not been raised, our preaching is useless and so is your faith" (1 Cor. 15:14). The resurrection of Christ is an essential part of God's plan of salvation.

Paul's second argument for the relevance of resurrection focused on the future reward offered to those who give their lives in service to Christ. "And as for us, why do we endanger ourselves every hour? . . . If I fought wild beasts in Ephesus for merely human reasons, what have I gained? If the dead are not raised, 'Let us eat and drink, for tomorrow we die'" (15:30, 32). The resurrection bursts the empty "beer-commercial" hedonism of Paul's day and of ours. "It *will* get better than this! You *will* go around again in life! Only next time it will last for all eternity and your eternal reward will depend on how wisely you lived life the first time." Resurrection forces believers to take a long-range view of actions and consequences.

Paul's third argument for the relevance of resurrection focused on the hope given to believers facing death. Paul reminded his readers that "the dead will be raised imperishable, and we will be changed" (15:52). Anyone who has stood at a graveside and watched the casket of a loved one lowered into the earth knows the powerful message of hope offered by the resurrection. We miss those loved ones who have died. But if they have put their trust in Christ, we will see them again one day.

Paul ended his message on resurrection by urging his readers to stability and faithfulness. "Therefore, my dear brothers, stand firm. Let nothing move you. Always give yourselves fully to the work of the Lord, because you know that your labor in the Lord is not in vain" (15:58).

Sometimes football games have been broadcast "tape delayed" —

the actual event was over before it was shown on TV. The hard-fought, close play may have kept those present on the edge of their seats. But if I know the outcome before watching, I find I am far less concerned about the ebb and flow of the game. I'm assured of the outcome in spite of the individual plays. Paul was telling the Corinthians that the outcome has already been decided. The resurrection *guarantees* that God's people will triumph in the end. Neither circumstances, nor external opposition, nor death itself can stand in the way. No matter how hard fought the struggle, we can have confidence.

1 Thessalonians 4:13-18

Though 1 Thessalonians appears later than 1 Corinthians in the New Testament, Paul actually wrote this letter about four years before 1 Corinthians. After a short ministry in Thessalonica, Paul fled to Berea and eventually landed in Athens. From there Paul sent Timothy back to Thessalonica to check on the spiritual health of this young church. Paul then moved from Athens to Corinth and wrote 1 Thessalonians from Corinth.

Though Paul only spent a few weeks in Thessalonica, he evidently thought it important to teach this young church about future things. In our English Bibles, each chapter of his letter ends with a reference to the return of Jesus Christ. While Christ's return was a source of hope, it also raised questions for these young Christians. Evidently some believers had died since Paul had left the city. Had those who died "missed out" on God's future program? The believers raised the question, and Paul addressed it in chapter 4.

Paul began by telling the believers that "we do not want you to be ignorant about those who fall asleep, or to grieve like the rest of men, who have no hope" (1 Thes. 4:13). Paul then painted a clear picture of the resurrection. "For the Lord himself will come down from heaven, with a loud command, with the voice of the archangel and with the trumpet call of God, and the dead in Christ will rise first. After that, we who are still alive and are left will be caught up together with them in the clouds to meet the Lord in the air. And so we will be with the Lord forever" (4:16-17).

Paul's description of the resurrection/rapture is one of the clearest statements on the actual sequence of events. The resurrection of the dead and transformation of the living is a hope for which believers have been waiting nearly two millennia. So what practical relevance could such an event have for the believers of Thessalonica? The passage provides two keys.

The imminence of the resurrection/rapture gives it relevance. Imminence does not mean that something *will* happen soon, but that something *could* happen at any time. While the event described by the Apostle Paul has not happened for almost 2,000 years, it *could have happened* at any time. Paul expected the event to happen in his lifetime. After explaining that the dead would rise first, Paul then said, "After that, *we who are still alive and are left* will be caught up together with them in the clouds to meet the Lord in the air" (4:17). The truth of the resurrection was relevant to the believers in Thessalonica because it could have taken place then. It's also relevant to us because it could take place today or tomorrow.

Paul's second key to the relevance of the resurrection can be found in his opening and closing comments. He began by saying he needed to explain this truth so believers would not "grieve like the rest of men, who have no hope" (4:13). He ended his discussion of the resurrection by saying, "Therefore encourage each other with these words" (4:18). The word for "encourage" (*parakaleō*) can also be translated "comfort." It is the same word Christ used to describe the Holy Spirit who would come to comfort believers following Christ's death, resurrection, and ascension (John 14:15-27).

Knowledge of the imminent resurrection of believers who had died and their reunion with those believers still alive was a great comfort. While believers still grieved the separation from a loved one who had died, their sadness was tempered by the realization that the parting was only temporary. Much like two parents crying when their son or daughter "leaves the nest" and moves far away, believers can grieve over their temporary separation. But, praise the Lord, the separation is not forever. Resurrection serves as a promise that a great "homecoming" will again reunite those loved ones in Christ.

Revelation 20:4-6, 11-15

The Book of Revelation forces one to decide how to interpret Bible prophecy. John's messages to the churches of his day (Rev. 2–3) are followed by his description of a time of terrible judgment for the earth (chaps. 6–18). These judgments climax in the triumphal return of Christ to earth as "King of kings and Lord of lords" (19:16). Following the defeat of Satan and his followers, John describes the resurrection of the dead. This resurrection includes Old Testament saints and those saints killed during the Tribulation. John's prediction of resurrection parallels that described by Daniel — supernatural activities with Michael the archangel standing for Israel (Dan. 12:1a; Rev. 12:7-9), terrible persecution of Israel (Dan. 12:1b; Rev. 12:13-17), divine intervention and deliverance (Dan. 12:1c; Rev. 19:19–20:3), and resurrection (Dan. 12:2; Rev. 20:4-6).

But the Apostle John provides new revelation. Daniel wrote that multitudes would be resurrected "some to everlasting life, others to shame and everlasting contempt" (Dan. 12:2). One might assume from Daniel that both the righteous and the wicked would arise simultaneously for their respective reward or judgment. However, the Apostle John reveals that these two groups are resurrected at two different times. The righteous are resurrected when Christ returns to earth to establish His kingdom (Rev. 20:4), but "the rest of the dead did not come to life until the thousand years were ended" (Rev. 20:5).

Often prophecies in the Old Testament appear as a single event when, in fact, they point to separate events. Interpreters call this *prophetic foreshortening.* Isaiah 9:6-7, for instance, announces, "For to us a child is born, to us a son is given" (first advent of Christ). The same verses predict that "the government will be on his shoulders. . . . He will reign on David's throne and over his kingdom" (second advent of Christ). Similar foreshortening can be seen in Daniel's prophetic history of the Gentile rulers in Daniel 11.

Foreshortening is often pictured as looking off into the distance at what appears to be a mountain with two peaks. As a traveler approaches the scene, he realizes that it actually consists of two separate mountains with a valley between. Daniel envisioned one mountain (the resurrection) with two peaks (the "righteous" and the ones destined to "shame"). Traveling ahead in prophetic revelation, John revealed two mountains (two resurrections) with a valley between (a thousand years separating the two parts of the resurrection).

Though John provides this additional revelation, his essential message remains the same as that spoken by Daniel over 600 years earlier. At the time of Christ's second coming the righteous "came to life and reigned with Christ a thousand years" (Rev. 20:4). The second phase of the resurrection is the resurrection of the unrighteous to appear before "a great white throne" (v. 11). At this resurrection "each person was judged according to what he had done. . . . If anyone's name was not found written in the book of life, he was thrown into the lake of fire" (vv. 13, 15).

Many disagree over when the events of Revelation 20 will happen, but all believe the chapter is describing still-future resurrections. Why did John include this information in his book? What relevance would these events have had for his readers, or for us?

John shows the relevance of the resurrection for believers when he specifically identifies one group of believers being resurrected, "those who had been beheaded because of their testimony for Jesus and because of the word of God. They had not worshiped the beast or his image and had not received his mark on their foreheads or their hands" (20:4). This resurrection includes martyrs who were killed for their faith in Christ. John specifically mentions these martyrs in Revelation 6:9 and 13:15-17.

God's promise of resurrection is a powerful encouragement to those facing death for their faith in Christ. It serves as a reminder that God can and will undo the worst that the world can do to them. Though the world might be able to cause their physical death, God can and will resurrect them at the appropriate time. And for those who are part of this resurrection of the righteous, "the second death has no power over them" (Rev. 20:6).

John also shows the relevance of the second resurrection. It is a resurrection unto judgment at God's great white throne. After reminding his readers of the immutable destiny of those who have not placed their trust in Christ (20:15), John ends his book with an appeal for individuals to make the decision that will determine their eternal destiny. "The Spirit and the bride say, 'Come!' And let him who hears say, 'Come!' Whoever is thirsty, let him come; and whoever wishes, let him take the free gift of the water of life" (22:17).

People want to know the future. This desire to know our destiny explains society's fascination with astrology and horoscopes, and the interest of some in prophecy (whether from the Bible or from other so-called seers like Nostradamus). The Bible recognizes this attraction. Why else would such prophecies be followed by clear offers of salvation to those listening to the message? Prophecy has an effect on evangelism because it shows the reader that God is in charge, that He has a plan for all individuals, and that a person's eternal destiny is determined by his or her response to God's Gospel message.

Practical Principles from This Study

So what practical benefit is there in studying Bible prophecy? There is great benefit if one studies prophecy the way God intended. God did not provide prophecy to "tickle our ears" or to enable us to construct complex charts. Every passage on the resurrection includes practical application for the here-and-now. God did not reveal everything that would happen in the future, but those events He did reveal have practical meaning for us today:

1. Prophecy *encourages* believers today by reminding them that God is in control and that they have an eternal destiny.

2. Prophecy *motivates* believers today by reminding them that God will reward them for faithful service.

3. Prophecy *comforts* believers today by reminding them that their troubles will someday end and that they will be reunited with those believing loved ones who have died.

4. Prophecy *challenges* believers today by reminding them that the world's standards are not God's eternal standards. Life is more than our current existence.

5. Prophecy *stabilizes* believers today by helping them see current events and circumstances from God's eternal perspective.

6. Prophecy *confronts* unbelievers today by reminding them that

263

God is in control of the universe and that He will judge those who refuse to put their trust in Him.

Does knowing about tomorrow help us live today? The answer is a resounding yes! As Peter explained after describing the future of this universe, "Since everything will be destroyed in this way, what kind of people ought you to be? You ought to live holy and godly lives as you look forward to the day of God and speed its coming. . . . So then, dear friends, since you are looking forward to this, make every effort to be found spotless, blameless and at peace with him" (2 Peter 3:11-12, 14). What you truly believe about the future will show in how you live today.

> "Pretribulationism teaches that the
> Rapture of the church
> (both dead and living saints)
> will occur before the seven-year
> Tribulation period."
> *(Basic Theology*, p. 482)

CHAPTER TWENTY-NINE

The Biblical Basis
for the Pretribulational
Rapture

Thomas Ice

C hurches today often neglect the study and preaching of biblical prophecy because they consider it a controversial and impractical topic. At the same time, they bemoan the apathy of believers and struggle to encourage people toward holy living. Churches caught in this trap need to consider that the teaching of the Rapture, woven throughout the fabric of the New Testament, addresses these issues and can provide motivation for godliness. No one Bible verse says precisely when the Rapture will take place in relation to the Tribulation or the Second Coming. However, this does not mean that the Scriptures do not teach a clear position on this matter.

Many important biblical doctrines are not derived from a single verse, but come from a harmonization of several passages into systematic conclusions. Some truths are directly stated in the Bible, such as the deity of Christ (John 1:1; Titus 2:13). Other doctrines, like the Trinity and the incarnate nature of Christ, are the product of harmonizing the many passages that relate to these matters. Taking into account all that the Bible says on these issues, orthodox theologians, over time, concluded that God is a Trinity and that Christ is the God-Man. Similarly, a systematic, literal interpretation of all New Testament passages relating to the Rapture will lead to the pretribulation viewpoint: that, at the Rapture, all living believers will be translated into heaven at least seven years before Christ's Second Coming.

Foundational Issues

Four affirmations provide a biblical framework for the pretribulational Rapture: (1) *consistent* literal interpretation, (2) premillennialism, (3) futurism, and (4) a distinction between Israel and the church.

Literal Interpretation

Consistent literal interpretation is the essential affirmation. The dictionary defines *literal* as "belonging to letters." A literal interpretation is "based on the actual words in their ordinary meaning . . . not going beyond the facts." Literal interpretation of the Bible explains the original sense of the Bible according to the normal and customary usages of its language. This can be seen in three areas. Grammatical (according to the rules of grammar), historical (consistent with the historical setting of the passage), and contextual (in accord with its context) considerations form the basis for this method.

Literal interpretation recognizes that a word or phrase can be used either plainly ("he died") or figuratively ("he kicked the bucket"). Either way, the meaning is understood directly from the text and the context. A "Golden Rule of Interpretation" has been developed to discern whether or not a figure of speech was intended.

When the plain sense of Scripture makes common sense, seek no other sense; therefore, take every word at its primary, ordinary, usual, literal meaning unless the facts of the immediate context, studied in the light of related passages and axiomatic and fundamental truths, indicate clearly otherwise (David L. Cooper, *The World's Greatest Library: Graphically Illustrated* [Los Angeles: Biblical Research Society, 1970], 11).

The principle of consistent, literal interpretation of the entire Bible logically leads one to the pre-trib position.

Premillennialism

The next principle foundational to pretribulationalism is premillennialism. Premillennialism teaches that the Second Advent will occur before Christ's thousand-year reign from Jerusalem upon earth, which is a necessary foundation for pretribulationalism. Postmillennialism or amillennialism by definition include a *post*-tribulational Rapture.

Futurism

The third contributing principle is futurism. Four possible views relate to the timing of prophetic fulfillment in history. The four views are simple in the sense that they reflect the only four possibilities in relation to time—past, present, future, and timeless. The *preterist* (past) believes that most if not all prophecy has already been fulfilled, usually in relation to the destruction of Jerusalem in A.D. 70. The *historicist* (present) sees much of the Church Age as equal to the Tribulation. Thus, prophecy has been and will be fulfilled during the current age. *Futurists* (future) believe that virtually all prophetic events will take place in the future Tribulation, Second Coming, or Millennium. The *idealist* (timeless) does not believe either that the Bible indicates the timing of events or that we can determine their timing in advance. Therefore, idealists think that prophetic passages mainly teach great ideas or truths about God to be applied regardless of timing. Pretribulationalism can be built only upon futurism.

Distinction between Israel and the Church

The final principle related to the pre-trib position is the biblical truth that God's single program for history includes two peoples, Israel and the church. This view has been systematized into what is often known as dispensationalism. While the basis of salvation (God's grace) is the same for Jew and Gentile, God's prophetic program has two distinct aspects. Presently, God's plan for Israel is on hold until He completes His current purpose with the church and raptures Christ's bride (the church) to heaven. After the Rapture, God will complete His unfinished business with Israel during the seven-year Tribulation period. An interpreter who does not distinguish passages intended for Israel from those intended for the church improperly merges the two programs, usually by seeing the church taking over the unfulfilled blessings prophesied for Israel in the Old Testament. Such a merger is incompatible with a pre-trib Rapture.

Specific Pretribulational Arguments

The fact of the Rapture is most clearly presented in 1 Thessalonians 4:13-18 which encourages living Christians that, at the Rapture, they will be reunited with those who have died in Christ before them. In verse 17 the English phrase "caught up" (NASB) translates the Greek word *harpazo,* which means "to seize upon with force" or "to snatch up." The Latin translators of the Bible used the word *rapere,* the root of the English term *rapture.* At the Rapture living believers will be "caught up" in the air, translated into the clouds, in a moment of time.

Contrasts between Comings

The Rapture is characterized in the New Testament as a "translation coming" (1 Cor. 15:51-52; 1 Thes. 4:15-17) in which the Lord comes *for* His church, taking her to His Father's house (John 14:3). But at Christ's Second Advent, He descends from heaven *with* His saints to set up His messianic kingdom on earth (Zech. 14:4-5; Matt. 24:30-31). The differences between these two events are harmonized naturally by the pre-trib position, while other views are not able to account comfortably for such differences.

Paul speaks of the Rapture as a "mystery" (1 Cor. 15:51-54), that is, a truth not revealed until it was disclosed by the apostles (Col. 1:26). Thus the Rapture is said to be a newly revealed mystery, making it a separate event. The Second Coming, on the other hand, was predicted in the Old Testament (Dan. 12:1-3; Zech. 12:10; 14:4).

The New Testament teaches about the Rapture of the church and yet also speaks of the Second Coming of Christ. These two events are different in a number of ways. Pretribulation scholar John F. Walvoord has noted the following contrasts between the translation at the Rapture and Christ's Second Coming to establish the kingdom (from *The Return of the Lord* [Grand Rapids, Mich.: Zondervan, 1955], 87–88).

Rapture/Translation	2nd Coming/Establish Kingdom
Translation of all believers	No translation at all
Translated saints go to heaven	Translated saints return to earth
Earth not judged	Earth judged & righteousness established
Imminent, any-moment	Follows definite predicted signs including the tribulation
Not in the Old Testament	Predicted often in Old Testament
Believers only	Affects all people
Before the day of wrath	Concluding the day of wrath
No reference to Satan	Satan bound

Both events mention clouds symbolizing a heavenly role in both, but other differences demonstrate that these are two distinct events. At the Rapture, the Lord comes *for* His saints (1 Thes. 4:16); at the Second Coming the Lord comes *with* His saints (1 Thes. 3:13). At the Rapture, the Lord comes only for believers, but His return to the earth will impact all people. The Rapture is a translation/resurrection event; the Second Coming is not. At the Rapture, the Lord takes believers from earth to heaven "to the

Father's house" (John 14:3); at the Second Coming believers return from heaven to the earth (Matt. 24:30).

The best harmonization of these two different events supports a pretribulational Rapture (which is signless and could happen at any moment), while the many events taking place during the Tribulation are best understood as signs leading up to the Second Coming.

The Time Interval between the Rapture and the Second Coming

Even though Scripture speaks of two events that are yet future, we still must ascertain when the Rapture will take place: Will it come before, during, or after the Tribulation?

Numerous items in the New Testament can be harmonized by the pre-trib time gap of at least seven years between comings. During this interval all church saints will appear before the Judgment Seat of Christ in heaven (2 Cor. 5:10). The interval allows for a time after the translation of all believers when multitudes left upon the earth will respond in faith to Christ. These Tribulation believers will have nonresurrected bodies at the Second Coming, will be the "sheep" mentioned in the judgment at the Second Advent (Matt. 25:31-46), and will expand the initial population base for the Millennium (Isa. 65:20-25).

The Imminent Coming of Christ

The New Testament speaks of our Lord's return as imminent, meaning that it could happen at any moment. Other things *may* occur before an imminent event, but nothing else must take place before it happens. Imminency passages instruct believers to *look, watch,* and *wait* for His coming (1 Cor. 1:7; Phil. 3:20; 1 Thes. 1:10; Titus 2:13; Heb. 9:28; 1 Peter 1:13; Jude 21). If either the appearance of the Antichrist, the Abomination of Desolation, or the unfolding of the Tribulation must occur before the Rapture, then a command to watch for Christ's coming would not be relevant. Only pretribulationalism teaches a truly imminent Rapture since it is the only view not requiring anything to happen before the Rapture. Imminency is a strong argument for the pre-trib Rapture and provides the believer with a true "blessed hope."

The Nature of the Tribulation

The Bible teaches that the Tribulation (i.e., the seven-year, 70th week of Daniel) is a time of preparation for Israel's restoration (Deut. 4:29-30; Jer. 30:4-11). While the church will experience tribulation in general during this present age (John 16:33), she is never mentioned as participating in Israel's time of trouble, which includes the Great Tribulation, the Day of the Lord, and the Wrath of God. Pretribulationalism gives the best answer to the biblical explanation of the fact that the church is never mentioned in passages that speak about tribulational events, while Israel is mentioned consistently throughout these passages.

The Nature of the Church

Only pretribulationalism is able to give full biblical import to the New Testament teaching that the church differs significantly from Israel. The church is said to be a mystery (Eph. 3:1-13) by which Jews and Gentiles are now united into one body in Christ (Eph. 2:11-22). This explains why the church's translation to heaven is never mentioned in any Old Testament passage that deals with the Second Coming after the Tribulation, and why the church is promised deliverance from the time of God's wrath during the Tribulation (1 Thes. 1:9-10; 5:9; Rev. 3:10). The church alone has the promise that all believers will be taken to the Father's house in heaven (John 14:1-3) at the translation, and not to the earth as other views would demand.

The Work of the Holy Spirit

Second Thessalonians 2:1-12 discusses a man of lawlessness being held back until a later time. Interpreting the restrainer of evil (2:6) as the indwelling ministry of the Holy Spirit at work through the body of Christ during the current age, supports the pretribulational interpretation. Since "the lawless one" (the beast or anti-Christ) cannot be revealed until the Restrainer (the Holy Spirit) is taken away (2:7-8), the Tribulation cannot occur until the church is removed.

271

Practical Implications

Like all aspects of biblical doctrine, teaching on the Rapture has a practical dimension. Dr. Renald Showers has summarized some of the practical implications of the pre-trib Rapture for a forthcoming book.

> The fact that the glorified, holy Son of God could step through the door of heaven at any moment is intended by God to be the most pressing, incessant motivation for holy living and aggressive ministry (including missions, evangelism, and Bible teaching), and the greatest cure for lethargy and apathy. It should make a major difference in every Christian's values, actions, priorities and goals.

As John writes, "Everyone who has this hope fixed on Him purifies himself, just as He is pure" (1 John 3:3). Our Rapture hope is said to urge a watchfulness for Christ Himself (1 Cor. 15:58); to encourage faithfulness in church leaders (2 Tim. 4:1-5); to encourage patient waiting (1 Thes. 1:10); to result in expectation and looking (Phil. 3:20; Titus 2:13; Heb. 9:28); to promote godly moderation (Phil. 4:5); to excite "heavenlymindedness" (Col. 3:1-4); to bring forth successful labor (1 Thes. 2:19-20); to experience comfort (1 Thes. 4:18); to urge steadfastness (2 Thes. 2:1-2; 1 Tim. 6:14; 1 Peter 5:4); to infuse diligence and activity (2 Tim. 4:1-8); to promote mortification of the flesh (Col. 3:4-5; Titus 2:12-13); to require soberness (1 Thes. 5:6; 1 Peter 1:13); to contribute to an abiding with Christ (1 John 2:28; 3:2); to support patience under trial (James 5:7-8); and to enforce obedience (2 Tim. 4:1).

The pretribulation Rapture is not just wishful "pie-in-the-sky, in the bye-and-bye" thinking. Rather, it is vitally connected to Christian living in the "nasty here-and-now." No wonder the early church coined a unique greeting of "Maranatha!" which reflected the primacy of the Blessed Hope as a very real presence in their everyday lives. *Maranatha* literally means "our Lord come!" (1 Cor. 16:22) The life of the church today could only be improved if "Maranatha" were to return as a sincere greeting on the lips of an expectant people.

"The knowledge of prophecy
provides joy
in the midst of affliction."
(*Basic Theology*, p. 440)

CHAPTER THIRTY

The Timing of the Millennium

Robert L. Thomas

The last book of the Bible has a distinctly practical purpose. Revelation even promises incentives for those who abide by its standards of behavior (Rev. 1:3; 22:7). The book's sequence ties the receipt of these blessings to the Millennium (mentioned six times in Rev. 20:2-7), and to the conditions of the new heaven and earth (Rev. 21) that come immediately after the thousand years (cf. Rev. 2:7 with 22:2; 3:12 with 21:2; 3:21 with 20:6). It is of no small consequence in the motivation for Christian living, therefore, to establish the timing of the Millennium. A future kingdom is spoken of by Christ (Luke 12:32; 22:29), Paul (1 Thes. 2:12; 2 Thes. 1:5), James (James 2:5), and John himself, particularly in the last chapters of Revelation. Expectation of this kingdom to come is an integral part of Christian experience now.

Those of postmillennial and amillennial persuasions usually identify the thousand-year period with what is happening presently to the church on earth. The Book of Revelation, however, pictures the present plight of Christians as one of persecution and suffering (Rev. 1:9; 2:7-11). The prospect that sustains them through this period of adversity is the imminent return of Christ to punish the disobedient (3:3, 16) and to reward the faithful during a future epoch (3:10, 20-21).

John's vision focuses on the kingdom Jesus will establish at His return. It is clearly a future kingdom with an initial phase that will extend for a thousand years upon the present earth. Three distinct lines of evidence demonstrate that this kingdom is yet future: the context of the book as a whole, the context of the seventh bowl, and the teaching of Revelation 20:1-10.

The Witness of Revelation's Broad Context

The context of the whole Book of Revelation supports a future Millennium. Early on, John speaks of sharing in the affliction, and kingdom, and endurance with his readers (Rev. 1:9). The grammatical construction and context of this phrase implies an emphasis on the "affliction" that relates to the "kingdom" and that requires "endurance" or "patient waiting."

To the overcomers in Thyatira and elsewhere, Christ promises a future "authority over the nations" (Rev. 2:26) based on their future destruction of them "with a rod of iron" (2:27). This is a promise of sharing in Christ's future rule over the nations (cf. 17:14; 19:14).

To the overcomers in Laodicea and elsewhere, Christ promises the privilege of sitting with Him on His future throne (Rev. 3:21). As with the rest of the promises to overcomers in Revelation 2–3, this one points to conditions described in Revelation 19–22. Christ's throne is different from the Father's throne in 3:21. The Father's throne is in heaven, and the other is on earth, belonging to Christ as the son of David in the future millennial reign. Because He is David's son, He will inherit David's throne (cf. Ps. 122:5; Ezek. 43:7). Christ emphasizes His own Davidic lineage and

His role as David's Lord (Matt. 22:42-45; Mark 12:35-37; Luke 20:41-44), and the Angel Gabriel explicitly states that Jesus will occupy David's throne when He comes in His future glory (Luke 1:32-33; cf. Dan. 7:13-14; Matt. 25:31; Acts 2:30; Heb. 2:5-8; Rev. 20:4). Revelation in particular emphasizes Christ's assumption of the Davidic throne (Rev. 1:5, 7; 3:7; 5:5; 22:16). As Acts 2:32-35 says, His resurrection and ascension have placed Him in a position to wait for the proper time to occupy that throne. He promises the overcomer a share in this earthly throne.

Revelation 5:10 refers to the future kingdom again: "You have made [i.e., will have made] them a kingdom and priests to our God, and they shall reign on the earth." The redeemed people of God will not only be a people over whom He reigns, but also will share in God's rule over the coming millennial kingdom (1 Cor. 4:8; 6:3). The phrase in Revelation 5:10, "they shall reign," uses the future tense of *basileusousin*, showing that this kingdom is the goal toward which the program of God is advancing (Rev. 20:4, 6). That believers will serve as delegated rulers means they will be the equivalent of kings in this forecast epoch. This fact, spelled out more particularly in relation to the Millennium and the new heavens and new earth (20:4; 22:5), reveals that believers will join with Christ in His millennial and eternal reign following His second advent.

Another reference to the future millennial reign comes in the song of the elders in Revelation 11:16-18. The broad perspective of this song encompasses the millennial reign (20:6), the wrath of the nations (19:19; 20:8), the wrath of God (19:11-21; 20:10), the judgment of the dead (20:12), and the reward of the faithful (21:1–22:5). The elders' song expands on the comparable announcement found in Revelation 11:15 that the kingdom of God will have arrived at a time anticipated in the song.

The future messianic kingdom is a foregone conclusion for John. It was future not only for him, but also for the entire period of the representative first-century churches whom he addressed. The kingdom's future state is expressed in all three types of literature in Revelation: the narrative (e.g., 1:9), the epistolary (e.g., 2:26-27), and the visional or apocalyptic (e.g., 5:10). The future establishment of God's kingdom on earth is a central theme of the book (see Robert L. Thomas, "Excursus 4: The Kingdom of

Christ in the Apocalypse," *Revelation 8–22, An Exegetical Commentary* [Chicago: Moody Press, forthcoming]).

The Witness of the Seventh Bowl

A second line of reasoning to demonstrate the future timing of the millennial kingdom comes from the context of the seventh bowl in Revelation 16. To establish the relevance of the seventh bowl to the timing of the Millennium, it is important to determine the extent of the judgment described by the bowl in the text of Revelation. Various suggestions have extended it from Revelation 16:17 (the obvious beginning point) through the end of chapter 18, or through Revelation 19:10, or through the end of chapter 19. But convincing evidence exists for concluding that the account of the bowl extends all the way through Revelation 22:5.

Evidence That the Seventh Bowl Includes Revelation 16:17–22:5

There are two direct pieces of evidence for this view. First, it is significant that the angel who shows John the vision of the New Jerusalem in 21:9–22:5 is one of the angels who administered the seven bowls of judgment. The text does not tell which of the seven it is; it could be the seventh angel. Suffice it to say, this agent belongs in a general way to the bowl series that is the same as the seven last plagues (Rev. 15:1). So what he reveals in chapter 21 must be part of the seven-plague series in chapter 16.

The second piece of direct evidence pertains to the introductory and concluding formulas for the descriptions of Babylon and the New Jerusalem (cf. Rev. 17:1-2 with Rev. 21:9-10 and cf. Rev. 19:9-10 with Rev. 22:6-9). These formulas coincide remarkably, even to the point of extensive identical wording. Therefore, if Babylon's delineation is part of the seventh-bowl account, then the detailed description of the New Jerusalem would also be.

Support for Extending the Seventh Bowl Through Revelation 22:5

Four additional features corroborate the direct evidence for the extended nature of the seventh-bowl description.

1. The first feature is the use of two perfect tenses of the Greek verb *ginomai* in Revelation 16:17 and 21:6. Translated "it is done" in the former case and "they are done" in the latter, the verb sounds the note of finality. The earlier use (16:17) connects conspicuously with the seventh bowl and anticipates the ultimate completion of the last plagues.

The use of *ginomai* in 21:6 probably looks back to the previous occurrence in 16:17. It announces the final days of the old creation. The words just spoken have been fulfilled, and a state of completion now exists. Since Revelation 21:9–22:5 is an expanded description of the New Jerusalem mentioned in 21:2, the words "they are done" extend the bowls' coverage to include that section too.

2. Further confirmation of the seventh bowl's proposed extent comes from a closer look at the battle of Armageddon. The regular interpretation of the sixth bowl assigns it the role of preparation for this great battle. The drying up of the Euphrates River and the mission of the three unclean spirits (Rev. 16:12-15) pave the way for the battle of the great day of God Almighty. The former action facilitates passage to the battle scene for the kings from the east, and the latter involves the kings of the whole earth in the conflict.

The sixth bowl does not include an account of the battle itself, however. The seventh bowl must do that. Its purview must extend far enough to tell of that battle. The battle for which the sixth bowl prepares is revealed in Revelation 19:17-21, so this section in chapter 19 has to be part of the seventh-bowl description. Failure to extend the bowl at least this far leaves the bowl series incomplete; that is, with preparations for a battle that never happens. This observation corroborates the extension of the bowl through the end of chapter 19.

3. A further confirmation of the extent of the seventh bowl relates to the "unholy trinity." The part played by the dragon, the beast, and the false prophet in preparation for the battle of Armageddon is explicit (Rev. 16:13). Under the sixth bowl they are instrumental in assembling a huge army to the battle site. The relegation of the beast and false prophet to the lake of fire comes in conjunction with the battle's conclusion (Rev. 19:20), but not

so with the dragon, otherwise known as the devil or Satan. The seven last plagues cannot conclude until this instigator of mass rebellion against God also reaches his place of destiny. His consignment to the lake of fire and brimstone comes at the conclusion of the Millennium. So the seventh bowl cannot end prior to Revelation 20:10. Only then will divine wrath have quelled human and diabolical rebellion for the last time.

The extended nature of the seventh bowl finds confirmation again. Instead of excluding the dragon from this last of the final plagues, this explanation includes him, along with the beast and false prophet, as part of the series that climaxes with a description of his doom.

4. A fourth element to confirm the seventh bowl's extent is the text's explicit identification of the seven last plagues with the seven bowls (Rev. 15:1, 6-8; 16:1; 21:9). Enlarging the seventh bowl to include the judgment of the Great White Throne at the end of Revelation 20 is the best way to do justice to the strong emphasis in 15:1 that this plague series is the very last one. Efforts to circumvent the plain statement about these plagues being ultimate are futile. No contextual feature supplies a reason for any type of limitation. If these plagues are the termination of God's wrath, they must include the assignment of all blasphemers (recounted in Rev. 16:9, 11, 21) to the lake of fire (seen later in Rev. 20:12-15).

This consideration along with the other evidences demonstrates how John intended the seventh bowl judgment to be explained in Revelation 16:17–22:5. Both the direct and the indirect evidence are convincing (see Thomas, *Revelation 1-7*).

The Description of the Seventh Bowl Proves a Future Millennium

As indicated above, the seventh bowl includes the Second Coming and the millennial reign of Christ. Few dispute that Christ's second coming is yet future. The Second Coming and the millennial kingdom are both part of the seventh bowl judgment. Since the Second Coming is still future, so too the Millennium must be future.

The present era is not part of the seven last plagues that conclude the wrath of God. If it were, there would be no future judgment of God, since His wrath already would have spent itself by the time Christ returns. This cannot be; so we conclude that the Millennium fits into God's plan for the future. The extent of the seventh bowl is a second evidence that the Millennium is yet future.

The Witness of Revelation 20:1-10

Revelation 20:1-10 also points to a Millennium as a future event.

The Necessity for Progression Instead of Recapitulation

Revelation 20:1-3. Some see Revelation 20:1-3 as a recapitulation of earlier accounts of Satan's deception (Rev. 12:9; 13:14; 18:23c). However, this event cannot be a recapitulation since Revelation 20:1-3 describes a time when Satan no longer is able to deceive the nations. Since the earlier passages describe Satan's deceiving on the earth, but Revelation 20:1-3 tells about his removal, to see them as the same event would be contradictory.

The events must be distinct since in the first case Satan acts on earth, and in the second instance he is bound. The only way that one could view Satan as bound before some time in the future would be to construe his binding as a restriction, not a cessation of his activity. Confinement to the abyss (20:3), however, requires a complete termination of his earthly activity. The uniform testimony of the New Testament is that Satan is not thus confined during the period between Christ's two advents (e.g., 1 Peter 5:8).

A further problem with concluding that this paragraph recapitulates the present era is its failure to adequately explain Satan's release at the end of the Millennium. If the Millennium were the current era, the restrictions currently placed on Satan could be removed at the end of this age. What these restrictions might be are unclear since it is plain that he has extensive freedom and is quite unrestricted already. So both the restrictions and the release are future, not present.

The effects of Satan's binding and imprisonment will be universal (Rev. 20:3). "The nations" who will be free from his deceptive ploys are not the same ones as Christ has destroyed at His earlier coming (19:11-21). These are nations who will emerge from faithful mortals who populate the Millennium at its beginning. The privilege of reigning with Christ will extend to those martyred by the beast, but it will also extend to the faithful of all ages. Such a future, chronologically limited kingdom on earth is necessary to allow for the fulfillment of Old Testament prophecies, and is in accord with the theological framework provided by Paul in 1 Corinthians 15:20-28.

Revelation 20:7-10. Some view Satan's effort at deception in recruiting a huge army (Rev. 20:8) as a recapitulation of the assemblage in Revelation 16:13-14. This cannot be because there are conspicuous differences between the two battles: the earlier gathering in chapter 16 is preparation for the battle of Revelation 19:17-21, and the recruiting in chapter 20 is preparation for the battle of Revelation 20:9. Chronological progression from Revelation 19:11-21 to 20:1-10 is exegetically sound and demonstrates once again that the Millennium is yet future.

The Necessity of Finding a Place for 1,000 Years

The sixfold appearance of the "thousand years" in Revelation 20:1-10 emphasizes the importance of this time designation. Efforts to explain the period as anything other than a thousand calendar years have failed. Explanations based on a theory that Revelation uses numbers symbolically are to no avail. Numbers in the book are demonstrably literal in essentially all cases. So one must find a specific period of one thousand years in Revelation to fix the timing of the Millennium.

Attempts to equate the thousand-year period with anything between the two advents of Christ have proven futile. No thousand-year period in the almost two-thousand year Christian epoch comes close to satisfying conditions such as are described in Revelation 20:1-10.

The Necessity of the Right Meaning for "Ezesan" ("Lived")

The expression "they lived" in Revelation 20:4 refers to bodily resurrection and necessitates a future Millennium. Attempts to avoid this interpretation have resulted in suggestions that this verb refers either to a spiritual resurrection only, to a bodily resurrection that is only apocalyptic and symbolic, to an apocalyptic unveiling of the reality of salvation in Christ, or to the new birth.

Virtually all interpreters acknowledge that the same form in Revelation 20:5 (*ezesan*, "they lived") refers to bodily resurrection. Wherever this Greek verb occurs in the New Testament in the context of bodily death, it always speaks of bodily resurrection (cf. John 11:25; Acts 1:3; 9:41). John plainly calls this a "resurrection" (Rev. 20:5), using a noun that occurs over forty times in the New Testament and almost always refers to physical resurrection. The same verb used elsewhere in Revelation is a frequent way of referring to bodily resurrection (Rev. 1:18; 2:8; 13:14).

The Necessity of the Right Meaning for "The Rest of the Dead"

"The rest of the dead" in Revelation 20:5 requires that a distinction be made between those raised prior to the Millennium and those raised afterward. Those raised following the Millennium are the ones excluded from the first resurrection—the wicked who are physically dead when Christ returns.

To have two resurrections, one for the righteous before the thousand years and the other for the wicked after the thousand years, requires that the Millennium be future. The past has not witnessed even one mass resurrection from the dead, much less two. Both resurrections are still ahead. One thousand years will separate the resurrection to everlasting life from that to shame and contempt (Dan. 12:2). The Millennium is yet future.

Millennial Motivation *for conclusion*

What keeps us going when our world is collapsing around us, or when we face severe physical or emotional penalties because of our faithfulness to Christ? When those we thought we could trust betray us, the present can look quite bleak. The doldrums of despair may beset us for a wide assortment of reasons, as they did John's first-century readers, but we can still press on because we know what is ahead. John used the promised participation in the coming kingdom to encourage Christians as they faced trials.

The hope of the Millennium is a theological truth that should be in the forefront of our thinking as we face the difficulties of life. Someday we will reign triumphantly with Christ in His millennial kingdom. Since we know that God controls the details of the future, we can be assured that nothing in the present lies outside the scope of His control. Just as surely as these present trials are part of God's plan for us, we know that someday we will join Christ in His victorious reign.

"The sufferings of the present time are not deserving of a comparison with the glory about to be revealed in us" (Rom. 8:18). Our hardships in this life become bearable and cease to be obstacles to living for Christ in light of what is ahead.

"For the Christian the Bible
provides clear and detailed teaching
concerning the future so that he may
know with certainty what lies ahead."
(*Basic Theology*, p. 439)

CHAPTER THIRTY-ONE

The Return
of the Lord
and the River of Life

Manfred E. Kober

Prophecy is big business; books on end-time topics abound. People are eager to learn about the future. Indeed, according to Ecclesiastes 3:11, God has "set eternity in their heart."

Prophecy, a prominent theme of Scripture, is history written in advance. Approximately one-fourth of the Bible was predictive at the time at which it was written. Though much of the prophetic Word has been fulfilled, especially with the first coming of Jesus Christ, vast portions of prophetic passages await future fulfillment.

The Lord promises special blessings to those who make an effort to understand His revelation concerning the future (Rev. 1:3;

22:7). Understanding the future enables the believer to live in the calmness of eternity now. On the one hand, a person's happiness now may be due in large part to the delightful prospects of the future. On the other hand, anxiety in the present is frequently the result of ignorance of the future. Prophecy ministers to the concerned believer and can be an effective witnessing tool to the unbeliever.

Though believers may recognize the value of prophecy, many wonder at its correct interpretation. For any passage of prophecy at least half a dozen different explanations might be found because different principles of interpretation result in varied understandings of biblical prophecy. Literal interpretation alone gives consistency and objectivity in the understanding of Scripture. Charles Ryrie put the matter succinctly.

> If God be the originator of language and if the chief purpose of originating it was to convey His message to man, then it must follow that He, being all-wise and all-loving, originated sufficient language to convey all that was in His heart to tell man. Furthermore, it must also follow that He would use language and expect man to use it in its literal, normal, and plain sense (*Dispensationalism Today* [Chicago: Moody, 1965], 88).

The New Testament itself records literal fulfillment of Old Testament prophecies. Over 300 prophecies concerning the first coming of Christ were literally fulfilled. As Ryrie notes, "This obvious but extremely significant fact argues for the validity and use of literal hermeneutics in all of biblical interpretation" (*Basic Theology*, 113).

Literal interpretation unlocks the secrets of prophecy. The dispensational interpreter who uses "the normal principle of interpretation *consistently* in *all* his study of the Bible" (*Dispensationalism Today*, 89) is able to understand and harmonize prophetic truth. By interpreting prophecy literally, the believer gains understanding and blessing. As a case in point, the literal or normal interpretation of two major prophetic passages, Zechariah 14 and Ezekiel 47, gives the reader a vivid picture of future events. Spiritualizing these passages brings only confusion. Interpreting them literally leads to clarity and conviction.

The Return of the Lord: Zechariah 14:1-11

The prophecy of Zechariah ends on the glorious note of the Savior's return and the establishment of His kingdom.

The Conquest of Jerusalem: Zechariah 14:1-3

The second advent of Christ is revealed throughout the Scriptures, beginning with Enoch before the Flood (Jude 14) to John at the end of the first century (Rev. 19). Zechariah 14 discloses numerous details which surround this climactic prophetic event.

The Second Advent concludes the Tribulation. The Day of the Lord will be upon the earth (Zech. 14:1), a time of judgment succeeded by a time of universal peace (Isa. 2:12; 4:1-2). Those who besiege Jerusalem will divide her spoil; representatives of all nations will destroy the city. Zechariah laments that "the city shall be taken, and the houses rifled, and the women ravished; and half of the city shall go forth into captivity, but the residue of the people shall not be cut off from the city" (Zech. 14:2). The prophet conveys a picture of Jerusalem's utter helplessness and hopelessness. Yet Israel's dire extremity becomes God's opportunity. The Lord Himself will come to the defense of Jerusalem to bring it that peace which its name, "city of peace," implies (v. 11). He will fight for His people as He has in the past (Josh. 10:14, 42; 23:3; Jud. 4:15, etc.).

The Coming of the Lord: Zechariah 14:4-11

Zechariah pinpoints the very place of the Lord's descent, "upon the Mount of Olives, which is before Jerusalem on the east" (Zech. 14:4). From this same mountain Ezekiel saw the glory of the Lord depart (Ezek. 11:23) and then saw the glory of the Lord return from the east (Ezek. 43:2). The Savior will return to the Mount of Olives, from which He ascended to heaven (Acts 1:11-12). Just as Christ's ascent was personal and literal, so will His descent be.

Various significant signs will accompany the return of Christ. First, an earthquake will cause a cleavage in the Mount of Olives, the hill dominating the skyline east of Jerusalem. Zechariah notes that "the Mount of Olives shall cleave in the midst thereof toward the east and toward the west, and there shall be a very great valley; and half the mountain shall remove toward the north, and half of it toward the south" (Zech. 14:4).

Second, there will be consternation among men. Israel will flee eastward from the terror of the earthquake and from the advancing armies through the new ravine which God literally calls "my mountain valley" (Zech. 14:5). To emphasize the fear Zechariah recalls a terrifying earthquake which occurred 200 years earlier (Amos 1:1) but was still remembered in his day.

Third, nature itself will convulse at the time of Christ's descent with His holy ones (Zech. 14:5), probably both angels (Ps. 89:5, 7) and saints (1 Thes. 3:13); and strange atmospheric conditions will prevail. "And it shall come to pass in that day that the light shall not be clear nor dark . . . at evening time it shall be light" (Zech. 14:6-7). The phrase, "the light shall not be clear," literally means "the glorious ones will congeal." Merrill comments that "the loss of light is explained by the congealing of the heavenly bodies, their 'thickening,' as it were to the point that they cannot shine" (Eugene H. Merrill, *An Exegetical Commentary: Haggai, Zechariah, Malachi* [Chicago: Moody Press, 1994], 351). The heavenly luminaries will cease to function normally.

At this point, Zechariah mentions the coronation of the King (Zech. 14:9). In fulfillment of prophecy (Ps. 2; 72:8-11; Isa. 54:5; Zech. 9:9-10), He will be recognized as the supreme sovereign over the earth. The mammoth earthquake to occur with the glorious advent of Christ will not simply split the Mount of Olives but will change the whole central highland ridge (Zech. 14:10). The entire area from Geba, some six miles northeast of Jerusalem, to Rimmon, thirty-three miles southwest of Jerusalem, will become an elevated plateau. The mountains around Jerusalem will become depressed while the city of Jerusalem will be elevated and exalted as the capital of the world for the next 1,000 years. Zechariah also mentions the expanse of the rebuilt city from the east to the west and from the north to the south. In fact, Zechariah 14:4-10 pictures enough detail to permit one to draw a general topographical map of Israel as it will appear for 1,000 years.

Zechariah concludes his description of the earthly capital by stating that "men shall dwell in it, and there shall be no more utter destruction; but Jerusalem shall be safely inhabited" (Zech. 14:11) by redeemed and restored Israel (Zech. 13:8-9).

The River of Life: Zechariah 14:8; Ezekiel 47:1-12

Woven throughout Old Testament prophecy is a constant theme of spectacular physical and geographical changes to occur when Christ returns. Zechariah 14 describes many features of this upheaval, including a new river to flow from Jerusalem into the desert (Zech. 14:8).

The Prophet Ezekiel concludes his temple vision (chaps. 40–46) with the description of this same miraculous, life-giving stream issuing from the temple. The river is also mentioned by Joel (Joel 3:18), some 250 years before Ezekiel, and by Zechariah after the Babylonian exile.

The Commencement of the River: Zechariah 14:8; Ezekiel 47:1-2

In Zechariah's prophecy, the river is said to originate in Jerusalem and to divide, one branch flowing into the Dead Sea, the other into the Mediterranean. In Ezekiel 47 only the river flowing eastward is described, as an angelic guide takes Ezekiel on a prophetic excursion along the river.

At the eastern front of the temple Ezekiel sees a spring emerging (Ezek. 47:1-2). The waters begin at the immediate dwelling place of Christ who is the source of all spiritual and physical life. The miraculous waters "trickled forth" at first, and yet, without any tributaries, increased in depth and volume.

The Course of the River: Ezekiel 47:3-5

The angel led Ezekiel along the riverbank, measuring the waters. After 1,750 feet (1,000 cubits) the waters were ankle-deep. In another 1,750 feet the waters had become knee-deep, then waist-deep at another 1,750 feet, until at another 1,750 feet the river was so deep that one could swim in it. In the distance from Jerusalem to the eastern slopes of the Mount of Olives (about 1½ miles), the trickle became a spring, the spring a brook, the brook a stream, and the stream a raging river. To accent the dramatic size and depth of the river, Ezekiel refers to it in verse 9 as "rivers," literally "a double river," because of its raging current.

The Changes Through the River: Ezekiel 47:6-12

The river continued to flow eastward, cascading into the Arabah (Ezek. 47:8), the desolate Jordan Valley rift extending from the Sea of Galilee southward to the Dead Sea and then to the Gulf of Aqabah. The river issued into the Dead Sea, healing its salty waters and rejuvenating the desert. The most inhospitable, arid, barren, desolate land on the face of the earth will become a fruitful land, lush with vegetation.

Along the banks of the supernatural yet literal river will grow "very many trees on the one side and on the other" (Ezek. 47:7). These marvelous trees shall be "for meat, whose leaf shall not fade, neither shall the fruit thereof be consumed: it shall bring forth new fruit according to his months, because their waters they issued out of the sanctuary; and the fruit thereof shall be for meat, and the leaf thereof for medicine" (v. 12). These trees will have an inexhaustible quantity of fruit all year long. The leaves of the tree will provide healing, apparently for those who were redeemed in the Tribulation and entered the Millennium in their physical bodies, and for their offspring.

The Dead Sea which will be healed is today a symbol of death and destruction. The stench of sulphur hanging in the air reminds one of the judgment of Genesis 19. Presently the Dead Sea can hardly sustain microorganisms, apart from some freshwater springs along its northwestern shores. As proof for the genuine healing, the sea will bring forth "a very great multitude of fish" (Ezek. 47:9). Fishermen will find the Dead Sea an ideal place for their trade, with an abundance of fish like those found in the Mediterranean Sea. Fishermen will spread their nets from En-Gedi ("fountain of a kid"), located on the middle of the western shore, to En-Eglaim ("spring of the two calves"), perhaps located along the northwestern shore near Qumran.

The swamps and marshes near the southern end of the Dead Sea "will not be healed; they shall be given to salt" (Ezek. 47:11). Though Ezekiel does not explain why the salt flats will remain, several explanations can be offered. Salt, essential for the preparation of food, will also be required for some of the memorial sacrifices offered in the temple (Ezek. 43:24; cf. Lev. 2:13). Further, the Dead Sea is an important source of minerals for Israel and possibly will be in the future. The Lord may also want to demonstrate to the rest of the world for 1,000 years how stagnant and lifeless the entire Dead Sea had been before the river of living water healed it.

The Controversy Over the River

Unfortunately many commentators spiritualize the river and thus cannot agree on its interpretation. The early church fathers saw the river as a symbol of baptism. Some see it as the stream of church history. Many speak of the river as emblematic of spiritual life, with some saints only ankle-deep or knee-deep Christians. Others identify the river with the stream of the Gospel, denying any literal future aspect of the prophecy. Derek Kidner, in relating the river with the river of paradise in Genesis 2, speaks of it simply as "vitality that flows from holy ground" (*Genesis: An Introduction and Commentary* [Downers Grove, Ill.: InterVarsity, 1967], 63), whatever that might mean.

Only the literal interpretation can do justice to magnificent prophetic passages such as Zechariah 14 and Ezekiel 47. It is demonstrably true in the interpretation of these and other passages that "*sane literal* interpretation . . . cannot fail to lead to happy results in exegesis. Spiritualizing and mysticalizing interpretation, on the other hand . . . are bound to produce endless confusion" (Merrill F. Unger, *Zechariah: Prophet of Messiah's Glory* [Grand Rapids: Zondervan, 1975], 239).

If one denies the literalness of the river, where does one stop? The events of the Second Advent outlined by Zechariah and Ezekiel are interrelated. The rebellion of the nations at Armageddon is followed by the ravishing of Jerusalem, which in turn is followed by the return of the Lord, the removal of the mountains, the revelation of the river, the redemption of nature, and the reign of Christ. The Germans have a proverb: "Wer A sagt der muss auch B sagen." He who says A also must say B. An interpreter who sees the return of the Lord as a literal event should also subscribe to a literal fulfillment of its accompanying events.

If the river is not literal, why would Zechariah and Ezekiel list so many actual geographical places in the context? Jerusalem, the Mount of Olives, the Arabah, the Dead Sea, En-Gedi, En-Eglaim, and the salt flats are quite specific locations.

If the river were not literal, why would other passages of Scripture mention the river as well? Psalm 46:4 mentions a river which will make Jerusalem glad. Joel 3:18's millennial prediction envisions a fountain coming out of the temple and watering the valley of Shittim in which the Dead Sea is located. In fact, the millennial changes predicted by Zechariah and Ezekiel are simply a microcosm of the healing of the curse that will take place all over the world.

Apparently every desert on earth will become lush and green. Joel speaks of other rivers of Judah flowing with water (Joel 3:16). Isaiah writes of waters breaking out in the wilderness, streams in the desert, and floods upon the dry ground (Isa. 43:19-20; 44:3). The wilderness will become a fruitful field (Isa. 32:15; 55:13). The changes described for the wilderness of Judea will be worldwide as deserts such as the Sahara, Gobi, and Mojave will become lush forests. The redeemed will be there to witness the transformation as the Redeemer saves the groaning creation from the curse of sin (Rom. 8:22). At that time the carol "Joy to the World" will take on its fullest meaning: "No more let sins and sorrows grow, nor thorns infest the ground. He comes to make his blessings flow far as the curse is found."

Implications

A thoughtful perusal of Zechariah 14 and Ezekiel 47 will prompt at least two major questions. First, what part will the believer have in the dramatic events surrounding the second advent of Christ?

Clearly Church Age believers will be with Christ. At the Rapture, Christ will summon every genuine believer into His presence (1 Thes. 4:13-18). The dead who are with Christ already and the living saints will receive their glorified bodies. The Bridegroom will take the church, His bride, to heaven to bestow rewards for faithful service (1 Cor. 4:5; 2 Cor. 5:10) and to decorate her with victor's garlands for the next event, the marriage of the Lamb (Rev. 19:1-10). At that glorious event the bride will be joined to the Bridegroom. From that point on the bride will be with the Bridegroom; whatever the Bridegroom does will be shared by the bride. As He returns in royal splendor at the end of the Tribulation, the saints will follow Him (Rev. 19:11-14). They will witness the destruction of His enemies, will accompany Him to the Mount of Olives, and will enter with Him triumphantly into Jerusalem. There they will revel in His regal presence and join Him in His righteous rule (1 Cor. 6:2-3).

Another question might arise as the Bible student envisions the literal regeneration of the desert and rejuvenation of the Dead Sea. Will the Church Age believer in his glorified body be able to sample the marvelous fruit from the trees and the abundance of fish from the Dead Sea? In other words, will there be food in our future? Here too the Scriptures permit a satisfying answer.

The resurrection body of the believer will be "fashioned like unto His glorious body" (Phil. 3:21). John predicts that, when Christ appears, "we shall be like Him" (1 John 3:2). Christ demonstrated to His doubting disciples that He had a physical body comprised of flesh and bones by eating broiled fish and honeycomb in their presence (Luke 24:42-43). Sometime later, on the shores of the Sea of Galilee, the Savior prepared a breakfast of fish and bread for Himself and His disciples (John 21:9-14). In fact, eating and drinking seems to have been commonly shared by the Savior with His disciples after His resurrection (Acts 10:41). So, whereas the glorified body with a new life principle (that of the Spirit) no longer needs food, the resurrected saint will be able to enjoy it.

The Savior also promised that fellowship in the kingdom would involve eating and drinking (Mark 14:25; Luke 22:30). The believer therefore is not deceiving himself when he anticipates a glorious time of fellowship with the Savior and the saints in the Millennium, enjoying the marvelous fruit and variety of fish predicted.

These millennial provisions will be replaced by even greater blessings after the new heavens and earth have been created. The believer's eternal home, a spectacular city, the New Jerusalem, will descend to earth (Rev. 21). A prominent feature of that city is "a pure river of water of life, clear as crystal, proceeding out of the throne of God and of the Lamb" (Rev. 22:1). Like the river described by Zechariah and Ezekiel for the millennial earth, the banks of that eternal river will produce "the tree of life, which bare twelve manner of fruits, and yielded her fruit every month" (Rev. 22:2). The tree of life in the original Paradise, forfeited by the first Adam, will bless humankind in the Millennium. Beyond that, it is part of the believer's glorious anticipation for his eternal home.

Afterwords

CHAPTER THIRTY-TWO

The Vocation of Charles C. Ryrie

Philip Hook

C harles Caldwell Ryrie was born on March 2, 1925, in Alton, Illinois. His father was a banker and a gentleman farmer, and his mother was a homemaker. Both were patrons of the arts. His older brother George became a banker while Charles followed the path of studies and music. Because of his education Charles was away from home during many of his teen and early adult years. This developed in him a reserved nature that lent itself to his lifelong fascination with scholarship. He was, and very much is, at home with his typewriter (now, computer) and his books.

Charles attended Stony Brook School on Long Island and Haverford College near Philadelphia. Attending college and seminary during World War II, when school was in session year round, accelerated his formal education.

While at Haverford, Ryrie majored in mathematics, intending to follow his father into banking and finance. However, an unusual series of circumstances altered that plan. Dr. Lewis Sperry Chafer, the founder of Dallas Theological Seminary, and his wife had often been guests in the Ryrie home when Charles was growing up. So, when Chafer came to Philadelphia on a speaking tour in 1943, Charles made an appointment to speak with him on April 23. As a result of that meeting, the young mathematician followed God's call into the ministry and transferred to Dallas Theological Seminary. Through an unusual series of circumstances, Ryrie was allowed to transfer credits back from Dallas Seminary to Haverford so that he graduated from college in 1946. He had completed his Th.M. (1947) and his Th.D. (1949) by the time he was 24 years old.

Ryrie's parents were generous with him and supported him financially through his schooling. His father gave him all the money necessary for his school expenses, only requiring that he account each month for how he had spent the money, down to the exact penny.

The Ryrie home engendered a commitment to excellence and to Christianity. His home also was a place of gentility and perfection, where any guest was honored. I remember well the first time that I visited the large home on the hill in the middle of Alton. We arrived in time for lunch. Since Mr. Ryrie was away, I was seated at his place at the head of the table. At the proper time, I was asked to step on a buzzer installed beneath the rug to indicate to the kitchen that we were ready to be served. I did not know that such service existed, and to my dismay, I couldn't find the necessary buzzer. Finally Mrs. Ryrie solved the dilemma by going to the kitchen herself to begin the meal (and probably to conceal her smile too).

Charles became an accomplished pianist, playing classical music with excellence and discipline. He would rarely play in public, but occasionally an audience would be able to marvel at a skill that equaled his ability in the Scriptures. Interestingly, this reticence to perform never influenced his professional speaking and teaching career. He simply chose to be a maestro of the Bible rather than of the piano.

Charles' first full-time job was teaching in the Bible Department and serving as Dean of Men at Westmont College, then a small Christian liberal arts college in Santa Barbara, California. At Westmont the meticulous habits that characterized his teaching career were developed. Always a careful student, he typed his teaching notes and kept them in special notebooks. His habit of recording his teaching material became a key means to his later development as an author.

His lectures were characterized by precision and simplicity. It was in teaching that his gift for making the profound issues of the Bible clear and precise was manifest. Students loved his classes. A second characteristic of Ryrie's teaching was his commitment to spending time with students. Readily available to all, he especially enjoyed time with young scholars and disciples who responded thoughtfully and actively to Scripture. Ryrie would often take them along on his speaking engagements and travels, both locally and internationally. Many of these students have since assumed significant positions in missions, ministry, and education. But always they are marked by their love for the Scriptures, their precision in interpretation, and their practical, clear purpose in speaking—the indelible marks of "time with Ryrie."

On several occasions I joined "Doc" on his vacation travels. One of his favorite approaches to leisure travel was to drive to the edge of town and flip a coin to determine which way to head out. This untypically carefree means of non-planning led us on different occasions to Florida and the warm beaches, or into the deserts of the western United States. My responsibility was to tend to the mechanics of the automobile, usually a well-loved, late-model car; he would graciously take care of the tab. I also earned my keep by helping him learn to swim and to water-ski—all in his boat, of course.

Another pattern that developed at this time was his love for foreign travel. He not only studied in Scotland and traveled extensively in Europe, but also made several trips to the Holy Land. He became an accomplished photographer and put together fascinating combinations of slides and commentary on Jerusalem, which he entitled "The City of Peace Is in Pieces." His travel lectures always were characterized by good photography, insightful commentary, and his special "turn of the phrase."

Most significant in Ryrie's development was a pattern of disciplined study that emerged from these early years. He honed his ability to sit down with books, the Book, and his typewriter, and to stay there until he had accomplished something of significance. This disciplined professional demeanor has stayed with him throughout his lifetime.

In 1951, Ryrie continued his education in Scotland where he pursued doctoral studies at the University of Edinburgh. Just as his education at Dallas Seminary produced one of his early books, *The Basis of the Premillennial Faith,* his time in Scotland spawned another of his works, *The Role of Women in the Church.*

Upon his return to the States, Dr. Ryrie accepted a new position as Professor of Systematic Theology at Dallas Theological Seminary. In a sense this was like coming home for Ryrie. Dallas Seminary was a place he had come to love, and a place that had shaped much of his thinking. He was comfortable here and the philosophy of education fit the way that he thought and taught. He was developing a way of thinking that was not just a theological education, but was a way of seeing the world and interpreting all of life. His courses were not just lectures in theology for his students, but were the foundation for his own life.

Ryrie's teaching at Dallas was characterized not only by his usual carefully crafted precision, but also by an increasing emphasis on grace. Dr. Lewis Sperry Chafer had been a mentor and a model for Ryrie in his formative years. Now that theme of grace that so typified Chafer's teaching found renewed and developed emphasis in Ryrie's own teaching. In the years since he had studied at Dallas, an emphasis on a legalistic separation had developed among some evangelicals. Ryrie brought to these discussions a tempered emphasis on the grace of God and freedom in Christ.

One of Ryrie's books seems to especially illustrate the emphasis in his thinking on careful application of the Scriptures: *Balancing the Christian Life.* Balance is the key, and is a necessary factor in fitting together the many perspectives on Christianity taken from the Bible and applied to the life of the believer. The chapter on money is an excellent illustration. Dr. Ryrie always taught that living by faith, with or without financial abundance, was a double miracle: both the giver and the receiver of funds have to live by faith to accomplish God's design.

The same interest in students which characterized Ryrie's Westmont career continued into his years at Dallas Theological Seminary. He would often invite several of us to his apartment to dialogue and study theology together. There was one rule: "Whatever you say, you must be able to defend, from your choice of words down to the tense of the verbs." These discussions would last for a couple of hours, and then another characteristic of Ryrie's would surface, and he would say, "It's 10 o'clock and it's bedtime." These visits were intense times that sharpened our skills and left Doc's stamp on all of us.

Ryrie's gift of giving was evident. Always a gracious and generous contributor to Christian ministries, he also cultivated a practice of supporting students anonymously and giving to their education. Each year he would pray over the list of students. When he was finished, his attorney would receive a list of names and a check. Days later, a receipt for tuition would be placed in the students' mail boxes. Few students ever knew that Ryrie was the one who provided their scholarship, and no one but his attorney knew the large number of students he helped. Today there are Christian workers all over the world who are the recipients of his prayerful generosity.

The years at Dallas Theological Seminary began the prolific part of Ryrie's career as an author. Each new course was the occasion for careful research, and often the result of his teaching was another book manuscript or a series of articles. One of the books written during these years was *Biblical Theology of the New Testament*.

After several years at Dallas Seminary, a new career beckoned. Ryrie was invited to become president of the newly formed Philadelphia College of Bible, a recent merger of the Bible Institute of Pennsylvania and Philadelphia School of the Bible. Though the schools were similar, they had separate traditions and characteristics and the merger was a stretching time of change for all who were involved. The alumni of each school watched vigilantly lest the traditions of their school be lost in the merger. Ryrie's leadership was always gentle and clear. Faculty meetings often were intense and differences were clarified. But the new president led with grace and acceptance, and a mutually acceptable course was implemented. The faculty and the students of these years were all influenced by Ryrie's style of leadership and fairness.

In 1962 Ryrie resigned and returned to Dallas Seminary as Dean of the Graduate School. There he entered an era of intense scholarly writing and teaching. During this period he wrote books such as *The Grace of God, Dispensationalism Today,* and *The Holy Spirit.* Under his leadership the graduate school expanded and grew. The seminary was at one of its high points, and its graduates were in great demand for teaching and leadership positions. Ryrie's mark of excellence was seen in most of the graduates in very special, sometimes subtle, ways.

The Ryrie Study Bible (Moody Press) probably has become the book for which he is best known. Ryrie's concise, clear interpretations and descriptions of biblical materials has made this companion/study Bible the book that many Christians would now choose if their library were suddenly limited to one volume. While Ryrie is clearly a dispensational, premillennial theologian, his study Bible is balanced in its interpretations and is usable by people of many theological persuasions. Ryrie made major additions to the *Study Bible* in 1993 by adding notes, helps, and graphics to this expanded edition (published in 1994). This makes this book an even more helpful tool to understanding the Bible. *The Ryrie Study Bible* is a monumental work of scholarship, and has firmly established Ryrie in the realm of excellence in Christian thinking and writing. His scholarly patience, ability to accomplish goals, and his love for simplified (but never simplistic) cognition about the Scriptures have merged in this work and have given Ryrie a significant place as a Christian scholar and author.

Since retiring from Dallas Theological Seminary, Dr. Ryrie has maintained a ministry of writing and speaking. He has served on a number of boards, including the board of CAM International, and has taught for many years at the Word of Life Bible Institute. More recently he has become adjunct professor of Bible at Philadelphia College of Bible.

Ryrie has maintained for many years a hobby of collecting ancient and original biblical manuscripts. He also has been involved in regular physical exercise, jogging, and swimming for fitness. Ryrie's musical talents and continuing interest in the piano are evident in his home: two pianos, his and his mother's, are the focus of his living room.

While his public ministry has been less prominent during recent years, his writing ministry has continued. *So Great Salvation* probably best typifies the refined theologian at work. Entering the intense contemporary discussions on the role of the lordship of Christ in salvation, Dr. Ryrie wrote one of the simplest, yet most profound discussions of this issue. Without animosity or rancor, he crafted a clear exposition of what it means to believe in Jesus Christ. He challenged the whole concept of "Lordship Salvation" with one question: "If I come to a fork in the road of my Christian experience and choose the wrong branch and continue on it, does that mean I never was on the Christian road to begin with? For how long can I be fruitless without having a lordship advocate conclude that I was never really saved?" (*So Great Salvation*, [Wheaton, Ill.: Victor, 1989], 48).

It is impossible to summarize the ministry of Charles Ryrie in so brief a space. Nor is it possible to assess accurately the impact of his life on so many of us. I was one of those men who somehow found himself privileged to be a student and friend of "Doc's." When he took an interest in me, I was a troubled teenager who had just been kicked out of freshman orientation week at Westmont College. As Dean of Men, Ryrie had every reason to send me home a failure. But he chose to deal with me in the Christlike grace which has always characterized his theology and his life. When people thank me for the ministry God has given me, I often think back to those days and thank God for "Doc" Ryrie's encouraging discipleship and example.

CHAPTER THIRTY-THREE

The Bible and Ryrie's Avocation

Decherd Turner

C harles C. Ryrie is admired and respected as a theologian, Bible scholar, author, and teacher. But there is a side of Dr. Ryrie that few have been privileged to see. He has assembled an extremely fine collection of rare Bibles and books. His deep love for the Word of God, his profound commitment to the exegesis of that Word, and his sense of the long tradition of biblical study have combined to develop a desire for having manuscripts and critical printed editions which form the foundations of his own scholarship. Just as great musicians must have the finest instruments, these are the tools with which Dr. Ryrie works. Here we will explain the goals and methods of collecting rare works, and to illustrate these through the Ryrie collection.

What Is the Purpose in Building a Bible Collection?

A good Bible collection should celebrate and document the unfolding of God's Word as conveyed through Hebrew, Greek, and Latin into modern languages, culminating in contemporary English.

What Are the Fifteen Fundamental Items in a Strong Bible Collection?

How does the Ryrie Collection comply?

1. A manuscript of an important part of the Old Testament. The Ryrie collection includes the text of Proverbs–Song of Songs on 180 vellum leaves, produced in France in the 13th century.
2. A Greek manuscript of the whole or substantial part of the New Testament. Ryrie's collection includes three major manuscripts:
   (a) The Gospels on 270 leaves produced in Constantinople in the mid-10th century;
   (b) The Gospels on 273 leaves produced in Constantinople in the 11th century;
   (c) A manuscript of Luke and John, ca. 13th century.
3. A Latin manuscript Bible.
   Ryrie owns a complete Latin text dated 1273.
4. An early printed Latin Bible (1455–1500).
   Ryrie's collection includes:
   (a) A leaf from the first printed book, the Gutenberg Bible, ca. 1455;
   (b) A Latin Bible printed by Koberger at Nuremberg, 1475;
   (c) A Latin Bible printed by Nicolaus Jenson, 1476;
   (d) One volume of a Latin Bible printed by Franciscus Renner de Heilbronn at Venice, 1482;
   (e) A Latin Bible printed by Johann Froben at Basel, 1491;
   (f) A Latin Bible printed by Johann Amerbach for Anton Koberger at Basel, 1500. Volume 3 of this set has a chained binding.
5. A Wycliffe manuscript.

Ryrie has a New Testament on 154 vellum leaves done about 1430.

6. An early printed Tyndale New Testament.

Not only does the Ryrie collection contain a 1552 Tyndale New Testament, printed by Richard Jugge, but his collection surpasses most others by having a copy of one of the rarest of Tyndale items—his translation of the Pentateuch (printed in Antwerp), 1530. This constitutes the first edition of the Pentateuch in English, and thus becomes the fourth biblical translation in English to be printed, and the second of which any complete copy survives. It was preceded only by two editions of Tyndale's New Testament (1525 and 1526 and no complete copy of either is known), and George Joy's translation of the Psalms, also 1530.

7. A sizable portion of the 1535 Coverdale Bible.

Ryrie's collection includes a 1535 copy (lacking only 7 leaves, but including a map) and is one of the finer surviving copies. Other Coverdales in the collection are the 1538 New Testament diglot (Latin and English) in parallel columns, and a reprint of the 1535 Bible printed in Zurich, 1550.

8. A Matthew Bible, 1537.

Ryrie owns a 1537 Matthew Bible along with a 1549 printing with revisions by Edmund Becke. This Bible contains the well-known note at the end of 1 Peter 3:7 on the words: "To dwel w' a wyfe accordinge to knowledge" in which occurs the sentence "And yf she be not obedient and helpfull unto him endeuoureth to beate the fear of God into her heade, that thereby she maye be compelled to learne her duitie and do it."

9. A Great Bible.

Ryrie has a copy of the 1539 (first edition) which Thomas Cromwell, as the King's vice-regent, ordered to be "set up in sum conuenient place wythin the said church . . . where as your parishoners may moste comodiously resorte to the same and read it." His collection includes four other printings: 1541, 1550, 1552, 1553.

10. An early Geneva Bible.

Ryrie's collection includes a copy of the first 1560, the first English Bible printed in Roman type, with verse divisions.

From 1560 to 1644 at least 144 editions were released. The collection also has editions printed in 1578, 1603, 1611.

11. An early Bishops' Bible.

Ryrie's collection has a 1568 (first edition), which was the most lavish in its production of any English folio Bible. (A folio edition has pages greater in size than 11 inches.) The collection also has editions printed in 1572, 1577, 1585, 1595.

12. A Rhemes New Testament 1582; Doway Old Testament 1609-10.

The collection includes both New and Old Testament first printings. This first Catholic translation's verbal patterns had considerable influence on some renderings in the forthcoming King James 1611 version. Further editions in his collection are the New Testament printed in 1600 and 1633; the Old Testament in 1635.

13. A King James 1611.

The Ryrie collection contains the most sumptuous copy of the 1611 I have ever seen. Also present are the first quarto (pages 9 by 12 inches), 1612; the first octavo (pages 6 by 9 inches), 1612; first edition, second issue, 1613-11; a true 1613 folio edition, and others.

14. A Baskerville Bible 1763; or the Bodoni Gospels 1962.

The Baskerville is included in the Ryrie collection. These Bibles reflect great typographic art. The Baskerville Bible of 1763 repeatedly has been identified as one of the most beautiful books in the world. The Bodoni Gospels has been termed one of the most magnificent books of our time.

15. A substantial "modern" version such as the Revised Version (New Testament 1881; Old Testament 1885), along with a selection of contemporary versions, of which there are many. *The Ryrie Study Bible: New International Version* is especially recommended.

What Is the First Test to Be Applied to a Proposed Addition?

Condition is particularly important in a Bible collection. The abundance of "old" Bibles enhances the temptation to settle for an inferior copy. On the other hand, with a critical eye to judge, many times an unsophisticated copy is more to be desired than a washed copy in a modern case binding.

A number of volumes in the Ryrie collection are superb examples of what fine condition means. (a) The rare Tyndale Pentateuch, 1530, probably is the finest copy extant. (b) The Ryrie King James 1611 has already been identified as the most elegant that I've ever seen in over fifty years of looking critically at copies of the first 1611 King James. This copy has survived relatively unscarred by the binder's knife; it is the largest recorded and includes frequent leaves with original deckle. (c) The sixth issue of the Great Bible, 1541, is a particularly fine copy. In other collections this edition usually exemplifies just how harsh the wear of time can be on a book. (d) In determining condition be sure to look beyond the cover. The Ryrie copy of the first complete Bible in Spanish, 1569, has a horrible modern binding (not the present owner's fault) but the inside is in beautiful condition.

What Is the Importance of "Provenance" in a Bible Collection?

Provenance is the story of how a book survived: Who owned it? When? What marks of ownership can be identified? Every book which survives has a particular story to tell, as does every person who lives to old age. The chief difference is that a person's life is relatively brief, whereas a book can span hundreds of years. The art of provenance is learning the book's own story of survival from whatever evidence it bears. The most obvious mark of its journey through time is the bookplates of former owners.

The Ryrie collection has several wonderful examples of provenance: (a) The celebrated King James 1611 can be traced to its very first residence, Losely Park, the house of Sir George More (1553–1632), treasurer in 1611 to King James' eldest son, Prince Henry. The volume's most recent appearance in public was the auction of the Louis H. Silver (book label present) collection in London, November 8, 1965, at which time it was purchased for the Ryrie collection. (b) The 1535 Coverdale was formerly in the celebrated Sir Leicester Harmsworth Library, and was auctioned in London, July 8, 1946. (c) On the last leaf of the manuscript of 180 vellum leaves of Proverbs–Song of Songs, a fifteenth-century hand records, "This book was acquired by brother Gille of the Royal Abbey of Royaumont from Jehan Guymier, library of Paris, by exchange made with him of four books of Kings and of Luke and John, glossed, which were duplicates in the library of Royaumont and did not have an equal to the present. Done the month of February in the year 1458." In its journey to its present home, this manuscript was in the library of Michael Tomkinson (book label present) of Franche Hall, Kiddermaster, England, and was auctioned in London in 1922, from whence it went into the collection of the great British palaeographer Eric George Millar. (d) The auction of the rare book collection of the General Theological Seminary in 1980 gave an opportunity to many private collectors to obtain desired items: the Ryrie copy of the first Great Bible, 1539, came from this collection.

What Constitutes "Taste" in Bible Collecting?

Taste in Bible collecting has most to do with the intellectual concept propelling the formation of the collection. In Bible collecting the range is so wide that both simple and complex goals can be within the reach of both the poor and the affluent. The chief rubric is that type of selective taste which proclaims, when the collection is examined, that the collector had a clearly defined purpose. The biggest danger in Bible collecting is that the collector will lose sight of his goal, and just become an accumulator.

In the sense of numbers, the Ryrie collection is not large. In the sense of quality, it is one of the closest knit collections built in the twentieth century. The collection has all the critical editions which are basic to the scholars' knowledge of the development of biblical text today. So carefully selected are the Ryrie volumes that they form an interlocking whole, like a jigsaw puzzle, no misfits, tight. Each item fits exactly between each of its neighbors.

What Constitutes "Technique" in Bible Collecting?

The appropriate technique is largely determined by the goal sought. A simple goal can be fun and intellectually rewarding: (a)

Bibles printed in a certain geographic area, (b) Scripture printed by the modern fine presses, (c) translations in contemporary versions of English, with many other possibilities. The collector can do this himself. However, the goal of doing, as far as possible, what Charles Ryrie did, would require great diligence and knowledge plus extensive travel. And the collector can't do it alone! He would need the very best book agent — an antiquarian bookseller with knowledge of availability of given volumes, one with knowledge of existing private and institutional collections, and one who, perhaps most valuable of all, is adept in the auction room. To this type of person come purchase possibilities which would never be made to the private collector.

Professor Ryrie searched extensively on his own, but quite frequently he used a few of the world's finest agents. He joins the rest of us in appreciative memories of the late John Fleming, Alan Thomas, and Warren A. Howell who served their clients so well.

Book collectors usually have one "Show and Tell" item which is used to arouse interest when exhibiting their collections. (Book collectors are crypto-showmen; they themselves become a part of the dramas their books profile.) Are Bible collectors exempt? Definitely not!

One of the great rarities in the Ryrie collection is the 1631 King James, known as the "Wicked Bible." The word "not" was left out of the seventh commandment, resulting in a reading, "Thou shalt commit adultery." (Possibly our time is ready for a reissue!) Of course, the elimination of the "not" was industrial sabotage, and indeed resulted in fiscal disaster for the printers involved. In an exhibition of his collection at the Bridwell Library, Dallas, in 1966, Professor Ryrie wrote concerning this item:

> I have opened my Wicked Bible to Exodus 20 and shown it to any number of people asking them to read the Ten Commandments aloud. Only about one in ten will read the Seventh Commandment as it is printed in the text that is open before them. The others will automatically insert the "not." Even on a second or third try they will not read what is there in front of their eyes. The inconceivability of a command in the Bible to commit adultery seems to guard their lips. And it

is unthinkable, but there it is—a Bible that not only permits but actually commands adultery, and that is why it is called the Wicked Bible.

Another item in this category is volume 3 of the Latin Bible printed for Anton Koberger by Johann Amerbach, 1500, which is a chained Bible with its original iron chain of 10 links and 2 rings measuring 11 inches, in an unusually fine state of preservation. Such an appearance speaks to us of an earlier day when books were few and the right to read was precious. Some of our current institutional libraries would do well to consider chaining some of their more important stack books (the last three I looked for had disappeared).

Entirely different as a "Show and Tell," because of a kind of awe which develops as the story is told, is the Eliot Indian Bible, 1663–61. The Ryrie copy is the Lilly Library duplicate copy auctioned in New York in 1962, which at one time had been in the Royal Society Library, London. John Eliot (1604–1690) came to New England and learned the Algonquin language so as to render greater service in his evangelistic work with the Indians. His magnificent achievement was the translation of the Bible, from the first verse of Genesis to the last word of Revelation, into a language previously unwritten—the first instance in history of such labor. It is, of course, the first Bible printed in the New World. About 1,000 copies were printed, and fewer than 50 exist today. Part of the strange mystique of this Bible is that no person living today can read it. Yet because of its wonderful "first" qualities, a copy brings stratospheric prices. The DAB described Eliot as "one of the most remarkable men of the Seventeenth Century in New England, and had the rare virtue of thinking of other souls besides his own." That spirit still surrounds a copy of his Bible.

What Second Step Should Bible and Other Book Collectors Take in their Collecting?

The first step is, of course, the collecting of the basic texts. The second step is collecting the great firstfruits of the analysis and examination of the basic texts by the earliest scholars, who in turn provide the foundational steps for contemporary academic labor.

The Ryrie collection is rich in these primary first sources. It includes: (a) The London Polyglot, 1655–1657, 6 volumes; (b) The first edition of the New Testament in Greek by Erasmus, 1516. Margaret Aston describes this event: "The appearance of Erasmus's New Testament was a historic moment for the world at large and for himself. It marked the achievement of an objective he had long been straining toward: the publication of the central document of the faith in its original apostolic language. . . ." (c) The Erasmus Greek Testament, 3rd edition, 1522, and others.

What Final Step Should a Bible (or Other Book) Collector Take?

Simply stated, focus on outstanding scholarship. Collect the works written by great scholars throughout the generations that have become fundamental texts for posterity. The Bible collector will seek the finest of this category.

The Ryrie collection includes: (a) John Calvin's *The Institutes of the Christian Religion*, first edition in English, 1561, as well as editions printed in 1574, 1582, 1585, 1599, 1634. This work was the most important doctrinal work of the Reformation and remains, for a large percentage of the Christian public, the fundamental structure of their faith. That great exhibition catalogue *Printing and the Mind of Man: A Descriptive Catalogue Illustrating the Impact of Print on the Evolution of Western Civilization During Five Centuries* devoted extensive space to *The Institutes*. "The *Institutio* was much revised, taking its final form in 1559; Calvin himself translated it into French in 1545, and thereby created one of the finest early prose writings in the language. It has been printed in innumerable editions and translations including Hungarian, Greek, and Arabic." (b) John Foxe's *Acts and Monuments of these Latter and Perillous Dayes, touching Matters of the Church,* first English edition, 1563. Most frequently called Foxe's "Book of Martyrs," it was for two centuries one of the most frequently read books in England. Once again, this book received extensive coverage in the *Printing and the Mind of Man* catalogue. "In 1571, a decree of Convocation ordained that copies were to be placed in all cathedral churches and that the houses of archbishops, bishops, archdeacons and resident canons should all have copies for the use of servants and visitors. There was no instruction that it should also be provided in parish churches, but it very often was, and chained examples (often seventeenth-century editions) survive not infrequently. The lively style of the book, not to mention the gruesome illustrations, which first appeared in the English edition of 1563, was thus given an opportunity to influence—and prejudice—the minds of people in all classes of society, including those who could not otherwise have afforded it." (c) *The Annals of the World, Deduced from the Origin of Time . . .* by Archbishop James Ussher, first edition in English and first complete edition, 1568, that established the date of creation (4004 B.C., the evening of October 22) along with other dates in the margins of many editions of the Bible. These dates ultimately came to be regarded as sacred as the text from which the chronology was deduced. Although Archbishop Ussher was severely attacked in the evolution controversy, book lovers hold him in high reverence. He was instrumental in preserving Irish antiquities and manuscripts, including the Book of Kells. (d) Henry VIII's *Assertio Septum Sacramentorum,* 1521 ("The Assertion of the Seven Sacraments") is termed by *Printing and the Mind of Man* (it is amazing to see how many Ryrie items are included in this important attempt to profile the last five centuries of Western civilization) as "one of the most fateful books in the history of western civilization." His reward from the Pope was a title—"Defender of the Faith" (even though he might have preferred being granted a divorce). The result was Reformation history!

What Will Happen to a Collection Upon the Death of the Collector?

This is a fundamental element in the collecting picture and, tragically, so many times is left out. From forty-two years of running bibliographic institutions and for the last five years an appraisal service, I can tell stories of bibliographic horror—all because the collector made no provision for his collection. Heirs were given precise directions concerning the house, bonds, other holdings, but no directions about the book collection. Book collectors have a reluctance-gene which frequently brushes aside the necessity for planning ahead in that area.

Even as Charles Ryrie has assembled these Bibles so carefully, he also has great concern that they continue to be available for future generations. Building his wonderful collection of rare Bibles has proven to be a source of great joy for Charles Ryrie. He has encouraged many of his students to appreciate deeply God's marvelous providence in preserving His Word for us. And he also has stimulated in many of his students a desire to preserve rare and unusual copies of the Bible for future generations to appreciate. There is no doubt that generations to come will reflect upon Charles' avocation with deep appreciation. As they admire, appreciate, and study these various volumes, we are sure that they too will feel a sense of awe and admiration—not just for the man who collected the volumes, but for the eternal truth recorded in these books.

It is unlikely that those who triggered Charles Ryrie's interest in collecting rare Bibles and related items had any idea of what their thoughtful gift would initiate. The genesis of this avocation occurred during his tenure as President of Philadelphia College of Bible. The members of a home Bible class that Ryrie had taught showed their appreciation by presenting him with a framed page from a first edition *King James Version*. From that simple beginning developed an intense and growing fascination with the heritage of our English Bible.

But Ryrie's avocation is more than a hobby pursued for his own private benefit. This carefully chosen compilation will provide pleasure and edification for years to come. The Ryrie collection surely meets all of the qualifications for excellence; its scope, quality, and technique exemplify an outstanding collection. But the distinguished provenance of this collection also includes the loving effort expended by Charles Ryrie in building it. As future generations enjoy and study this collection, we are sure that Dr. Ryrie's first and foremost desire is that they will glorify God, who has given us His Word and who has preserved it for us. And we are sure that these generations also will appreciate the diligence, scholarship, and passion for excellence of Charles Ryrie.

CHAPTER THIRTY-FOUR
Expressions of Appreciation

Gary Vincelette

I was drying up in my seminary study of theology. How could that be? I needed to do something radical. I asked if I could be transferred into Dr. Ryrie's section on the Holy Spirit. They probably shouldn't have done it, but they did. I'm still grateful. Dr. Ryrie made the discipline of systematic theology come alive for me inductively from text to theology. He made it appear so simple, so clear, so understandable. During my first year of class with Dr. Ryrie, my daughter was hospitalized with seizures. My wife and I were deeply touched at his leading our systematic theology class in prayer many times for her, and he rejoiced with us at her recovery.

At my ordination examination I was asked, "Which book has

made the most significant contribution to your life?" My immediate answer was, "*Balancing the Christian Life* by Dr. Ryrie." In Austria when we discussed which one-volume systematic theology to translate into German for TEE courses behind the Iron Curtain and in Austria, we chose *Basic Theology*. Ryrie's teaching and books, more than any other man's, have provided my wife's and my foundation for systematic theology. And we do not stand alone in this. My children in college, as well as Annette and I, have well worn the pages of your Study Bible. Annette and I thank you, Dr. Ryrie, for your discipline of study, research, and writing.

Charles C. Tandy

While I was still a young anesthesia resident at Parkland Hospital in Dallas in 1957, I was invited to attend a newly formed Sunday School class — the Medical-Dental Class — at First Baptist Church. The new teacher was a young theologian who had recently returned to Dallas Theological Seminary. For the next ten years I had the gift and pleasure of having Charles Ryrie as my mentor. For the first time, the Bible had meaning and relevance to me as an individual.

In 1978, I was invited to a small luncheon in Dallas on the occasion of the publication of *The Ryrie Study Bible*. I am convinced God produced that study Bible through Dr. Ryrie for me! I have been told that a few others have also found meaning for their lives from his clear illumination of God's Word.

Robert P. Lightner

Charles Ryrie first impressed me as my professor in several courses in Systematic Theology at Dallas Theological Seminary. I was attracted by his deep, precise thinking and his clear, well-outlined presentations. He never wasted words. The balance he brought to theological issues was refreshing and made me want to do the same.

In the forty years I have known and worked with Charles Ryrie, I have found him to be faithful to the Lord and to His Word. He has been a mentor as my friend, professor, employer, colleague, and department chairman. I have watched this man under happy times and sad times, stressful times and relaxed times, in professional and nonprofessional settings, and have always found him to be Christlike, seeking to manifest the fruit of the Spirit in his life. God has blessed me with Charles Ryrie's friendship and partnership.

Richard E. Elkins

I first met Charles at Westmont College in 1948. He had just finished graduate studies at Dallas Seminary and had come to teach Bible and Greek. During the next three years God used him to establish in me a sound theological bent and to equip me for the coming years of service on the mission field. His influence was not merely educational. For me and for many others he was an example of how a man or woman of God should live. Under his guidance I grew both academically and spiritually, and he became more than a teacher. He was a close friend who was always ready to help and to offer godly counsel.

When my wife and I joined Wycliffe Bible Translators, Charles became one of our first partners and has faithfully continued in this partnership until the present. Eternity alone will reveal the extent of how God has used his participation with us and with many others in the lives of people around the world.

Howard P. McKaughan

It was some fifty years ago that I met Charles Ryrie. He had recently started his studies at Dallas Theological Seminary. He had begun to help with a weekend ministry at a housing project. Sunday School, church, and a young people's group were meeting regularly, and Charles played the piano—a safe, nonthreatening responsibility.

Then I asked him to give the object lesson for the thirty or so youngsters in Sunday School—a simple task involving about ten minutes. I didn't realize it at the time, but Charles was petrified. He said he definitely could not give that lesson—not him. But I wouldn't take no for an answer, and he had to prepare that object lesson. No one knew how uncomfortable this shy, twenty-year-old was. How could he get in front of those squirming youngsters and make himself heard? How could he give them a really meaningful lesson? It was too much to ask. Though at first he didn't think he could do it, he did give that lesson. He probably remembers to this day what it was, though I do not.

That first traumatic experience led to giving more such lessons, and eventually Charles wrote several "Easy to Get Object Lesson" books. Though reluctant at first, he still met the challenge and then built the experience into important contributions for others. Charles has been an inspiration all of these years because he has taken the simplest task seriously, and then found a way to use it to help others. We are deeply grateful to God for him.

Elliott E. Johnson

It is an honor to be included among those who recognize the contribution of Charles Ryrie. I first met Dr. Ryrie when I was a seminary student as a recent graduate engineer. From a distance I appreciated the care and conviction with which he thought, wrote, and taught. As his student I often agonized over the precision of his thought, but in time, as a colleague, I grew to respect him for a simple, but not simplistic, statement of theology.

While Charles Ryrie was a dignified teacher, he was also honest, creative, and not threatened. He ministered to me in the fresh and vital way he preached the Word, and later as a colleague, I appreciated the candor with which he spoke in personal discussions and the growing maturity in his own expression of the truth.

Renald E. Showers

I did not have the privilege of taking courses with Dr. Ryrie. For several years I had looked forward to studying under him, but the year I was to enroll as a student at Dallas Theological Seminary, he left to become the president of Philadelphia College of Bible. I was so disappointed that I postponed going to Dallas for one year.

I began to get to know Dr. Ryrie on a personal level while courting my wife who baby-sat his children. In later years it was my privilege to minister together with him on more than one occasion, both overseas and in the States. Through those experiences and his writings I finally was able to sit under his ministry and to benefit greatly from his excellent gift of teaching. God has used Dr. Ryrie to enrich my life and ministry.

Wesley R. Willis

My relationship with Charles Ryrie has extended over many years and through a wide variety of relationships. I first became acquainted with him as my college president. In seminary he became my professor, and then increasingly as my friend. When Elaine and I served as short-term missionaries with CAM International, we met in Guatemala when Dr. Ryrie was a board member. When I began teaching at a Bible college we developed a new relationship (one in which he would tease me, a Christian Education prof, about colored pencils and overhead transparencies). When I served in publishing at Scripture Press Publications, I became responsible for assisting and encouraging (and occasionally even badgering) Charles in his writing ministry. In recent years we have worked on several writing projects together. Now I am privileged to know him as a faculty member who serves under me. Through all the years my admiration has grown for Charles.

I have marveled at Charles Ryrie's consistency in every relationship. His walk with the Lord, his faithfulness in ministry, his uncanny ability to simplify without becoming simplistic, and his commitment to act upon his convictions (his theology directs his behavior) all demonstrate that consistency. Unquestionably he has the gift of teaching. This comes through his classroom ministry, his preaching ministry, and his writing. And millions of Christians are richer spiritually because of his multifaceted ministry. Thank you, Charles Ryrie.

Kenneth Boa

Wisdom is seeking the assistance of a mentor. *Greatness* is seeking to *be* a mentor. Dr. Charles Ryrie played such a role in my life. He believed in my potential and ministered to me unselfishly in many ways, both personally and spiritually. He was always available with help and advice at critical decision points in my life and ministry. His encouragement to students went beyond the realm of the theoretical: he succeeded in engaging the mind and heart together through the ultimate example of his own actions.

I welcome this opportunity to express my deep gratitude for his faithfulness in proclaiming God's kingdom, not through mere words, but through the very fruit of his relationship with Jesus

Christ. In the same way, I pray for myself and others that we might honor this great man by offering up our lives as mentors to the next generation.

Glenn R. Goss

What always stood out to me in Dr. Ryrie's teaching was his clarity, whether in lectures, in addresses or messages, or in his books. There was never any question about the point he was making. It was never masked by side issues or unrelated material. The truth was presented, and the scriptural support was laid out fully.

His exams were known for their clarity as well. They usually were not long. Dr. Ryrie evidently felt that if you did not know the definitions, supporting Scripture, and the key points of doctrine, no amount of verbiage would make a good theological composition. And, as is normally the case, he was right.

G. Robert Kilgore

I have had the privilege of knowing Dr. Ryrie in four different contexts: as a student at Philadelphia College of Bible when he was president, at Dallas Theological Seminary when he chaired the Theology Department, as a member of CAM International during the years he chaired the board of the mission, and now as a faculty member at PCB where he currently serves as adjunct faculty.

In each of these his consistency as a friend stands out. As a professor his wise counsel to me as a struggling student forced me to deal with key issues of lifestyle and my understanding of God. His passion for the effectiveness of our mission and its missionaries took him to Central America on several trips where he provided those of us wrestling with our own ministries a larger view of the whole mission—the whole world. More than anything else, his ability to penetrate through seemingly complex discussions and to help determine the real core issues has made him a valuable friend, counselor, and example.

Joseph Y. Wong

Three things come to mind when I think of my mentor. There is his practical, meaningful spirituality as evidenced in his stewardship of money. Even in his selection of automobiles he demonstrated practical spiritual stewardship, "where the rubber meets the road."

Then there is the development of his charges. From the individualized attention (and stern rebuke when needed) to his individual students, to the design of a course for his doctoral students virtually guaranteeing their success, his mentoring was the envy of the students in all other programs. Thanks for letting us serve you as graders and disciples, for that has marked our own ministries in patient, detailed, and pointed service. My wife and my three children also have been blessed with our association. Blessing upon you as an educator of educators.

Last is his consistency in his spirituality. His monumental works will enrich the church until our Lord returns. And his steadfast commitment to principles, convictions, and exegetical details, even in tough personal life and relational difficulties, will challenge me to be consistent, to persevere, and to live unto the Lord.

Frederic R. Howe

My friendship and many pleasant memories of association with Charles began in 1955, when I was a student in the Th.D. program at Dallas Seminary. What I learned to respect and appreciate so much in Charles was his quiet and careful workmanship in the classroom, and his penetrating analyses of theological issues. I was privileged to have Charles' instruction in both biblical and systematic theology. He introduced us to the discipline of biblical theology and set a positive tone, balancing this field with other theological disciplines. We all remember the beautifully organized and interesting subject matter in those biblical theology courses. However, we also were exposed to Charles' abilities as a discussion leader, mentor, and guide in smaller classes dealing with advanced systematic theology matters as well.

In 1973 I returned to DTS to serve under Charles, who was then department chair. It was through these closer contacts that I gained even more admiration and respect for this quiet-spoken, steady leader. I remember many department meetings, held informally over the lunch table in a small basement room in Lincoln Hall #2.

Charles calmly set the pace, honoring us as team workers, and blending the efforts of widely differing personalities into a unified effort. Instead of arbitrarily assigning teaching loads, Charles sought for and honored our preferences. It is indeed with gratitude and fond memories that I reflect upon the influence of God's servant, Charles C. Ryrie.

J. Dwight Pentecost

After forty years of association with Charles Ryrie I still stand in constant amazement at his unique ability to make the deepest truths of the Word simple, clear, and understandable. He grasps these truths not only with a keen mind but with a warm heart as well. This knowledge is communicated with a Christlike humility that befits a servant of Jesus Christ. The insights he has gained into Scripture can only come as one walks in a close relationship with the Savior and is guided by the Holy Spirit. Those who love the Lord and His Word are deeply indebted to Charles Ryrie for sharing the fruits of his study with us.

John R. Master

"Why does Dr. Ryrie call me an alligator?" puzzled two-year-old Stephen before he learned the appropriate rejoinder, "After a while, crocodile!" So developed Charles Ryrie's warm relationship with our oldest son, in typical Ryrie style meeting this child as an individual at his level. Years later, he shared our middle son's excitement in catching a fly ball, even though Daniel had cut Dr. Ryrie's class to go to the game. Our youngest son can hardly wait to take a class from him. I hope he has that opportunity, for I well remember learning from Charles Ryrie an even deeper love for the Word of God and the doctrines derived from it.

My seminary education was an absolute delight. Along with my classroom education, I was blessed with the personal discipling ministry of some of the faculty, including Charles Ryrie. Whether swimming, riding bikes, or simply talking, he shared and modeled his careful application of God's Word. Janet and I have treasured his counsel at every turn in our ministry.

Scholarship, balance, and love—Charles Ryrie has gifted us with all of these and with the sheer joy of his close friendship. God has wonderfully impacted my life and that of my whole family through this godly man.

Robert Gromacki

Dr. Ryrie says so much in so little and he states it so well. He makes the complex simple. Ever since 1956, my first year at Dallas Seminary, I have been impressed with his clear presentation of biblical truth, marked by graphic illustrations. I was overwhelmed to discover that he had written books on object lessons for children and that he had taught junior church. He could communicate to any audience. What a role model for me to follow.

I have a treasure in my personal library. It is *The Ryrie Study Bible* (KJV), graciously sent to me by Dr. Ryrie himself and inscribed: "For Dr. Robert Gromacki, May our Lord bless you always. Charles C. Ryrie, 2 Cor. 3:5." God has blessed me with the privilege of knowing Dr. Ryrie and having his influence in my life.

Thomas R. Edgar

When I began study at Dallas Theological Seminary, Dr. Charles C. Ryrie was already well-known and had written several books. In seminary his classes were just like his books — clear, succinct, practical, and to the point. Dr. Ryrie very clearly states and argues for the position he holds. His classes and writings are aimed at communication of the truth. Since seminary days I have continued to profit from his writings, appreciating his ability to discern the real problem and make the issues clear. He has had a direct ministry to me and countless others over a long period of time, through the classroom, speaking, and writing.

Just as significant a ministry has been his theological commitment. He has not wavered or shifted his theological position or beliefs due to academic and cultural pressures, as many others have. His testimony has always been clear, consistent, and straightforward. Thus he has had a strong ministry, not only through classes and writing, but also by the consistency of his theological testimony. He presents each of us with a challenge to do the same. Hats off to a gentleman and a scholar!

Zane C. Hodges
Over the years I have known Dr. Charles C. Ryrie as a teacher, as a colleague, and as a friend. I have been impressed with his personal integrity, his theological stability, and his deep commitment to the grace of God.

Ron Blue
In our family Dr. Ryrie is still known as the "good peanut man." Dr. Ryrie carried cashews for protein needed to counteract his hypoglycemia. However, to our three-year-old daughter he was the wonderful man who gave "peanuts" to a hungry child of missionaries in Spain.

Dr. Ryrie is not only a renowned theologian; he is a man of compassion. It is fitting that his first published work was on object lessons for children. Deeply committed to the Word, he has the unique ability to clarify the most complex theological truths, a mark of a true scholar. Dr. Ryrie has been a marvelous teacher, a much respected president of the CAM International Board, a trusted faculty colleague at Dallas Seminary, and most of all a much loved friend.

Keita Takagi
One grand heritage of Dallas Theological Seminary which I particularly appreciate is its emphasis on a crystal clear presentation of the Gospel message of salvation. Personally, I am greatly indebted to Dr. Charles C. Ryrie for this emphasis. I recall the following hypothetical story which Dr. Ryrie related in one of his theology classes in order to help students gain a succinct grasp of the terms of salvation:

You have often sought the opportunity to present the Gospel to Mr. A, one of your friends. One day as you walk along, you come upon Mr. A, who lies seriously injured at the side of the road. An ambulance will arrive in a matter of minutes, but Mr. A may not live even that long. Now is your chance to share the Good News. What would you say? Would it be: "Right now, tell God all the sins you ever committed," or "Completely forsake your sins and evil ways," or "Grieve over your sins," or "Make recompense now for your sins," or "Give God control of every area of your life"?

Or would you say: "Believe in the Lord Jesus Christ as your Savior. He has already paid the penalty for your sins on the cross."

Upon returning to Japan following my graduation from Dallas Seminary, I was shocked to find out that most of the evangelistic messages in my country were tainted by "Lordship salvation." To promote the "free grace" position, God led me to write a book in Japanese titled, *Shinjiru Dakede Sukuwareruka* (Tokyo: Word of Life Press, 1980), which became one of the best-selling books on Christian doctrine in Japan. Without my training under men like Dr. Ryrie, I would not have been used to benefit the Lord's work in Japan like this.

Arnold G. Fruchtenbaum

I have been positively influenced by Dr. Ryrie by his writings and by his classroom instruction. The first book I ever read by Dr. Ryrie was *Dispensationalism Today*. This particular work by Dr. Ryrie gave me an understanding of what the real issues were, as well as the hermeneutical presuppositions held by those who taught these subjects erroneously. It not only gave me an adequate knowledge in counteracting inaccurate replacement theology I had been taught, but also gave me a framework to positively present why I believed what I believed.

In the classroom, Dr. Ryrie was the first one who actually made systematic theology exciting for me. I had systematic theology classes in college but found them to be rather boring and unexciting with little purpose in practical spiritual living. Studying systematic theology under Dr. Ryrie changed my whole perspective on this field and showed how theology can have practical ramifications.

But more than sharing biblical and theological knowledge, Dr. Ryrie truly showed me how to live the balanced spiritual life as I was able to observe, both inside and outside the classroom, how his own daily life was integrated with his teaching. To me he became the example of one who lived what he preached and taught. To him I owe a great debt.

Joel T. Andrus

Though I've known Dr. Ryrie ever since he and my dad attended Dallas Seminary together, it wasn't until my own seminary days that he really became a mentor to me. That mentoring took place primarily in the classroom, where I learned a great deal not only about theological content, but about theological thinking. I learned that words were important and needed to be chosen carefully. I learned the value of knowing central texts for various truths. I learned the goodness of saying things succinctly. His exams were designed to allow very little space to give an answer, and he didn't want the answer carried over onto the back side of the page. If you couldn't say it in the space provided, you didn't know it well enough. And you were graded accordingly. Some classmates, who actually knew much more than I, never did quite catch on to that.

But his mentoring also took place outside the classroom. Not only did he answer my questions and challenge my thinking, but he greatly encouraged me. I struggled with many feelings of inadequacy. To know that he had confidence in me did more than anything else I ever experienced to keep me pushing on. I'll never forget the week before graduation. I had accepted a call to the Martensdale Community Church in Iowa, where I am still pastor. But I was scared, being very conscious that I didn't possess many of the skills of my classmates. He met me one afternoon out on the commons in front of Mosher Library. After listening to my fears, he responded by simply saying, "But, Joel, you can preach the Word. Just go be faithful in doing that." And that's what I've been doing for more than twenty-six years.

Stanley D. Toussaint

For some forty years it has been my privilege to know Dr. Charles Ryrie in several capacities. First, I benefited enormously as a student in several of his courses on biblical theology at Dallas Theological Seminary during the '50s. At the same time I was serving as a youth pastor in a small Dallas church. Dr. Ryrie was a favorite with our young people. Whenever I would ask our teenagers who they would like as a special speaker, it was always Charles Ryrie. I was much impressed by this, a world-class theologian so beloved by young people.

When we served together on the faculty of Dallas Seminary, Charles Ryrie was always most supportive and a dear friend and colleague. I have missed his presence there in later years. It is indeed a high honor and privilege to be a part of this work in honor of Dr. Charles C. Ryrie. May he continue to minister to the church of Jesus Christ for many years to come.

Stephen J. Nichols

A teacher, according to the dictionary definition, is one whose occupation is to instruct. And a mentor is a trusted counselor or guide. There are many, including myself, who are very grateful for Dr. Ryrie, our teacher, our mentor, and our guide.

Dr. Ryrie is an extraordinary teacher. I will never forget the clarity with which he expounded the doctrine of imputation. He reconstructed a courtroom scene in the classroom by using students to demonstrate first, the penalty for sin and then, the wonderful payment that was made on our behalf.

He also is a mentor and guide, even counseling through his writings. Since recently reading *Transformed by His Glory*, my thinking about God and my relationship to Him have not been the same. He has guided through the example of his life. His graciousness and warmth and his love for the Lord, the Word, and theology serve as a great model to follow. Thank you, Dr. Ryrie, for being a teacher and a mentor.

Jeffrey L. Townsend

The first time I met Dr. Ryrie was an unscheduled visit to his Dallas Seminary office during my first semester at the school. After my nervous knock, I opened the door to find Dr. Ryrie eating a lunch of dry Chinese noodles and melon balls, both out of plastic baggies. Immediately the humility of this esteemed man struck me. Thus began a twenty-plus year mentoring relationship.

The greatest gift God gave to the church in Charles Ryrie is his ability to define deep truths clearly. The second is Dr. Ryrie's unswerving commitment to presenting truth, with unwarranted extremes and implications excluded. The qualities of clarity and balance served Dr. Ryrie well as teacher and author. If I were marooned on a desert island with just one book, I pray it would be *The Ryrie Study Bible*. If by God's grace two books could be granted, then add *Basic Theology*.

I have appreciated Dr. Ryrie's personal interest in my life and his sage advice. I recall a naive concern that a church I considered pastoring wanted to pay me too much. Dr. Ryrie gave me this advice, "Maybe God knows you will need more money than it appears now that you will need." I took the call and the money, and needed every dime! Thank you, Dr. Ryrie, for your interest in my life and ministry.

Paul Benware

As a student, I knew that each theology class could likely produce some stimulating or profound thoughts. So I was not disappointed in the senior theology class one day when the good doctor said, "Keep it simple stupid" (K.I.S.S.). And while being mildly offended by the partially accurate designation, we got the point — our theology must be clear and understandable when we minister. Obscure, complex, verbose pronouncements might impress a few, but they do little good in actually helping God's people. So many of us are indebted to him for making theological truth both clear and applicable, penetrating our minds and hearts. Dr. Ryrie's exhortation to those in that senior class gives new meaning to the Apostle Paul's exhortation to greet the brethren with a holy K.I.S.S.

Albert T. Platt

It has been my privilege to enjoy interaction with Dr. Charles Ryrie for many years in various contexts. Early on, he was finishing graduate study at Dallas Theological Seminary while I was beginning the Th.M. work. In fact, in those days he played the piano for our seminary chorus. By the time I returned to the Th.D. program during furlough time from ministry with CAM International, Dr. Ryrie was on the faculty at Dallas offering great classes in the theology of the New Testament.

Though I have always admired and appreciated his teaching and delight in the clarity and ease with which he explains even the most difficult concepts, it was his great contribution to CAM International that is so indelibly stamped upon my heart and mind. As chairman of the Board of Directors, his was the strong word for soundness in doctrine. His reminder that a doctrinal statement is only as strong as the men who hold it challenged us all. What a delight and comfort as president of the mission to call my friend, Dr. Charles Ryrie, and go over those issues which affected CAM. He is retired from the Board and I from the presidency, but the friendship and the telephone call consultations continue with the same deep appreciation.

Charles H. Dyer

My first exposure to Dr. Charles Ryrie was as a student in Bible college. After plodding through scores of ponderous theology textbooks, I found *Dispensationalism Today* a breath of fresh air. That clear, persuasive style taught me an important lesson: Scholarship is not synonymous with obtuseness. A true scholar can take the deep truths of God's Word and present them in a way that is understandable to all. Dr. Ryrie is such a scholar.

I had the privilege of sitting under Dr. Ryrie's teaching at Dallas Theological Seminary. Once again, his clarity of teaching was astounding, and was punctuated at times by his dry wit and humor. He had the uncanny ability to take a complex argument and distill its essence. And he approached theology using the Bible.

Charles, thanks for your contribution to the body of Christ. Let me close by "Ryrie-izing" you, using your own brand of brevity and insight: "Charles Ryrie: Sharp mind! Keen wit! Crisp writing! Kind heart!"

Thomas Ice

Dr. Charles C. Ryrie is an example to our generation that knowing and doing are both important in the eyes of God. Dr. Ryrie has demonstrated that the Bible is to be both understood and applied. It is to be understood so that believers can be directed by the will of God. It is to be practiced, because it is the truth.

It has been said that true genius is the ability to make clear through simplification. Dr. Ryrie has been a blessing to the church because of his gift of boiling down truth to its essentials. As a theologian he is able to recognize the essentials of an issue, state them clearly, and propose a clear biblical solution. Those of us lacking this skill have benefited greatly from the ministry of Dr. Ryrie in so many different areas of theology.

Biblical doctrine for Dr. Ryrie is the very truth of God to be applied in the life of all believers. Dr. Ryrie has been an example to his students as one who depends upon the Word of his Lord even through difficult trials. We have seen Dr. Ryrie demonstrate through his own life that the theology he espoused in the classroom also works in the real world.

Along with many others, I can honestly say I have only fond memories of our much beloved brother in Christ, Dr. Charles Ryrie.

Robert L. Thomas

It's hard to think of Dr. Ryrie as a seventy-year-old. My recollections of him go back to his youthful days when he first joined the faculty of Dallas Seminary. Despite his relative youthfulness, his meaningful instruction of God's truth made a powerful impact on my life. I owe him an eternal debt of gratitude for the part he has played in allowing the Lord to use him in shaping me into a vessel for service.

Manfred E. Kober

When reflecting on my six years as Dr. Ryrie's student at Dallas Theological Seminary, and my association with him since the 1960s, three major features stand out. I am impressed with his clarity of expression, his conciseness of presentation, and his compassion for others.

Whether in class or in his books, Dr. Ryrie's ability to express himself clearly helped make difficult theological concepts understandable. His writing ministry includes everything from object lessons for children to the definition of theological terms on the Moody Study Graphs of Bible Doctrine. Without fail, his presentations enable even lay people and children to understand divine truth.

As a student, I have always appreciated his conciseness of presentation. After studying with verbose professors at the University of Erlangen, I appreciated Dr. Ryrie's use of Occam's Razor: "Multiplicity ought not to be posited without necessity." His purposeful brevity and studied simplicity have endeared him to all who have heard or read him.

Lastly, I appreciate Dr. Ryrie for his sterling Christian character. He embodies the best of evangelical scholarship and genuine spirituality. His commitment to sound doctrine is coupled with a compassion for others.

A few summers ago, during the Iron Curtain era, Dr. Ryrie taught in West Germany and was able to accompany me on a visit to my relatives and to pastors in Eastern Germany. Before the memorable trip he asked if I could use any of his study Bibles for distribution to East European pastors and made a sizable quantity of his Bibles available. We carefully and safely took them to overjoyed pastors. His interest in them turned to a loving concern once he met them. After a dozen years he still prays for them. They, in turn, still speak about the godly and gracious professor from Texas who visited them. That's how they remember him and that's why those of us who know him delight to honor him.

Philip Hook
It is impossible to summarize the ministry of Charles Ryrie in so brief a space. Nor is it possible to assess accurately the impact of his life on so many of us. I was one of those men who somehow found himself privileged to be a student and friend of "Doc's." When he took an interest in me, I was a troubled teenager who had just been kicked out of freshman orientation week at Westmont College. As Dean of Men, Ryrie had every reason to send me home a failure. But he chose to deal with me in the Christlike grace which has always characterized his theology and his life. When people thank me for the ministry God has given me, I often think back to those days and thank God for "Doc" Ryrie's encouraging discipleship and example.

Decherd Turner
There is a worldwide organization which has as its motto: "The Love of Books Unites Us." That is a perfect reflection of my relationship with Charles Ryrie. We come at many things from different perspectives, but there is such a strong bond between us as book lovers that other areas of difference fade away.

It has long been established that there is a clear relationship between the worth of a collection and its owner: "Show me the

books, and I'll tell you about the man." Well, look at the books.
Charles' books are the fundamental writings of our civilization,
whenever possible in the finest condition, each carefully selected,
each an important part of the cultural picture, each geared to fit in
with the others so that the strongest possible whole is constructed. The collection is complete—a great picture. That tells all about
Charles Ryrie.

CHAPTER THIRTY-FIVE

Reflections

Charles C. Ryrie

Anumber of years ago I was preaching a series of sermons at a U.S. Army base in Germany. One evening I spoke on Matthew 20:1-16, that intriguing story about the workers hired at different times of the day to work in a vineyard. After the service we were having a social time in the chaplain's home. His wife was enthusiastic about the message, for the point that stood out to her (which I do not remember having mentioned at all) was this: we are not only saved by grace, but we serve by grace. Whether we are allowed to serve one hour, three, six, or the full day, it is by grace.

I suppose that mentally I knew that, but it never struck me as it did that night. Our Lord is not especially privileged to have me or any of us serve Him; we are the ones privileged to do so by His grace. And looking back over sixty-five years in God's family and fifty-two years in His service, I realize He has given me a full day's worth by His grace. And for that I am deeply grateful.

That night in the chaplain's home, I was also reminded of a supernatural phenomenon observed many times during these years of ministering the Word of God. It is this: the Holy Spirit may use a text, which I may consider unlikely or even irrelevant, to bring help to someone. No matter how well I think I know the needs of people, He knows them completely, and He can and will use the Word to speak to those needs. I have tried to learn the often hard lesson that if the Lord has led me to use a particular passage, I should not change just because someone appears in the audience whose special need I know, or because the host pastor suggests needs that I feel may not be met by that passage. The Word of God is living, active, and profitable to warn, enlighten, and make wise. Preach the Word.

As I have grown older I am more and more convinced that the best thing I can do for people is to urge them to expose themselves to the Bible. All the books, tracts, arguments, sermons, and seminars, useful as they may be, don't hold a candle to the ability of the Word to lead people to faith and then to Christlikeness. Read the Word. Love the Word. And live the Word.

The perspective of age also makes it easier to prioritize what's important in life. Close to the top of my list are my friends, scattered through the world. To the Masters and the Willises, in whose hearts this project was conceived and through whose efforts it was guided to publication, I am especially grateful. They have been close and supportive friends for more years than they might wish to acknowledge. To the authors, most former students and all special friends, who undoubtedly represent others who could and would have contributed as well, I thank you so very much. I hope your articles will help many others. To Mark Sweeney, a longtime friend, who published the book, thanks not only for doing this one but also for being involved in my publishing life in many ways and for many years. And to our Lord who made it all possible, thank You.

CONTRIBUTORS

Joel T. Andrus, Th.M.
  Pastor, Martensdale Community Church, Iowa
Paul Benware, Th.M., Th.D.
  Professor of Bible and Theology, Moody Bible Institute
Ron Blue, Th.M., Ph.D.
  President, CAM International
Kenneth Boa, Th.M., Ph.D.
  Divisional Director, Search Ministries; President,
  Trinity House Publishers
Charles H. Dyer, Th.M., Th.D.
  Assistant to the President and Professor of Bible Exposition,
  Dallas Theological Seminary
Thomas R. Edgar, Th.M., Th.D.
  Professor of New Testament and Department Head,
  Capital Bible Seminary
Richard E. Elkins, Ph.D.
  International Translation Consultant,
  Summer Institute of Linguistics
Arnold G. Fruchtenbaum, Th.M., Ph.D.
  Co-Director, Ariel Ministries
Glenn R. Goss, Th.M., Th.D.
  Professor of Bible, Philadelphia College of Bible
Robert Gromacki, Th.M., Th.D.
  Distinguished Professor of Bible and Greek, Cedarville College;
  Pastor, Grace Community Baptist Church,
  Washington Court House, Ohio
Zane C. Hodges, Th.M.
  Editorial Director and Partner, Redencion Viva Publishers,
  Dallas, Texas
Philip Hook, Th.M, Th.D.
  Professor of Biblical Studies, LeTourneau University

Frederic R. Howe, Th.M., Th.D.
  Professor Emeritus of Systematic Theology,
  Dallas Theological Seminary
Thomas Ice, Th.M.
  Executive Director, Pre-Trib Research Center,
  Washington, D.C.
Elliott E. Johnson, Th.M., Th.D.
  Professor of Bible Exposition, Dallas Theological Seminary
G. Robert Kilgore, Th.M.
  Associate Professor and Chair, Division of Professional
  Education, Philadelphia College of Bible
Manfred E. Kober, Th.M., Th.D.
  Professor and Chairman of the Department of Theology,
  Faith Baptist Bible College and Theological Seminary
Robert P. Lightner, M.L.A., Th.M., Th.D.
  Professor of Systematic Theology, Dallas Theological Seminary
John R. Master, Th.M., Th.D.
  Professor of Bible and Chair, Division of Biblical Education,
  Philadelphia College of Bible
Howard P. McKaughan, M.A., Th.M., Ph.D.
  Emeritus Professor of Linguistics, University of Hawaii
Stephen J. Nichols, B.S.
  Graduate Student, Westminster Theological Seminary
J. Dwight Pentecost, Th.M., Th.D.
  Distinguished Professor of Bible Exposition, Emeritus,
  Dallas Theological Seminary
Albert T. Platt, Th.M., Th.D.
  President Emeritus, CAM International
Renald E. Showers, Th.M., Th.D.
  Minister at Large, The Friends of Israel Gospel Ministry
Keita Takagi, Th.M.
  Pastor, Suita Bible Gospel Church, Osaka, Japan
Charles C. Tandy, M.D.
  Chairman, Department of Anesthesiology,
  Methodist Medical Center, Dallas, Texas
Robert L. Thomas, Th.D.
  Professor of New Testament Language and Literature,
  The Master's Seminary

Stanley D. Toussaint, Th.M., Th.D.
  Senior Professor of Bible Exposition, Emeritus,
  Dallas Theological Seminary
Jeffrey L. Townsend, Th.M.
  Senior Pastor, Woodland Park Community Church, Colorado
Decherd Turner, B.A., B.D., Litt.D., D.H.L.
  Retired Librarian
Gary E. Vincelette, Th.M.
  Director of Theological Education and Leadership
  Development, Eastern Europe, Send International
Wesley R. Willis, Th.M., Ed.D.
  Senior Vice President and Dean of Undergraduate Studies,
  Philadelphia College of Bible
Joseph Y. Wong, Th.M., Th.D.
  Vice President, Educational Development,
  Multonomah Bible College